JESUS AND THE DEAD SEA SCROLLS

JESUS AND THE
DEAD SEA SCROLLS

Revealing the Jewish Roots of Christianity

JOHN BERGSMA

IMAGE
NEW YORK

Library of Congress Cataloging-in-Publication data is available upon request.

ISBN 978-1-9848-2312-0
Ebook ISBN 978-1-9848-2313-7

Printed in the United States

Book design by Virginia Norey

4 6 8 10 9 7 5

First Edition

To James C. VanderKam,
who introduced me to the Scrolls

CONTENTS

Introduction   xi

PART ONE:
INTRODUCING THE DEAD SEA SCROLLS

Chapter 1: The Archeological Find of the Twentieth
Century   3

Chapter 2: Waiting for the Messiah   15

PART TWO:
BAPTISM AND THE SCROLLS

Chapter 3: The Scrolls, John the Baptist, and
Baptism   31

Chapter 4: The Scrolls, John the Apostle, and
Baptism   44

Chapter 5: Baptism Today 68

PART THREE:
THE EUCHARIST AND THE SCROLLS

Chapter 6: Did Qumran Have a "Eucharist"?   81

Chapter 7: When Was the Last Supper?   93

Chapter 8: Putting It All Together: Reading the Last
Supper in Light of the Scrolls   110

PART FOUR:
MATRIMONY, CELIBACY, AND THE SCROLLS

Chapter 9: Celibacy in the Scrolls   125

Chapter 10: Marriage in the Scrolls   140

PART FIVE:
HOLY ORDERS AND THE SCROLLS

Chapter 11: Priesthood and the Scrolls   161

Chapter 12: Priesthood in the Gospels   172

Chapter 13: Priesthood in the Early Church   182

PART SIX:
THE CHURCH AND THE SCROLLS

Chapter 14: Did St. Paul Write Anything About the Church?   191

Chapter 15: The Scrolls, the Reformation, and Church Unity   206

Chapter 16: The Essenes and the Early Church: What Is the Relationship?   221

Acknowledgments   229

Notes   231

Introduction

ABOUT TWO THOUSAND YEARS AGO, A HOLY MAN AROSE among the Jews of Palestine. He gathered around himself disciples and founded a community based on what he called the "new covenant" between God and Israel. Entrance to this community was through a ritual of water washing in which the Holy Spirit forgave one's sins. After the death of the founder, the community continued to celebrate a daily meal of bread and wine, as they awaited the return of the Son of David and the coming of the kingdom of God.

The story sounds familiar, but we are not talking about Jesus and the Church. The holy man we are discussing is a mysterious figure known as the "Teacher of Righteousness," and the community he founded made its home at a place called Qumran on the northwest shore of the Dead Sea. Thousands of years later, in the caves around Qumran, we would discover the remains of their library, which we call the "Dead Sea Scrolls."

How could two such similar communities arise at about the same time in the land of Israel? And what is the relationship between the two? Did one come from the other? Did Jesus imitate the men at Qumran, and is Christianity a "copycat" phenomenon? Those are some of the questions we hope to address in this book.

One of the most interesting aspects of the Dead Sea Scrolls for modern readers is the light they shed on the time period of Jesus and the early growth of the Church. The Scrolls are the only Jewish documents we possess *that were physically copied during the lifetime of Jesus or even earlier.* They provide an amazing window into the thoughts and practices of a very devout Jewish religious community that was flourishing at the same time John the Baptist, Jesus, Paul, and the other apostles were active in Israel and the early Church was growing.

My purpose in this book is to use the Scrolls to give us a window into the thought and practice of the Judaism of Jesus' day. After nearly twenty years of studying and teaching about the Scrolls, I've become convinced that they illuminate many passages of the New Testament that are otherwise confusing or hard to understand. They also help us to see how many of the beliefs, teachings, and practices of early Christianity are much more firmly rooted in Judaism and the Old Testament than we have generally recognized. This material needs to be better known by both believers and unbelievers alike, because it can debunk a great deal of misinformation about the nature of this remarkable movement in human history we call "Christianity" or "the Church."

One piece of misinformation that the Scrolls debunk is the idea that large parts of the Gospels must have been invented by second- and third-generation Christians and then written back into the life of Jesus. While few practicing Christians believe this, it is a view often found among scholars. For example, scholars used to date the entire Gospel of John around A.D. 160, because they did not believe its language or its picture of Jesus could have been composed by a Jew of Jesus' own lifetime.[1] But since the discovery of the Scrolls, many began to realize that the Gospel of John, out of all the New Testament books, has the *most* similarities in language and concepts with these pre-Christian Jewish documents from the Dead Sea![2] For this and other reasons, it's now widely agreed that, at the very least, the Gospel of John was written by a Jew who lived in the land of Israel close to the lifetime of Jesus.[3] The Scrolls help us to see the same thing about many other books, stories, and teachings of the New Testament. They enable us to look through Jewish eyes at the New Testament documents and the early Church, recognizing them as thoroughly embedded in the religious world of first-century Israel.

Since the purpose of this book is to help modern Christians (and other interested persons) understand the light the Scrolls shed on the origins of the Christian faith, I begin with a general overview of the discovery and contents of the Scrolls, and then organize the rest of the book around the central practices of Christianity. The early Christians called these practices "the mysteries" (Greek *mysteria*), a term later translated into Latin as *sacramenta,* giving us the word "sacraments." The various modern Christian denominations number and order the sacraments differently, but I have structured this book around four commonly recognized ones: Baptism, Eucharist, Matrimony, and Holy Orders. In each part of the book, the goal will be to use the Scrolls to help us better understand ancient Judaism, the New Testament, and the origins of these Christian practices. Finally, since the Church itself has been called a "mystery" and even "the universal sacrament of salvation," the last part of the book allows the Scrolls to shed light on the Church itself as a sacred society offering salvation to its members.[4]

Ultimately, this exploration is not merely an exercise in intellectual curiosity for me. Any way one looks at it, Christianity is an amazing human phenomenon. Over 2 billion people—about one in every three on the globe—claims some kind of relationship with a two-thousand-year-old Jewish teacher from Nazareth named Jesus. All these people have inherited from Jesus certain common practices, like sacred washing in water (Baptism) and a ritual meal of bread and wine (Eucharist). But there is a remarkable diversity in the understanding of what these practices mean. I myself am something of an American Christian "mutt," having worshipped in a wide variety of churches in my upbringing. In some churches I belonged to, Baptism was an optional, symbolic profession of one's faith in Jesus performed by adults. In other churches, Baptism was an infusion of the Holy Spirit absolutely necessary for salvation, and therefore performed even on infants. I have been in churches where communion was a quarterly ceremony in which Wonder bread and grape juice were consumed to remember Jesus, and in churches where the holy sacrifice of Calvary under the appearance of bread and wine was the central act of every worship service. Most Christians have a sense that this disagreement over the meaning of even these basic practices of our faith is at best unfortunate and at worst tragic. The Scrolls are not going to solve those differences, but they will help us better understand how Jesus, the Apostles, and the first generation of Jewish Christians understood their faith and its rituals. My hope is that this may become a place of common ground, or at least a common starting point, for contemporary Christians to move toward unity in their faith and practice.

PART ONE

INTRODUCING
THE DEAD SEA SCROLLS

CHAPTER 1

The Archeological Find of the Twentieth Century

FOR GOOD REASON, THE DISCOVERY OF THE DEAD SEA Scrolls has been called "the greatest archeological find of the twentieth century."[1] It began in the winter of 1946–47, when Bedouin shepherds were searching for hidden treasure in a cave on the northwest shore of the Dead Sea.[2] They were hoping to find gold, and were disappointed with the three old scrolls they found in a jar. They couldn't realize, of course, that one of the scrolls they found was a complete and nearly pristine copy of the Book of Isaiah in Hebrew, dating to around 125 B.C., or about *a thousand years older* than any complete biblical book in Hebrew previously known to scholars! Far more valuable than gold, the scrolls the Bedouin discovered would eventually prompt the State of Israel to spend tens of millions of dollars building a bunker-like museum to house them in a carefully climate-controlled environment. The Bedouin ended up selling the first several scrolls they found to an antiquities trader for twenty-four British pounds (about a hundred dollars at the time), but when these ancient writings came to the attention of professional scholars, the true value of the find quickly became apparent, and the rush was on to search the northwest coast of the Dead Sea for additional scrolls. In the years 1949 to 1956, dozens of exploratory missions by both native Bedouin and Western scholars located a total of eleven scroll-bearing caves in the limestone cliffs surrounding the ruins of an ancient dwelling called Qumran. Years of archeological excavations at Qumran revealed a complex of buildings inhabited by a religious community of men in the last centuries B.C. and first century A.D.—in other words, in the centuries just before and during the life of Jesus. The scrolls in the caves were the remains of their library, which once consisted of about a thousand handwritten manuscripts on parchment (leather) and papyrus (reed paper). About a quarter of these documents were copies of books found in the Bibles of modern Jews and Christian Old Testaments, like Genesis, Exodus, Isaiah, and the Psalms. But three-quarters of the scrolls were nonbiblical religious writings composed or treasured by the community of Jews that lived at Qumran. It didn't take scholars long to identify this community with one of the three sects that dominated first-century Jewish culture according to our ancient classical (Greek and Latin) sources. Two of these sects, the Sadducees and the Pharisees, are well known even to modern readers because they appear frequently in the Gospels and other New Testament writings. However, it was to the third and least-known of the sects, the Essenes (ESS-seenz), that the Qumran community belonged. Although Essene characters can be found in the Gospels, they are never called by that name, and the group was largely forgotten by Jewish and Christian culture until the discovery of the Scrolls brought them into public consciousness once more.

One of the most important sources on the Essenes is the Roman military commander and geographer Pliny the Elder (A.D. 23–79), who attempted to describe the known world in an encyclopedic work he called *Natural History.* In the section of the work devoted to Israel, he describes Galilee and moves south down the Jordan River, eventually getting to the north end of the Dead Sea, about which he says this:

On the west side of the Dead Sea, but out of range of the nox-
ious exhalations of the coast, is the solitary tribe of the Essenes
which is remarkable beyond all the other tribes of the whole
world as it has no women and has renounced all sexual desire,
has no money, and has only palm trees for company. Day by
day the throng of refugees is recruited to an equal number by
numerous accessions of persons tired of life and driven there
by the waves of fortune to adopt their manners. Thus, through
thousands of ages (incredible to relate) a race in which no one
is born lives on forever—so prolific for their advantage is other
men's weariness of life!

Lying below the Essenes was formerly the town of Engedi,
second only to Jerusalem in the fertility of its land and in its
groves of palm trees, but now like Jerusalem a heap of ashes.[3]

Much has been written about this passage because it fits very
well with the caves and buildings found at Qumran, which is located just where Pliny places his "tribe of the Essenes": on the
western shore of the Dead Sea, south of Jericho and north of Ein
Gedi.[4] The rest of the coast has been scoured by archeologists
without turning up the remains of any settlement that could rival
Qumran as the Essene city that Pliny describes. Pliny's description
of an all-male community also fits the archeology of the site, as
the ancient cemetery adjacent to it consisted almost exclusively of
individual graves with male skeletons, and almost no female-
gendered artifacts were discovered within the buildings or caves.[5]

Pliny is the only ancient author who describes an Essene settlement specifically on the shores of the Dead Sea, but other authors
tell us much more about the Essenes in general. In fact, one such
author, Flavius Josephus (A.D. 37–100), usually known simply as
Josephus, is such an important source on the Essenes that it would
be good to say a little bit about him before going further.

Josephus was born Joseph son of Matthias around A.D. 37 in the region of Jerusalem. His father was a priest and his mother a descendant of the royal house of Israel. His family was part of the Jewish elite, and when war broke out between Rome and Judea in A.D. 66, he was appointed the military governor of Galilee. Josephus was an able commander but was eventually defeated and captured by Vespasian, the Roman general. After his capture, Josephus threw in his lot completely with the Roman victors, and later served as advisor and translator for Vespasian's son Titus, who commanded the Roman armies during the fateful siege that ended in the destruction of Jerusalem in A.D. 70. When Vespasian later became Roman emperor, he heaped honors on Josephus and granted him a pension. Josephus took the name of the imperial family (Flavian), styling himself Flavius Josephus in Roman society. He lived out his days in Rome, writing two massive works, *The Jewish War,* an account of the disastrous revolt of the Jews from A.D. 66 to 70 and the events leading up to it, and *The Antiquities of the Jews,* a history of the Jewish people from creation to his own day, much of which is based on the Bible.

Josephus gives not one but three lengthy descriptions of the Essenes in his works, as well as numerous incidental references.[6] He classifies the Essenes along with the Pharisees and Sadducees as one of the three primary Jewish sects, or "philosophical schools," on the analogy of classical philosophical schools like the Pythagoreans, Stoics, and Epicureans. The Sadducees consisted of the chief priests and other wealthy aristocrats who controlled the Temple and the capital city, Jerusalem. Focused on blessings in this life, they accepted only the five books of Moses (the Pentateuch) as Scripture, and rejected anything not explicit in them, like an afterlife, angels, or spirits.[7] The Pharisees were a more scholarly movement that emphasized the study of Scripture and wanted all Jews to live by high standards of ritual purity. They accepted a larger group of sacred books similar to the modern Jewish Bible or Protestant Old Testament, and Josephus himself ended up identifying with them. Despite that, he seemed more fascinated with the Essenes, as he records far more information about them than about the other two sects.

"Essene" probably derives from the Hebrew word *'ôssîm,* "doers," meaning "doers of the law," although other etymologies have been proposed.[8] The Essenes accepted a larger number of inspired books than the Sadducees or Pharisees, including writings that are now considered apocryphal by Jews and most Christians, such as the *Book of Jubilees* and the various books that make up *1 Enoch.* Like the Pharisees, they also accepted angels and demons, heaven and hell, judgment and resurrection, and the authority of oral tradition. But Josephus mentions other peculiarities of this group: They lived a life of poverty and held goods in common, rejecting private property and indulgence in physical pleasures. Most eschewed family life and lived in celibate male community, sharing a common table and living a common life. They devoted themselves to the study of Scripture, and especially to prophecy, having many prophets among them and being renowned for the accuracy of their predictions. They dressed in simple white garments and every day underwent a sacred bath followed by a common meal hosted by a priest who blessed the bread and wine.

Fascinatingly, almost everything that Josephus says about the Essenes can be corroborated or at least correlated with passages from the Scrolls or the archeological remains of the buildings and caves at Qumran.[9]

For example, Josephus describes the Essenes as practicing a daily ritual washing, and more ritual baths were found at Qumran than at any comparable site from the time period—enough to accommodate hundreds of men bathing in a short amount of time.

Another example is Josephus's description of the Essenes as consisting of basically two orders: one celibate and the other marrying:

120. These Essenes reject pleasures as an evil, but esteem continence, and the conquest over our passions, to be virtue. They
neglect wedlock, but choose out other persons' children, while
they are pliable, and fit for learning; and esteem them to be of
their kindred, and form them according to their own manners.

160. Moreover, there is another order of Essenes, who agree
with the rest as to their way of living, and customs, and laws,
but differ from them in the point of marriage, as thinking that
by not marrying they cut off the principal part of the human
life, which is the prospect of succession; nay rather, that if all
men should be of the same opinion, the whole race of man-
kind would fail.[10]

Strikingly, a central passage from one of the constitutional documents among the Dead Sea Scrolls (the so-called Damascus
Document) reflects this very division into two orders:

In short, for all who conduct their lives by these laws, *in perfect
holiness,* according to all the instructions, God's covenant
stands firm to give them life for thousands of generations.
    But if they live in camps according to the rule of the land
and marry women and beget children, then let them live in
accordance with the Law, and by the ordinance of vows according to the rule of the Law.[11]

This fascinating passage describes two ways of life for those in
the movement.[12] First, there is the path of "perfect holiness" (Heb.
tamîm qôdesh). The word "perfect" here (*tamîm*) has the sense of
"complete" or "whole." Such a lifestyle involved abstention from
many things, including sexual intercourse, which—according to
Mosaic Law—made one ritually unclean. Thus, one who engaged
regularly in the marital act could not be "*completely* holy." There-

fore, the men of "perfect" or "complete holiness" rejected the married life, but the document assures them that, though they have no natural progeny, they will gain eternal life "for a thousand generations."[13]

On the other hand, those who married and lived in Essene communities scattered throughout Israel—described as "camps" in the "land"—were held to a lower standard of religious behavior. It was enough for them to "live in accordance with the Law"—which really meant in accordance with the Essene *interpretation* of the laws of Moses, which frequently differed from those of other sects.

In the time of Jesus and the Apostles, there were Essene communities in all the significant towns and cities of Israel, including Jerusalem. We don't know how many belonged to the marrying order and how many to the celibate, but the classical authors give the impression that the majority were single men living in community. All the evidence suggests that Qumran was such a community, where the men slept in the natural caves and used the buildings for work, prayer, meals, study, and the copying of sacred books. The large number of books they wrote, preserved, and collected represents an incredible expenditure of time and money in ancient society, and thus it is reasonable to suppose that Qumran served as a center of learning for the larger Essene movement. We now turn to a quick overview of some of the more important books in their impressive library.

The Most Important Scrolls Found

As mentioned in the previous section, the remains of what once were a thousand individual scrolls were found in the eleven caves at Qumran. A quarter were "biblical" scrolls, and the rest, with some exceptions, were writings of the sect itself. Scholars give a technical name to each scroll, usually consisting of the number of the cave in which it was found (e.g., "1Q" means "first Qumran cave") followed by a name or acronym (for famous scrolls) or the number of its discovery (for most scrolls). Most of them are in such fragmentary condition that we can only make educated guesses about what they contained, but the following are ten of the best-preserved and most important scrolls in the collection:

1. The Great Isaiah Scroll (1QIsaiah^a, the first copy of Isaiah found in Cave 1). This complete copy of the Book of Isaiah in almost pristine condition is the longest, best-preserved, and among the oldest copies of any biblical book found at Qumran. Dating from c. 125 B.C., it is the most photographed of the Scrolls, since it still *looks* like a scroll, whereas the vast majority of the rest of the Scrolls consist of small scraps of inscribed leather pieced together by scholars. It contains the Hebrew text of the Book of Isaiah in a form similar to the traditional Jewish text (the "Masoretic Text") still chanted in synagogues today.

2. The *Community Rule* (1QSerek-ha-Yahad, or simply 1QS). This document is arguably the oldest example of the rule genre in Western civilization. A "rule" in this sense is the constitution of a religious order or sect, like the Rule of St. Benedict or the Rule of St. Francis. Buddhist monasticism also has rules. The *Community Rule* of Qumran regulated the common life of a community of Jewish men living in the buildings on the site. Their lives, like the lives of monks in other religions, consisted of a daily routine of prayer, work, study of Scriptures, worship, and the necessities of life, like eating and sleeping. In subsequent chapters, we will quote frequently from the *Community Rule* and discuss the life and beliefs of this monastic community in great detail.

3. The Damascus Document (CD). This document was originally called the Covenant of Damascus, and is still typically abbreviated "CD" by scholars. It describes the history, aims, and some of the constitutional laws of the larger Essene movement to which the Qumran community belonged. Many of its terms and concepts are also found in the *Community Rule*. Several fragmentary copies of this text were found among the Scrolls. Western scholars recognized it immediately, because a more complete copy of it had already been discovered in the document storage room (*genizah*) of one of the oldest synagogues in Cairo, Egypt, in 1897.

4. The War Scroll (1QM, for *Milhamah*, Hebrew for "battle" or "war"). This apocalyptic document describes the Qumran community's view of what Christians call "Armageddon," that is, the final battle of the forces of Good and Evil at the end of history. The Qumranites had it all planned out, to the very specifics of which tribes of Israel would lead the charge into battle on each day of the final war, the decoration of their banners, and the weapons they would use.

5. The Temple Scroll (11QTemple). This scroll purports to be instructions from God to Moses concerning how to govern the Jerusalem Temple. The Qumranites did not agree with how the chief priests in Jerusalem were governing the Temple in their own day; they believed instead that the Messiah would give control of the Temple to the Essenes in the latter days. Thus, the Temple Scroll describes the rules they planned to implement when the Temple was under their control.

6. 4QMMT, short for *Miqsat Ma'asei Ha-Torah,* meaning "Some of the Works of the Law." This text is a letter from the men of Qumran to the Pharisees in Jerusalem concerning

twenty or so different issues of ritual purity, including how to handle leather, dogs, corpses, liquids poured from one vessel to another, and similar matters. The Pharisees were too loose in their practice of the ritual laws of Moses, so the men of Qumran wrote to exhort them to greater diligence.

7. The *Pesharim,* such as 1QpHab (Pesher Habbakuk), 4QpNah (Pesher Nahum), and 4QpPs[a] (Pesher Psalms). *Pesher* is Hebrew for "interpretation," and the plural of *Pesher* is *Pesharim.* The *Pesharim* is the collection of commentaries on biblical books found among the Scrolls. Some of the best-known *Pesharim* are those on Nahum, Habakkuk, and the Psalms. These *Pesharim* interpret the prophetic books of the Bible as predicting key historic events in the life of the Qumran community, but use jargon understood only by community members. They speak of a "Teacher of Righteousness" who founded the community, and his conflict with hostile characters like the "Wicked Priest" and the "Man of Lies." Scholars have used the *Pesharim* to try to reconstruct the history of the community based on these cryptic references to fulfilled prophecies, but the reconstructions are uncertain.

8. The Psalms of Thanksgiving (1QHodayot[a] or 1QH[a] is the most important copy). Better known to scholars by their Hebrew name *Hodayot* ("Thanksgivings"), these are extrabiblical psalms of praise composed probably by the founder (or one of the founders) of the community, perhaps the "Teacher of Righteousness" mentioned in the *Pesharim.* The author was aware of having a divine mission to serve and lead the true community of God's people, almost like a messianic self-consciousness. Scholars have often been intrigued by the possible parallels to Jesus' self-awareness of his messianic vocation.

9. The Melchizedek Document (11QMelchizedek). One of the last scrolls discovered, 11QMelchizedek brings together various biblical texts and interprets them as predicting the return of the priest-king Melchizedek (Gen 14:18) at the end of time, when he would declare a Year of Jubilee for all the righteous. Based on the biblical Jubilee Year (Lev 25:10), which freed slaves and restored sold land to its original owner, the end-times Year of Jubilee proclaimed by Melchizedek would free the righteous from their debt of sin and from their slavery to the Devil.

10. The Rule of the Congregation (1QS^a, meaning "the first appendix to 1QS"). This is an end-times, or "eschatological," document, describing how the entire nation of Israel would be governed and organized when the Messiah (or Messiahs) arrived. This is a short document, and there is only one copy extant, which was written as an appendix to the *Community Rule* from Cave 1. In essence, with the coming of the Messiah, the rules of the community would be adjusted and extended to cover the whole nation of Israel.

We now have a brief but sufficient overview of the religious community that lived at Qumran, and the contents of the library they left us. The question remains to be answered, however, why they had withdrawn from society and chosen to live in this hostile and remote location.

The Dead Sea Scrolls, largely discovered between 1946 and 1956, are the remains of the library of a religious community of Jewish men that flourished on the northwest shore of the

Dead Sea in the last centuries B.C. and first century A.D. This community belonged to the larger Essene movement, a branch or sect of ancient Judaism that strove for holiness through a demanding, ascetical lifestyle. The documents recovered among the Scrolls included books of the Bible, religious rules, apocalyptic literature, hymns, prophecies, and commentaries on Scripture.

For Further Reading

Collins, John J. *The Dead Sea Scrolls: A Biography.* Princeton: Princeton University Press, 2013. A clear, readable introduction by an expert in the field.

Schiffman, Lawrence H. *Reclaiming the Dead Sea Scrolls.* Philadelphia: Jewish Publication Society, 1994. A lengthy and robustly Jewish introduction to and interpretation of the Scrolls.

VanderKam, James C. *The Dead Sea Scrolls Today.* 2nd ed. Grand Rapids, MI: Eerdmans, 2010. A reliable, easy-to-read overview of Qumran and the Scrolls.

VanderKam, James C., and Peter W. Flint. *The Meaning of the Dead Sea Scrolls: Their Significance for Understanding the Bible, Judaism, Jesus, and Christianity.* San Francisco: HarperCollins, 2002. A thorough, technical introduction to the Scrolls for the more advanced reader.

CHAPTER 2

Waiting for the Messiah

THE MEN OF QUMRAN WERE LIVING OUT IN THE DESERT waiting for the Messiah to show up. Isaiah 40:3 says, "A voice is crying out: 'In the wilderness prepare the way of the Lord, make straight in the desert a highway for our God.'" The Qumranites took this literally. They took "the way of the Lord" and the "highway for our God" as references to the route the Messiah and his entourage would take when he processed up to the Holy City in the last days. From the perspective of Jerusalem, the spiritual center of Judaism, the "wilderness" and "desert" were directly east, consisting of the wasteland on the way down to the Dead Sea. Some biblical prophets had also predicted that the Lord would return to Jerusalem from the East when all things were restored.[1] So the men of Qumran headed directly east from Jerusalem until they hit the Dead Sea, and there they set up camp to await the coming of the Messiah, along the route they expected him to take. Their sentiments were very similar to those of the American spiritual that says, "Oh, when the saints go marching in! I want to be in that number, when the saints go marching in!"

The term "Messiah" comes from the Hebrew word *mashiach*, "someone anointed with oil," from the verb *mashach*, "to anoint with oil." The Greek equivalent is *christos*, from the verb *chriô*. The literal English translation of *mashiach* or *christos* would be

"Anointed One." In ancient Israel, religious or civil leaders were often anointed to mark the beginnings of their careers of leadership. Kings and priests were always anointed at the starts of their reigns, and sometimes prophets as well. Late in the history of Biblical Israel, when the kingdoms of Israel and Judah were in steep decline, prophets arose who promised that at some time in the future, an anointed leader would arise to restore the people to their former glory. In the few centuries before the birth of Jesus, it became common in Judaism to combine some or all of the various prophecies into one general expectation that a final Anointed One, a "Messiah," would arise to restore Israel. Opinions varied as to whether this Messiah would primarily be a prophet, a priest, or a king—or fill multiple roles.[2]

Some have argued that the Qumran community was itself founded by a Messiah figure. Their own writings refer frequently to a certain "Teacher of Righteousness" who organized them and established their doctrine. Many scholars think this Teacher was the high priest of the Jerusalem Temple who was forced out by the Maccabean king Jonathan Apphus. Jonathan illegitimately claimed the office of High Priest for himself in 152 B.C. The legitimate High Priest was then exiled and founded the community by the Dead Sea to preserve fidelity of faith and practice until God acted to restore the legitimate priesthood and kingship.[3] Another theory is that the Teacher was the founder not just of Qumran but of the larger Essene movement of which Qumran was a part.

It is also widely believed that this Teacher of Righteousness composed many of the unique thanksgiving psalms found among the Scrolls, especially the Thanksgiving Hymns document (Hodayot).[4] These psalms reveal the intimate relationship the Teacher had with God, and his self-consciousness of having a unique, divinely given vocation to lead God's people. Many have observed similarities between this Teacher and Jesus of Nazareth, as both were conscious of God's unique call on their lives, and both founded communities by establishing a new covenant with representatives of the people of Israel. The scholar Michael O. Wise even published a book on the Teacher of Righteousness called *The First Messiah*.[5]

However, for all the formal similarities between the Teacher and Jesus, it is not correct to characterize the Teacher as a "Messiah." He never claimed that title, nor did the Qumranites apply it to him. The Teacher himself seemed to be waiting for the Messiah, and he taught the men of Qumran to do the same. For example, the Damascus Document warns about backsliders as follows:

> They shall not be reckoned among the council of the people, and their names shall not be written in their book from the day the Beloved Teacher dies until the Messiah from Aaron and from Israel appears. (CD 19:35–36)

As this statement indicates, after the death of the Teacher, they were actually expecting *two* Messiahs, a priestly one from the line of Aaron and a royal one from the line of David. They termed these two messiahs "the Messiah of Aaron and the Messiah of Israel." A section of the *Community Rule* instructs the Qumranites to stay faithful to their founding vision until these two Messiahs appear:

> They shall govern themselves using the original precepts by which the men of the Yahad began to be instructed, doing so until there come the Prophet and the Messiahs of Aaron and Israel. (1QS 9:10–11)

Scholars call this expectation of two messiahs "diarchic messianism" (die-ARK-ick MESS-ee-ahn-izm). It's probably based on several prophetic texts that affirm God's faithfulness to the royal and priestly dynasties of Israel. For example, Jeremiah 33 insists that the House of Levi will never lack a man to function as priest before the LORD, and the House of David will never lack a man to serve as king. The implication of this promise is that God will one day restore both houses. Likewise, the prophet Zechariah famously sees a vision of two olive trees, which represent two "sons of oil" who stand by the LORD (Zech 4:14). These could easily be interpreted as two Messiahs, royal and priestly, to arise in the future.

Diarchic messianism seems to have been the dominant expectation at Qumran. But at least one document appears to represent a "minority report," an alternative messianic expectation focused on the return of the mysterious biblical figure Melchizedek, who was both a priest and a king (Gen 14:18–20). This document was found in Cave 11, and since the content focuses largely on Melchizedek, scholars call it "11QMelchizedek."

Although 11QMelchizedek is in fragmentary condition, we can read it well enough to realize that it is a prophecy that combines several biblical texts related to the Year of Jubilee and applies them to Melchizedek, who will return at the end of time.[6]

The ancient Israelites celebrated the Year of Jubilee every forty-nine years by blowing a trumpet throughout the land, proclaiming the forgiveness of outstanding debts, the return of all family property sold for debt, and the release of all debt-slaves. Every Israelite was to return to his property, and have his property returned to him.

Unfortunately, over the centuries, the Israelites observed the jubilee sporadically if at all. In time, the prophets saw it more as an end-times expectation than a living law.[7] Isaiah foresaw an anointed "servant of the LORD" who would announce an end-times Jubilee Year:

The Spirit of the Lord GOD is upon me, because the LORD has anointed me to bring good tidings to the afflicted; he has sent me to bind up the brokenhearted, to proclaim liberty to the captives, and the opening of the prison to those who are bound; to proclaim the year of the LORD's favor. (Isa 61:1–2)

Likewise, Daniel prophesied that a Messiah would arrive after a perfect set of ten jubilee cycles, bringing to an end the travails of Jerusalem. The angel Gabriel tells him:

Seventy weeks of years are decreed concerning your people and your holy city, to finish the transgression, to put an end to sin, and to atone for iniquity, to bring in everlasting righteousness, to seal both vision and prophet, and to anoint a Holy of Holies.[8] Know therefore and understand that from the going forth of the word to restore and build Jerusalem to the coming of Messiah, a prince,[9] there shall be seven weeks and sixty-two weeks.[10] It shall be built again with squares and moat, but in a troubled time. And after the sixty-two weeks, Messiah shall be cut off, and shall have nothing. (Dan 9:24–26 RSV *alt.*, cf. LXX; emphasis mine)

"Seventy weeks of years" are 490 years, or ten jubilee cycles of 49 years each.[11] The English of Daniel 9:24–26 used here follows all the ancient translations of this passage, which describe the "Messiah, a prince" as coming "seven and sixty-two weeks" (that is, 69 weeks of years or 483 years) after the decree to rebuild Jerusalem. Read this way, the Messiah appears one "week of years" before the final culmination of the whole 490-year period. In other words, the Messiah shows up shortly before all things are fulfilled.

The prophecy 11QMelchizedek combines both these passages

of Isaiah and Daniel, as well as verses from Leviticus 25, the jubilee law, and connects them to the return of Melchizedek:

Reading Fragmentary Scrolls

Most of the Scrolls are in fragmentary condition, with large pieces of text missing, or only small pieces of text still present. Sometimes, however, scholars are able to reconstruct, or at least make an educated guess at, the words that are missing. The standard practice is to place these reconstructed words inside brackets [ ], but in this book we print them in a lighter font. The document 11QMelchizedek has many holes, but scholars have been able to fill in much of the missing text because of frequent biblical quotations and the repetition of characteristic phrases.

And concerning what Scripture says, "In this year of jubilee you shall return, every one of you, to your property" (Lev 25:13) . . . the interpretation is that it applies to the Last Days and concerns the captives, just as Isaiah said: "To proclaim the jubilee to the captives" (Isa 61:1) . . . and whose teachers have been hidden and kept secret, even from the inheritance of Melchizedek, for . . . and they are the inheritance of Melchizedek, who will return them to what is rightfully theirs. He will proclaim to them the jubilee, thereby releasing them from the debt of all their sins. This word will thus come in the first week of the jubilee period that follows nine jubilee periods. Then the "Day of Atonement" shall follow at the end of the tenth jubilee period, when he shall atone for all the Sons of Light and the people who are predestined to Melchizedek. (11QMelch 2:1–8)

We see how the ancient sage interprets the jubilee law (Lev 25:13) in light of Isaiah's jubilee prophecy (Isa 61:1) and works in the chronology of Daniel's ten jubilees. However, Melchizedek's jubilee won't be about money debt; it will release people from the "debt of all their sins." Furthermore, they will be freed not just from earthly slavery but from bondage to the Devil, as the document explains later:

> Therefore Melchizedek will thoroughly prosecute the vengeance required by God's statutes. In that day he will deliver them from the power of Belial, and from the power of all the spirits predestined to him. (11QMelch 2:13)

The Essenes seemed to have a very high view of Melchizedek, because they interpreted passages of Isaiah speaking about God as applying to this ancient priest-king:

> It is written concerning him, "who says to Zion 'Your God reigns'" (Isa 52:7). "Zion" is the congregation of all the sons of righteousness, who uphold the covenant and turn from walking in the way of the people. "Your God" is Melchizedek, who will deliver them from the power of Belial. Concerning what Scripture says, "Then you shall have the trumpet sounded loud in all the land of . . ." (Lev 25:9, modified). (11QMelch 2:23–25)

Summing up, 11QMelchizedek presents an alternate view of the end-times, focused not on the twin Messiahs of Aaron and Israel but on a single priest-king figure, the almost-divine Melchizedek, who will proclaim a supernatural jubilee freeing God's people from the debt of sin and slavery to Satan.

We see parallels in the Gospels. For example, it is absolutely fascinating to read the first few chapters of Luke while keeping in mind the Essene expectations about the Messiah. In fact, the background of the Scrolls may illuminate some of the unique and unusual features of Luke. For example, Luke opens with the lineage and origins of *John the Baptist,* not Jesus, and the early chapters turn into a kind of double biography of Jesus and the Baptist. Luke alone of the Gospel writers lets us know of John's *priestly lineage* through his father, Zechariah, who was a practicing priest in the Temple, and high enough in status and bloodline to be among those who were candidates to burn incense in the Holy Place, a noble duty (Luke 1:8–9). Why does Luke pay so much attention to the circumstances of John's birth and his early life and ministry? There are many possible reasons, but when we read this Gospel with Essene eyes, John looks very much like the promised "Messiah of Aaron," a priestly Messiah who "anoints a Holy of Holies," namely Jesus himself, who is the replacement of the Temple. To Jesus, then, falls the role of the Messiah of Israel, and Luke includes Jesus' Davidic genealogy (Luke 3:23–31; cf. 1:27, 32, 69; 2:4) to drive home the point. The Essenes also knew the royal Messiah had to be from David's line:

> And the one who sits on the throne of David shall never be cut off, because the "ruler's staff" (Gen 49:10) is the covenant of the kingdom, and the thousands of Israel are "the feet," until the Righteous Messiah, the Branch of David, has come. For to him and to his seed the covenant of the kingdom of His people has been given for the eternal generations, because he has kept [. . .] the Law with the men of the Yahad. (4Q252 5:2–5)

Notice that the Essenes understand the Messiah to be heir of the "*covenant* of the kingdom," recalling that David's kingdom was established by a divine covenant (2 Sam 5:3; 2 Chr 13:5; Ps 89:3–4). The connection of Davidic kingdom and covenant will also show up in Luke at the Last Supper, but we will look at that in chapter 8.

Getting back to Luke's introduction, as we read through the Infancy Narratives (Luke 1–2), we see a surprising number of connections with the Qumran literature. For example, at the Annunciation, the angel Gabriel tells Mary:

> "And behold, you will conceive in your womb and bear a son, and you shall call his name Jesus. He will be great, and will be called the Son of the Most High; and the Lord God will give to him the throne of his father David, and he will reign over the house of Jacob forever; and of his kingdom there will be no end." (Luke 1:31–33)

This sounds a lot like a messianic prophecy that was found among the Scrolls and dated to the reign of Herod the Great (37 b.c.–4 b.c.), or shortly before the birth of Jesus:

> Great will he be called and he will be designated by his name. He will be called son of God, and they will call him Son of the Most High. . . . His kingdom will be an eternal kingdom, and all his paths in truth. He will judge the earth in truth and all will make peace. The sword will cease from the earth, and all the provinces will pay him homage. The great God is his strength, he will wage war for him; he will place the peoples in his hand and cast them all away before him. His rule will be an eternal rule.[12] (4Q246 1:9–2:9)

Mary responds to Gabriel, "How can this be? For I do not know a man" (Luke 1:34), which is a bit of an odd reply. The Benedictine Bible scholar and archeologist Bargil Pixner argued that "I do not know a man" refers to a vow of celibacy, and that Mary was part of the Essene movement, who were the only sect to practice celibacy.[13] This is possible, but very speculative. We don't have any clear evidence of female celibacy among the Essenes.

As we continue reading Luke's account, we find that he describes the parents of Jesus and John as spontaneously composing spiritual songs that begin with a statement of praise and resemble the biblical psalms (see the "Magnificat," 1:46–55; and the "Benedictus," 1:68–79). We have no record of the Pharisees or Sadducees composing new songs in the biblical psalm tradition, but ample attestation of this practice at Qumran, where we have dozens of "Thanksgiving Hymns" (better, "Thanksgiving Psalms") composed by the Teacher of Righteousness and perhaps others as well. The songs of Mary and Zechariah in Luke 1 would appeal in form and theme to Jews of an Essene background, as would Jesus' remarkable wisdom (Luke 2:46–47), almost all of John's actions and teaching (3:1–20, see later in this chapter on John the Baptist), and Jesus' reception of the Holy Spirit in the water (3:21–22).

However, it is at Jesus' first sermon at his hometown of Nazareth that we observe some rather specific connections with Essene expectations. Here is Luke's account:

> And he came to Nazareth, where he had been brought up; and he went to the synagogue, as his custom was, on the sabbath day. And he stood up to read; and there was given to him the book of the prophet Isaiah. He opened the book and found the place where it was written, "The Spirit of the Lord is upon me, because he has anointed me to preach good news to the poor. He has sent me to proclaim release to the captives and recovering of sight to the blind, to set at liberty those who are oppressed, to proclaim the acceptable year of the Lord" (Isa 61:1–2). And he closed the book, and gave it back to the attendant, and sat down; and the eyes of all in the synagogue were fixed on him. (Luke 4:16–20)

Everyone was looking at Jesus, because when he sat down, it was a sign that he was about to preach. Unlike Christian preachers, Jewish rabbis preached from a chair, sometimes called "the seat of Moses" (Matt 23:2), the idea being that they continued Moses' teaching ministry. There was tension in the air, because he had just read a passage that all Jews considered significant, but the Essenes in particular connected with Melchizedek and the proclamation of the final jubilee. What will Jesus say about this passage?

And he began to say to them, "Today this scripture has been fulfilled in your hearing." (Luke 4:21)

In other words, "I am the one Isaiah is describing here: the one anointed by the LORD to proclaim the jubilee and restore Israel. I am the fulfillment of the passage!"

That was absolutely electrifying, especially for Jews formed in Essenism, who associated Isaiah's "one anointed by the Spirit" with a nearly divine Melchizedek! Was Jesus of Nazareth the Melchizedek who was to come? Yet talk is cheap! Can he back up words with deeds?

Well, let's look at what Jesus does just a few days later, in the same chapter of Luke:

And he went down to Capernaum. . . . And in the synagogue there was a man who had the spirit of an unclean demon; and he cried out with a loud voice, "Ah! What have you to do with us, Jesus of Nazareth? Have you come to destroy us? I know who you are, the Holy One of God." But Jesus rebuked him, saying, "Be silent, and come out of him!" And when the demon had thrown him down in the midst, he came out of him, having done him no harm. And they were all amazed and said to one another, "What is this word? For with authority and power he commands the unclean spirits, and they come

out." And reports of him went out into every place in the surrounding region. (Luke 4:31–37 RSV)

Didn't the Essenes say about Melchizedek, "In that day he will
deliver them from the power of Belial, and from the power of all
the spirits predestined to (Belial)"? (11QMelch 2:13)

And then in the next chapter, Jesus performs another action
associated with divine authority:

On one of those days, as he was teaching. . . . And behold, men
were bringing on a bed a man who was paralyzed, and they
sought to bring him in and lay him before Jesus; but finding no
way to bring him in, because of the crowd, they went up on the
roof and let him down with his bed through the tiles into the
midst before Jesus. And when he saw their faith he said, "Man,
your sins are forgiven you." And the scribes and the Pharisees
began to question, saying, "Who is this that speaks blasphe-
mies? *Who can forgive sins but God only?*" When Jesus perceived
their questionings, he answered them, "Why do you question
in your hearts? Which is easier, to say, 'Your sins are forgiven
you,' or to say, 'Rise and walk'? But that you may know that the
Son of man has authority on earth to forgive sins"—he said to
the man who was paralyzed—"I say to you, rise, take up your
bed and go home." And immediately he rose before them, and
took up that on which he lay, and went home, glorifying God.
And amazement seized them all, and they glorified God and
were filled with awe, saying, "We have seen strange things
today." (Luke 5:17–26 RSV; emphasis mine)

Did not the Essenes say of Melchizedek, "He will proclaim to
them the jubilee, thereby releasing them from the debt of all
their sins"? (11QMelch 2:6)

So we can see that an Essene reading Luke's Gospel would find the figures of John and Jesus answering to the expectation of the "Messiahs of Aaron and Israel." Further, he would see Jesus fulfilling everything that was expected of the godlike Melchizedek! After all, Jesus proclaims the fulfillment of the jubilee in Isaiah 61:1–2, and follows through by releasing people from the power of *Satan* and *sin*.

There are many possible explanations for why the early chapters of Luke have so many connections with the Scrolls—some believe that the families of Jesus and John were involved in some way with the Essene movement.[14] But regardless, we can certainly say that for Jews who were raised in Essenism or shared the Essene messianic expectations, the Gospel of Luke makes for compelling reading, and the figure of Jesus appears boldly as one who fits the criteria of the expected Anointed One of Israel.

To this day, the Christian Church is a community waiting for the arrival of the Messiah. This expectation has many expressions, from the popular Left Behind books of Protestant author Tim LaHaye to the prayer used by Catholics at every Mass: "Deliver us, Lord, we pray, from every evil . . . as we await the blessed hope and the coming of our Savior, Jesus Christ." But before the Church was founded, the Essenes were already a "community in waiting." This spirit of messianic expectation is a major common feature of both movements. In subsequent chapters, we will see other common characteristics that are even more specific.

The devout men of Qumran were waiting in the desert for the appearance of the Messiah, in accordance with Isaiah 40:3. Actually, they expected two Messiahs, a royal and a priestly. But one of their documents focuses messianic hope on a mysterious Melchizedek, who will arise at the end of time to proclaim a supernatural Jubilee Year. Someone shaped by Qumran beliefs would find the Gospel of Luke fascinating reading, because the way Luke describes John the Baptist and Jesus answers many of these expectations.

For Further Reading

Abegg, Martin. "The Messiah at Qumran: Are We Still Seeing Double?" *Dead Sea Discoveries* 2, no. 2 (1995): 125–144.

Collins, John J. "Ideas of Messianism in the Dead Sea Scrolls." Pages 20–41 in *The Dead Sea Scrolls and the Christian Faith.* Edited by James H. Charlesworth and Walter P. Weaver. Harrisburg, PA: Trinity Press International, 1998.

Knohl, Israel. "Melchizedek: A Model for the Union of Kingship and Priesthood in the Hebrew Bible, 11QMelchizedek, and the Epistle to the Hebrews." Pages 255–262 in *Text, Thought and Practice in Qumran and Early Christianity: Proceedings of the Ninth International Symposium of the Orion Center for the Study of the Dead Sea Scrolls and Associated Literature.* Edited by Daniel R. Schwartz et al. Studies on the Texts of the Desert of Judah 84. Leiden: Brill, 2009.

PART TWO

BAPTISM
AND THE SCROLLS

CHAPTER 3

The Scrolls,
John the Baptist, and Baptism

BY ALL ACCOUNTS, JOHN THE BAPTIST WAS A SENSATION IN his own time. In an age before reality TV or shock-jock radio, John's politically incorrect diatribes against leaders of Church and State were religiously profound, yes—but also great entertainment for the populace. The powerful effect this ancient Jewish prophet had on the society of his day is reflected in how frequently he is mentioned in the Gospels, often at key moments in Jesus' ministry. Ancient Christianity recognized his importance, and both the Western (Latin) and Eastern (Greek) Churches traditionally have granted him more feast days than anyone but Mary, Mother of the Lord. In European Catholic church buildings, shrines to the Blessed Mother and the Baptist (not St. Joseph) traditionally flanked the main sanctuary. Is he still important to contemporary culture? Let's look at it in this way: based on statistics about world Christianity, we can estimate that every third human being on the planet has undergone a water washing for the forgiveness of their sins at some point in their life, and arguably this widespread human cultural practice can be traced historically back to the influence of John the Baptist.

What can the Dead Sea Scrolls tell us about him?

In my opinion, quite a bit.

Perhaps the greatest expert on the Gospel of John in the twentieth century, Fr. Raymond Brown, once remarked that "virtually everyone who has studied the Qumran texts in the light of the New Testament has recognized the startling Qumran parallels in the narratives concerning John the Baptist; almost every detail of his life and preaching has a *possible* Qumran affinity."[1] Indeed, the circumstantial case that John had contact with the Essenes at Qumran is very strong.[2] The Essenes were the only sect of the Jews that produced prophets, observed strict asceticism, and practiced celibacy; and all that describes John: a celibate, ascetic prophet preaching repentance before an imminent judgment—a message also found abundantly in the Scrolls. But many of the connections between John and the Essenes are much more specific.

First of all, they were active in the same area. We know from the Gospels that John preached and baptized "in the wilderness of Judea" (Matt 3:1), which refers to the desert areas to the east and downhill from Jerusalem. The fact that great crowds from Jerusalem and Judea went out to him virtually requires that John was ministering along the southern Jordan River, not far from the Dead Sea, the most accessible section of the Jordan for the Jerusalem populace.[3] John probably spent part of his ministry in the territory of Perea across the Jordan from Jericho, as this place was a major trade route in antiquity. Goods and people crossed the Jordan here to the Jericho region and thence up to Jerusalem. Many Jews from Galilee would travel through this area in order to get to the Temple, because they preferred to cross the Jordan in the north and travel south through Perea and recross here rather than stay on their own side of the river and have to walk through hated Samaria, home of people they thought had impure blood and heterodox beliefs. So John the Baptist ministered in a strategic location where he would have access to thousands of Jews (and Gentiles, too) crossing the Jordan from one side to the other. Not coincidentally, this was also the general area where Joshua encamped the Israelites before invading the Promised Land, and Elijah was assumed into heaven. John may have wished to evoke the memory of both those events. Certainly, John intentionally dressed like Elijah with "a garment of haircloth, with a girdle of leather about his loins" (see 2 Kings 1:8). Camel's hair was coarse, and rarely used for garments, but more commonly for tents.

Our point is, at times in his ministry, John would have been baptizing as little as a half day's walk from Qumran. Both John and the Qumranites placed great emphasis on washing with water in conjunction with repentance for sins. We have seen that the Qumranites washed even daily but were insistent that without interior conversion, the ritual was ineffective:

> Through an upright and humble attitude his sin may be covered, and by humbling himself before all God's laws his flesh can be made clean. Only thus can he really receive the purifying waters and be purged by the cleansing flow. (1QS 3:8–10)

In the Damascus Document, the Essenes describe themselves repeatedly as the "repentant ones of Israel" (e.g., CD 6:5 *et passim*). Although the Qumranites washed daily, there is reason to think that the initial baptism they received upon swearing the oath and joining the covenant community was particularly dramatic and functioned as a sign of conversion, similar to the baptism John preached. However, John baptized anyone—not just devout Jewish men but the common people, women, and even Gentiles—without any process of initiation. There is a plausible reason for both the similarities to and differences from Qumran washing, but more on that in a moment.

The parallels between John and Qumran don't stop. For both the Baptist and this baptizing community, the Book of Isaiah was central to their theology, especially Isaiah 40:3:

A voice cries in the wilderness: "Prepare the way of the LORD, make straight in the desert a highway for our God."

Either John identifies himself with this verse or others identify him with it in all four Gospels.[4]

Unsurprisingly, the Qumran community also adopted this verse as central to their identity. When describing the repentant ones of Israel who founded their community, the *Community Rule* says:

When such men as these come to be in Israel, conforming to these doctrines, they shall separate from the session of perverse men to go to the wilderness, there to prepare the way of truth, as it is written, "In the wilderness prepare the way of the LORD, make straight in the desert a highway for our God" (Isaiah 40:3). (1QS 8:12–14)

As we saw earlier, this verse inspired the Qumranites to settle where they did. From the perspective of Jerusalem, Isaiah's "wilderness" is directly east, down toward the Dead Sea. Moreover, there was biblical reason to believe that God and/or the Messiah would return to Jerusalem one day from the East.[5] So the men of Qumran went directly east from Jerusalem until they hit the Dead Sea, and there they set up their community intent on "preparing the way for the LORD," which they probably associated with the coming of the messiah (or messiahs) in the eastern wilderness.

John claimed that he was preparing the way for one who was to come after him, who would "baptize with the Holy Spirit and with fire" (Luke 3:16). We've seen that the Qumran community likewise expected one or more messiahs to appear shortly, and the wicked would be judged by fire (1QS 4:13), while the righteous would be cleansed by the Holy Spirit (1QS 4:21). For the Essenes, God's glory was surrounded by "the fire of the great Spirit of perfect holiness" (4Q405).[6] No other Jewish sect put such emphasis on a soon-to-come judgment and the role of the Holy Spirit.

Is it just *coincidence* that John and the Qumranites are both "preparing the way for the LORD in the wilderness" within a few miles of each other, practicing baptism of repentance for the forgiveness of sins before the judgment and the outpouring of the Spirit?

But the plot thickens. Certain facts about Qumran give satisfying answers to otherwise very curious and inexplicable facts about John's person.

First, his diet. Mark records that John "ate locusts and wild honey" (Mark 1:6). What is the significance of that? These are both naturally occurring and ritually clean foods, to be sure, but why was he not eating normal human fare? Some suggest it was just a unique form of asceticism, and that is surely possible. But there is a more compelling answer. John is not the only desert-dwelling holy man eating off the land known to us from this time period. The historian Josephus recounts how, as a teenager, he endured a three-year apprenticeship to a very Baptist-like Jewish ascetic who lived in the same region where John was active. Josephus writes:

> When I was informed that one, whose name was Banus, lived in the desert, and used no other clothing than grew upon trees, and had no other food than what grew of its own accord, and bathed himself in cold water frequently, both by night and by day, in order to preserve his chastity, I imitated him in those things, and continued with him three years. (*Life* §11)

John, Banus, and the Qumranites were all living in the same area, practicing water washing and celibacy. John and Banus, in particular, were eating off the land. That cannot *merely* be a necessity of living in the desert region, because thousands of travelers moved through this area for trade and pilgrimage, and urban centers where human fare could be begged or borrowed (e.g., Jericho) were not far off. Elsewhere in his writings, Josephus provides us the clue to explain this peculiar behavior. When describing how a man was initiated into the Essene order, Josephus records the following:

> Before he is allowed to touch their common food, he is obliged to take tremendous oaths. . . . (*War* 2:139) But for those that are caught in any heinous sins, they cast them out of their society; and he who is thus separated from them, does often die after a miserable manner; for as he is bound by the oath he hath taken, and by the customs he hath been engaged in, *he is not at liberty to partake of that food that he meets with elsewhere, but is forced to eat grass,* and to famish his body with hunger till he perish; for which reason they receive many of them again when they are at their last gasp, out of compassion to them, as thinking the miseries they have endured till they come to the very brink of death, to be a sufficient punishment for the sins they had been guilty of. (*War* 2:143–144)

Again, is it just coincidental that Josephus describes those expelled from Qumran as being forced to wander around "eating grass"—apparently, anything edible in the environment—and that we have historical record of two men with strong connections with the practices of Qumran—John the Baptist and Banus—doing just that? Apparently, the oaths of membership to the covenant community of Qumran included a commitment never again to partake of food prepared outside the community. But a loophole to this vow was edible aspects of the environment that weren't prepared by anyone, and perhaps didn't qualify as "food" according to their oath. I suspect both Banus and the Baptist had been expelled from Qumran—I'll suggest why a little later.

But while we are still on this subject, it's further worth noticing that the Qumran documents actually prescribe a procedure for eating locusts. The Damascus Document declares: "Fish may not be eaten unless they are split open while living and their blood poured out, but all species of locust must be put in fire or water while they are alive, because that befits their nature" (CD 12:14–15). While locusts have been considered food and even a delicacy in different cultures and at different times, the only evidence we have of anyone in Israel eating locusts in the time of Jesus comes from the Dead Sea Scrolls and the Gospel passages about John the Baptist.[7]

The connections don't stop. The Scrolls may also explain another curious statement made about John. Luke summarizes his childhood and youth by saying, "And the child grew and became strong in spirit, and he was in the wilderness till the day of his manifestation to Israel" (Luke 1:80). Luke makes it sound like John grew up in the Judean desert; but did Zechariah and Elizabeth really shoo the young John out the door at age five to fend for himself in a barren wasteland? How does a child raise himself in such conditions? Josephus, however, mentions this about the Essenes:

> They neglect wedlock, but choose out other persons' children, while they are pliable, and fit for learning; and esteem them to be of their kindred, and form them according to their own manners. (War 2:120)

Could Zechariah and Elizabeth have sent their son to be raised by the Essenes, perhaps the very community at Qumran? Maybe, and there are additional reasons why they might have. Zechariah and Elizabeth were both from priestly families, and Zechariah's pedigree was good enough that he was a candidate for the solemn task of burning incense within the Temple (Luke 1:9). We know from the Scrolls that the Qumranites were excessively concerned with matters of priesthood, and were in fact led by "Zadokites," descendants of the high priest Zadok, who served under Solomon. According to Ezekiel, only priests descended from Zadok were qualified to serve in the Temple (Ezek 40:46). The legitimacy of the Jerusalem priesthood may have been an issue between the Essenes and other Jews. The Qumranites may have defended higher standards for the pedigree of the priesthood and recruited from among the priestly clans, and Zechariah may have sympathized with their position. In addition to these considerations, Zechariah and Elizabeth were already quite old when John was born, and they may have found it a relief to entrust his upbringing to others, or they may even have passed away while he was still young.

Although a century ago it was common for scholars to argue that Luke simply made up the Infancy Narratives (Luke 1–2), it is now clear that he was using Jewish sources for these chapters.[8] For example, the songs of Mary and Zechariah (the Magnificat and Benedictus) are clearly translated from Hebrew (or Aramaic) into Greek.[9] Luke was able to write idiomatic Greek, but the terms used in the Magnificat and Benedictus only make sense in Hebrew. Mary says: "He has helped his servant Israel, in remembrance of his mercy, as he spoke to our fathers." To "remember one's mercy" is a Hebrew idiom that doesn't make sense in Greek (or in English, for that matter). The terms "mercy" (Heb. *hesed*) and "covenant" (Heb. *berith*) are sometimes synonyms in Hebrew, and "to remember one's mercy" means "to remember one's covenant" (i.e., the obligations one has to one's covenant partner). Luke is translating word for word a Hebrew source, not creating something fictitious in Greek. In the previous chapter, we saw other parallels between Luke's opening chapters and the Hebrew documents at Qumran, such as this remarkable first-century-B.C.

oracle that sounds so much like Gabriel's annunciation to Mary in Luke 1:31–33:

> Great will he be called and he will be designated by his name. And he will be called son of God, and they will call him son of the Most High. . . . His kingdom will be an eternal kingdom, and all his paths in truth. He will judge the earth in truth and all will make peace. . . . His rule will be an eternal rule. (4Q246)[10]

Getting back to John the Baptist, we can make one final connection between him and the Essenes: his criticism of Herod Antipas's marriage to Herodias, which resulted in his beheading (Mark 6:18).

In general, the Essenes were stricter than all other Jewish sects in the regulation of marriage. The laws of Leviticus 18 forbid the marriage of nephew to aunt; the Essenes reasoned that what was true of one gender was true of the other, therefore their Damascus Document forbids marriages between niece and uncle (CD 5:7–11). And this is precisely the situation between Herod Antipas and Herodias, who were uncle and niece.

Furthermore, both Antipas and Herodias divorced their original spouses in order to marry each other, and there are passages of the Scrolls that seem to oppose multiple spouses in a lifetime. In a passage that criticizes a group cryptically called "the Shoddy-Wall Builders" (probably the Pharisees), the Damascus Document says:

> They are caught in . . . fornication, by taking two wives in their lifetimes, although the principle of creation is "male and female He created them" (Gen 1:27) and those who went into the ark "went into the ark two by two" (Gen 7:9) and concern-

ing the prince it is written, "He shall not multiply wives to himself" (Deut 17:17). (CD 4:20–5:2)

It is striking that the prohibitions of uncle-niece marriages as well as multiple marriages in a lifetime—especially for the "prince" or leader of the people—are next to each other in the Damascus Document (cols. 4–5). Herod Antipas's marriage to Herodias violated both principles, and John the Baptist vigorously opposed it (Luke 3:19).

So what are we to make of all the similarities between John the Baptist and Qumran? We can venture a scenario that admittedly can't be proven but does fit with all the known facts:

John the Baptist received some or all of his education from the Essenes at Qumran, either being sent to them by his parents at a young age or else joining them voluntarily when he was older. He got the characteristic features of his theology from them. However, John also studied the prophet Isaiah, who was greatly honored by the Qumran community—and through this study he eventually found himself at odds with the community that had formed him. For the prophet Isaiah clearly prophesied a coming salvation for *all nations,* in other words, *all the Gentiles.* For example, since in Hebrew and Greek the word for "nation" and "Gentile" is the same, the end of Isaiah can be read as follows:

> "I am coming to gather all Gentiles and tongues; and they shall come and shall see my glory, and I will set a sign among them. And from them I will send survivors to the Gentiles . . . that have not heard my fame or seen my glory; and they shall declare my glory among the Gentiles." (Isa 66:18–19 RSV *alt.*)

But when John pointed out this and similar passages of Isaiah to the superiors of the Qumran community, they wanted nothing to do with it. "No, there is no place in the world to come for the

Gentiles! There can only be separation between us and them! Not even the grain they grow can be brought into the Temple for offering!"

But John was insistent that God's message of salvation should go out to all the people, not just an elite among Israel—and the argument led to his expulsion from the community.

"Very well," thought John. "If the community will not prepare the way of the Lord by preaching repentance to all the people, I will do it myself." So, staying faithful to the oaths he had sworn at Qumran, he ate unprepared foods, continued his ascetic lifestyle, and began to preach at the fords of the Jordan, to the large numbers of people passing through on business or pilgrimage. When those he baptized asked how they should live the rest of their lives, John encouraged the ethic of simplicity and equality he had learned at Qumran: "He who has two tunics, let him share with him who has none, and he who has food, let him do likewise" (Luke 3:11 RSV *alt.*). For the Qumranites had all food and clothing in common, and each had only one tunic. But unlike the Qumranites, John turned no one away, not even the hated Roman-friendly tax collectors, whom he told: "Collect no more than is appointed you" (Luke 3:13). Nor the Roman soldiers themselves, whom he told, "Rob no one by violence or by false accusation, and be content with your wages" (Luke 3:14). In this way, John the Baptist truly *did* prepare a way for a Lord who would also preach to "tax collectors and sinners" (Matt 11:19).

Wrapping Up on John the Baptist

So that's my opinion of John the Baptist. Along with well-respected scholars like Otto Betz, Jean Cardinal Daniélou, James Charlesworth, and many others, I think he was educated with the Essenes and then left (in my opinion, was expelled) in order to preach more widely the message of baptism for repentance of sin. This is a plausible theory based on a large body of circumstantial evidence.[11]

What can we know for sure? We can say with certainty that, in light of the Dead Sea Scrolls and our other sources about the Essenes, John the Baptist fits extremely well in the time period and the geography in which the Gospels describe him. John the Baptist is no fiction created by the early Church. He is a living, breathing—indeed, shouting—historic figure of first-century Palestine who, through his relationship with Jesus and Jesus' disciples, had an enormous impact on world culture. In fact, one of the ways he affected world culture was his influence on another man of the same name, whose life and writings we will explore in the next chapter.

There are striking similarities between the teachings and lifestyle of John the Baptist and those of the Qumranites. John may have been raised or formed in the community and then left to pursue a ministry to a wider audience. The Dead Sea Scrolls help us to see that John the Baptist, as described in the Gospels, fits well into the historical reality of first-century Judaism in the land of Israel.

For Further Reading

Betz, Otto. "Was John the Baptist an Essene?" Pages 205–214 in *Understanding the Dead Sea Scrolls: A Reader from the Biblical Archeology Review.* Edited by Hershel Shanks. New York: Random House, 1992.

Brownlee, William H. "John the Baptist in the New Light of the Ancient Scrolls." Pages 33–53 in *The Scrolls and the New Testament.* Edited by Krister Stendahl. New York: Harper, 1957.

Charlesworth, James H. "John the Baptizer and the Dead Sea Scrolls." Pages 1–35 in *The Bible and the Dead Sea Scrolls, Volume 3: The Scrolls and Christian Origins.* The Second Princeton Symposium on Judaism and Christian Origins. Edited by James H. Charlesworth. Waco, TX: Baylor University Press, 2006.

CHAPTER 4

The Scrolls,
John the Apostle, and Baptism

THE GOSPEL OF JOHN HAS LONG BEEN CONSIDERED THE
last written, and most profound, of the four Gospels. John the
Baptist plays a prominent role in this Gospel, especially in the first
chapter, in which the author moves slowly from a mystical reflection on Jesus as the preexistent Word of God (John 1:1–18) into
historical time, with John the Baptist exercising his ministry on
the shores of the Jordan, not far from Qumran (John 1:19–42).
The Gospel tells us that John was standing with two of his disciples one day and, seeing Jesus pass by, identified him as the "Lamb
of God" (John 1:29)—a rich phrase that evoked the image of the
Passover Lamb; Isaac, son of Abraham, who almost became a
human sacrificial "lamb" (Gen 22:9); and the mysterious suffering servant of Isaiah 53, who "like a lamb led to slaughter" (v. 7)
is silently sacrificed for the people of God.[1] The two disciples leave
John and follow "Jesus the lamb of God" (John 1:37). The Gospel
identifies one disciple as Andrew, the brother of Peter, who later
finds Peter and brings him to Jesus (v. 40). But the other disciple
in this scene is conspicuously left unnamed, inviting the curiosity
of the reader. Who is this unidentified disciple who was with Andrew? And how does the author of this Gospel know so well the
intimate details of this event? If he knows the very words that
John the Baptist and Jesus spoke on this occasion, surely he knows

the name of the other disciple also. Why then does he not identify this other disciple—unless it is *the author himself,* and he knows this incident so well because he was there with Andrew when it occurred!

I would argue that the author of the Gospel of John is using a literary technique to invite the reader to suspect that Andrew's partner is the author himself, whom the Church traditionally has identified—correctly, in my view—as the Apostle John, the son of Zebedee.[2] If this is so, then John the Apostle was originally the disciple of John the Baptist, and the Baptist, we have argued, was formed in the community at Qumran. This scenario would explain why—as we shall soon see—the Gospel of John exhibits the strongest parallels to the Dead Sea Scrolls in language and concepts of any of the New Testament writings.[3] Although John's Gospel, obviously, is distinctly Christian and departs far from Essenism in many ways, nonetheless it seems strongly influenced by Essene language and worldview.

A century ago, the world of John scholarship was dominated by a German scholar by the name of Rudolf Bultmann, one of the most skeptical individuals ever to make a significant impact on New Testament studies. Bultmann regarded all the Gospels as fictional—"mythology" was his favorite term—and especially the Gospel of John. He argued that the unique features of this Gospel, like its peculiar emphasis on light and darkness, were from an esoteric branch of Platonic philosophy that influenced Christian thought in the second century (A.D. 100s), and thus the Gospel of John was written long after the ministry of Jesus, and reflected virtually nothing of the actual words and deeds of the Lord.

That's why it was a shock to John scholars when the Scrolls began to be published, and they discovered that words, phrases, and concepts thought to be from Greek philosophy were actually used in Judaism up to a century or more before the birth of Christ.[4] Specifically, the Scrolls are marked by a black-and-white,

good-versus-evil, us-versus-them kind of thinking that scholars
refer to as "dualism." Many of the dualistic expressions found in
the Scrolls also occur in the Gospel of John, but they are almost
absent from other ancient literature.

For example, the Qumran Scrolls emphasize the radical difference between the "Spirit of Truth," which is essentially the same
as God's Spirit or the Holy Spirit, and the "spirit of falsehood."
The *Community Rule* promises that God will purify the repentant
ones by the Spirit of Truth:

> By His truth God shall then purify all human deeds. . . . Like
> purifying waters, He shall sprinkle each with a *Spirit of Truth,*
> effectual against all the abominations of lying and sullying by
> an unclean spirit. Thereby He shall give the upright insight
> into the knowledge of the Most High and the wisdom of the
> angels, making wise those following the perfect way. (1QS
> 4:21–23)

This Spirit of Truth is opposed by a "spirit of falsehood," which
results in all manner of sin:

> The operations of the *spirit of falsehood* result in greed, neglect
> of righteous deeds, wickedness, lying, pride and haughtiness,
> cruel deceit and fraud. (1QS 4:9)

Outside of the Scrolls, the term "Spirit of Truth" occurs only in
the *Testaments of the Twelve Patriarchs,* an apocryphal work with
many similarities to the Scrolls and Essene theology, and in the
Gospel of John. At the Last Supper, Jesus says:

> And I will pray the Father, and he will give you another Coun-
> selor, to be with you forever, even the *Spirit of Truth,* whom
> the world cannot receive, because it neither sees him nor knows

him; you know him, for he dwells with you, and will be in you. (John 14:16–17; see also John 15:26; 16:13; 1 John 4:6)

The First Letter of John contrasts this Spirit of Truth with the "spirit of falsehood" we know from Qumran:

We are of God. Whoever knows God listens to us, and he who is not of God does not listen to us. By this we know the *Spirit of Truth* and the *spirit of falsehood.* (1 John 4:6)

Distinguishing between the Spirit of Truth and the spirit of falsehood is not as easy as one might expect, and human beings can be deceived. Therefore both John and the Qumranites emphasize the importance of testing the spirits:

Beloved, do not believe every spirit, but *test the spirits* to see whether they are of God; for many false prophets have gone out into the world. (1 John 4:1)

When anyone enters the Covenant—to live according to all these ordinances, to make common cause with the Congregation of Holiness—they shall *test their spirits* as a community, each member taking part. (1QS 5:20–21)

The contrast between truth and falsehood in both John and Qumran is also described as "light" and "darkness." These images run throughout both literatures. For example, at Qumran, those who follow the truth are "Sons of Light." The *Community Rule* describes itself as a document for their instruction:

A text belonging to the Instructor, who is to enlighten and teach all the Sons of Light about the character and fate of humankind. (1QS 3:13)

In John, the words are similar, but it is Jesus and not the law *per se* that is the source of the light:

> "While you have the light, believe in the light, that you may become *sons of light*." (John 12:36)

One characteristic of the sons of light is that they "do the truth," "witness to the truth," and "walk in truth." We find these expressions in both the Scrolls and John:

> They are to *do the truth* together with humility, charity, justice, lovingkindness, and modesty in all their ways. (1QS 5:3–4)

> But he who *does the truth* comes to the light, that it may be clearly seen that his deeds have been wrought in God. (John 3:21)

Likewise:

> When these things exist in Israel, the council of the *yahad* [community] will be established in truth—to be an everlasting plantation, a holy house for Israel, and a foundation of the Holy of Holies for Aaron, *witnesses of the truth* for justice, elected by grace to atone for the land. (1QS 8:4–6)

> For this I was born, and for this I have come into the world, *to witness to the truth*. Everyone who is of the truth hears my voice. (John 18:37)

> For I greatly rejoiced when some of the brethren arrived and *witnessed to the truth* of your life, as indeed you *walk in the truth*. (3 John 1:3)

And as for you, you shall *walk in the truth* together with all who seek Him. (1Q418 2:11)

Keep in mind that John wrote the Gospel in Greek, but phrases like "do the truth," "witness of the truth," and "walk in truth" are not good Greek and sound unnatural in the language. These are "Hebraisms," because John is thinking in the rhythms of biblical Hebrew but writing in Greek.[5]

Another important theme the Scrolls and John share is the love that members of the community ought to have for one another. In the Scrolls, one should love the community members and hate those outside:

The instructor is to teach them both *to love all the sons of light*—each commensurate with his lot in the council of God—and to hate all the sons of darkness, each commensurate with his guilt. (1QS 1:9–11)

No one should speak to his brother in anger, even if he sins against him:

Each man should reprove his neighbor in truth, in humility, and in *merciful love for one's fellow.* No one should speak to his brother in anger or muttering. (1QS 5:24–25)

In John, more than the other Gospels, we see this emphasis on love of the community members for one another:

A new commandment I give to you, that you *love one another;* even as I have loved you, that you also *love one another.* By this all men will know that you are my disciples, if you have *love for one another.* (John 13:34–35)

If anyone says, "I love God," and hates his brother, he is a liar;
for he who does not love his brother whom he has seen, cannot
love God whom he has not seen. And this commandment we
have from him, that he who loves God should *love his brother
also*. (1 John 4:20–21)

The notable difference in John's writings, however, is the absence of hate for those outside.

There are dozens and dozens of similarities in language between
John and the Scrolls, especially between John and the *Community
Rule*. In fact, there is a central section of the *Community Rule*—an
instructional document titled "For the Instructor: For Educating
and Teaching the Sons of Light about the Nature of All the Sons
of Men"—that has about a dozen clear parallels to the Gospel of
John in just a column and a half of text! There we find typical
Johannine expressions like "Spirit of Truth," "Holy Spirit," "sons
of light," "eternal life," "light of life," "walking in darkness,"
"wrath of God," "blindness of eyes," "fullness of grace," "works of
God," and "the evil works of men." One scholar has suggested
that this passage must have been memorized by members and had
a strong influence on their worldview and habits of speech.[6] John
the Apostle may have picked up these habits of thought and word
from his onetime mentor, the Baptist.

It's all well and good to show that there are similarities of language between John's Gospel and Letters and the Scrolls, especially the *Community Rule*, but similar language can be superficial.
On a deeper level, can we understand the Gospel of John as the
work of someone who—apart from the obvious impact of Jesus
on his life—was also profoundly influenced by John the Baptist
and Essene thought? The answer could be yes, because *Baptism* is
a recurrent theme in John more so than the other Gospels, and
viewing his Gospel through Essene eyes makes sense of passages
that otherwise are hard to understand.

Baptism in the Gospel of John

Let's take a quick tour of the theme of Baptism in the Gospel of John.

In the first chapter, we note that John the Baptist is the first human being mentioned in this Gospel, and he is introduced in epic fashion: "There was a man, sent from God, whose name was John. This man came for a witness, to witness about the light." The very phrase "witness about the light" has an Essene ring to it.[7] The rest of the chapter includes a discussion of the meaning of John's Baptism (1:24–28), a flashback of Jesus' Baptism by John (1:29–34), the promise that Jesus will baptize with the Holy Spirit (1:33), and the information that at least two (if not more) of Jesus' first disciples had previously been disciples of the Baptist (1:35–42). Thus, we can say that the Baptism theme is strong at the beginning of the Gospel.

In John 2, we have the accounts of the Wedding at Cana and the Cleansing of the Temple. Both are illuminated by knowledge of the Scrolls and Essenism.

At the Wedding in Cana, Jesus turns the water in six stone jars into wine. Archeologists have recovered many jars and other vessels made of stone from Qumran. Jews used stone vessels because, according to Mosaic Law, they could be cleansed and reused when they contracted ritual uncleanliness, whereas clay vessels had to be destroyed. The stone vessels we recovered from Qumran were mostly quite small, because it is hard to find large, high-quality rocks from which to sculpt a vessel, and it takes a great deal more work and effort to grind and hollow a vase, for example, out of solid rock than to form the same item on a potter's wheel. The stone jars in John 2 were enormous, holding twenty to thirty gallons. It took a great deal of time or money or both to make a single vessel like this, much less six. This tells us that the household hosting this wedding was probably wealthy, and spent their wealth (time and treasure) on making sure they were keeping the ritual laws of Moses. This may have been an Essene household, although the Pharisees, too, were very concerned about these matters.

The number six, the material stone, and the liquid water are also symbolic. Six is one short of seven, the number of perfection and divinity. Stone recalls the tablets of stone of Moses (Exod 24:12) and the stony hearts of the people of Israel (Ezek 36:26). Water will keep one alive, but unlike wine, it doesn't bring a lot of joy. The six stone jars of water, then, symbolize the old covenant and its external "baptisms," which could not bestow the joy of the Holy Spirit (Acts 13:52; Gal 5:22). Jesus transforms this water into wine, a symbol of transforming the old covenant into the New, through the gift of the Holy Spirit, with which Jesus will "baptize" (John 1:33). So one of the many messages of the Wedding at Cana narrative (John 2:1–11) is that Jesus is superior to the water washings of the old covenant, which John knew so well from his youth.

The next narrative is the account of the Cleansing of the Temple (John 2:13–22). Here, too, the Scrolls shed light. We might think that Jesus' indignation at what was going on in the Temple was unique to him, because all other Jews were loyal to the Jerusalem Temple and its customs. But from the Scrolls we realize that one of the three major sects of Jews had significant issues with the Temple to the point that they would not participate in its rites, because it was being run according to an incorrect interpretation of the law, and possibly because the priesthood itself was illegitimate.[8] Like the Essenes, Jesus opposed the way the Temple was being run, although not for exactly the same reasons.

After Jesus cleanses the Temple, the Judeans demand of him, "What sign will you show us for doing this?" And Jesus responds, "Destroy this Temple and in three days I will raise it up." The Judeans balk: "It has taken us forty-six years to build this Temple, and you will raise it up in three days?" But John explains: "He spoke of the Temple of his body" (John 2:18–21).

Now, here is a classic case where, without the Scrolls, we would be sorely tempted to think that the author of the Gospel writes later Christian theological ideas back into the words and the deeds of Jesus. The idea that Jesus' body could be a Temple seems so foreign to Judaism and such a uniquely Christian theological concept that it surely must be out of place in the actual ministry of Jesus in the late A.D. 20s, right? Actually, no. From Qumran, we know that the community members already believed themselves to be a "Temple of Adam" (Heb. *miqdash 'adam;* 4Q174 1:6), a phrase that could also be understood as a "Temple of a Man" or "Temple of Humanity." Indeed, they saw themselves as a replacement for the Holy of Holies, the most sacred part of the Temple!

> When these things exist in Israel the Community council shall be founded on truth, to be an everlasting plantation, *a holy house for Israel* and the foundation of *the Holy of Holies* for Aaron, witnesses of the truth for justice and elect by the grace (of God) to atone for the land. . . . This [i.e. the Community] is the tested rampart, the precious cornerstone that does not . . . shake or tremble from their place. (It will be) *the most holy dwelling for Aaron* . . . and it will be *a house of perfection and truth* in Israel in order to establish . . . a covenant in compliance with the everlasting decrees. (1QS 8:4–9)[9]

Notice here all the Temple language that is applied to the community: "holy house for Israel," "Holy of Holies for Aaron," "precious cornerstone," "most holy dwelling for Aaron," "house of perfection and truth." Another Scroll identifies the Temple that David wished to build for God (2 Sam 7:10–11) as the Qumran community itself:

This "place" is the house that they shall build for Him in the
Last Days, as it is written in the book of Moses: "A temple of
the Lord are you to prepare with your hands; the Lord will
reign forever and ever" (Exodus 15:17–18). This passage describes the temple that no man with a permanent uncleanness shall enter. . . . Strangers shall not again defile it, as they
formerly defiled the Temple of Israel through their sins. To
that end He has commanded that they build Him a *Temple of
Adam,* and that in it they sacrifice to Him proper sacrifices.
(4Q174 1:2–7; emphasis mine)

As we mentioned, the phrase "Temple of Adam" could also be
translated "Temple of a Man." Furthermore, it is a small step from
understanding a community to be a Temple of human beings to
understanding the *leader* of the community, who represents and
embodies the community, as being the Temple in a particular
sense. Jesus' response to the Judeans in John 2 presumes that he
thinks of himself as a "Temple of a Man," as the leader of a new
temple community. Furthermore, while Qumran claimed to be
the "cornerstone," Jesus applies this image to himself personally:
"Have you never read in the scriptures: 'The very stone which the
builders rejected has become the head of the corner'?" (Matt
21:42).[10] As leader of the new temple community, Jesus is the
embodiment of the Temple in a unique way.

The connection with Baptism is a bit indirect, but it is through
Baptism that Jesus cleanses our body-temples and makes our bodies into temples of the Holy Spirit (cf. 1 Cor 6:19). The Temple
cleansing is a physical image of the spiritual cleansing Jesus enacts
on each one of us in Baptism.

Before we move on to discuss more Baptism passages in John,
let me take a time-out to comment on the use of the term "Jew"
in John. Everyone knows that throughout John, Jesus is in arguments with a group most English translations call "the Jews." The

Greek word is *ioudaioi,* more accurately rendered "Judeans." In the first century, this was not always a religious category, unlike our modern word "Jew." In the first century, you could be a *ioudaios* or "Judean" for simply geographical reasons, as distinguished from the Galileans, who lived up north, or the Samaritans, who lived in the center of Palestine.

One of the interesting things about the Dead Sea Scrolls is that the Qumranites never call themselves "Judeans" (in Hebrew, *yehudim*). Rather, they always refer to themselves as "Israel" or some variation thereof ("sons of Israel," "repentant of Israel," "congregation of Israel," "the multitude of Israel").[11] There are a number of reasons of for this. Technically speaking, a Judean (Gk. *ioudaios;* Heb. *yehudi*) was a descendant of Judah, one of the Twelve Tribes of Israel. But the Essenes and the Qumran community aspired to be the restoration not merely of Judah but of the ancient twelve-tribe nation of Israel that was joined together by Moses under the Sinai Covenant. So they always call themselves "sons of Israel" (or variants thereof) and hoped for the restoration of all twelve tribes. The name "Essene" was given to them by outsiders, and never occurs either in the Dead Sea Scrolls or in the New Testament. "Essene" was probably a Greek corruption of the Hebrew *'ossim,* "doers," short for "doers of the law" (cf. Rom 2:13).[12] But they called themselves "Israel," and the New Testament authors sympathized with them.

Jesus shared with the Essenes the hope for the restoration of Israel. His choice of twelve Apostles was deliberately symbolic of his intention to restore the Twelve Tribes of Jacob. There was, after all, a Jewish prophecy that in the end-times the twelve patriarchs would be resurrected—and in a sense, Jesus was doing just that with the Twelve.[13] Furthermore, in the Gospel of John, the term "Judean" almost always refers to people opposed to Jesus, whereas the terms "Israel" and "Israelite" are always positive. For example, when Jesus first sees Nathaniel, he says, "Behold! Here is truly an

Israelite in whom there is no deceit!" And Nathaniel responds, "You are the King of Israel!" (not "King of the Jews") (John 1:47–49). This doesn't prove that Nathaniel was an Essene, but what Jesus says to him certainly resonates with the Scrolls, which emphasize being the "true Israel" and strongly warn against deceit.[14]

So, in light of the Scrolls, we should change our translations of the Gospel of John. Everywhere Greek *ioudaios* occurs in John, it should be translated "Judean" rather than "Jew." The issue in John is not that Jesus is a "Christian" in constant debate with "Jews." That is pathetically anachronistic. Rather, Jesus is perceived to be a Galilean from Galilee, the rural, hilly area in northern Israel that was less wealthy and urbanized (like West Virginia for Americans), and the "Judeans" from the region around Jerusalem (the New York of ancient Israel) see him as an outsider and a threat to their religious-economic system. Furthermore, Jesus did not see Judea—ruled as it was by the Herodians, Sadducees, and Pharisees—as the sole heir of Biblical Israel. He looked forward to a great restoration of Israel, which he was inaugurating with his twelve Apostles.

Now, let us return to the subject of Baptism. Unsurprisingly, Baptism comes up again in the next chapter of John (John 3). Here we find Nicodemus, a Pharisee and member of the Jewish ruling council (the Sanhedrin), coming to see Jesus at night. In response to Nicodemus's questions, Jesus tells him, "Unless one is born of water and the Spirit, he cannot enter the kingdom of God" (3:5). When Nicodemus responds, "How can this be?" (3:9), Jesus gets a little frustrated. "Are you a teacher of Israel, and yet you do not understand this? . . . If I have told you earthly things and you do not believe, how can you believe if I tell you heavenly things?" (3:10–12).

For most of my life I was unable to understand Jesus' frustration with Nicodemus. It was obvious that "being born of water and the Spirit" referred to Baptism, so Jesus was stressing the need for this sacrament. But how could he expect Nicodemus to get that? The Church hadn't been established yet, the sacraments weren't being administered on a regular basis, and Nicodemus was a Jew. So how could Jesus get frustrated with Nicodemus for not understanding something he could not be expected to know about? I was sorely tempted to agree with those scholars who said this conversation never took place in the life of the historical Jesus, but was just a creation of early Christian theology written back into the life of the Lord.

But here the Scrolls help out, once again. We know that the Qumranites believed that the Holy Spirit moved through their community, making their ritual washings efficacious:

> For only through the spirit pervading God's true society can there be atonement for a man's ways, all of his iniquities; thus only can he gaze upon the light of life and so be joined to His truth by His holy spirit, purified from all iniquity. Through an upright and humble attitude his sin may be covered, and by humbling himself before all God's laws his flesh can be made clean. Only thus can he really receive the purifying waters and be purged by the cleansing flow. (1QS 3:6–9)

We can see the connection between the Spirit and water in this passage, which the Qumranites derived from various prophecies in the Old Testament. Isaiah correlates the outpouring of water with the outpouring of the Spirit:

> For I will pour water on the thirsty land, and streams on the dry ground; I will pour my Spirit upon your descendants, and my blessing on your offspring. (Isa 44:3)

Ezekiel identifies a divine water sprinkling with a cleansing that will result in a "new spirit":

I will sprinkle clean water upon you, and you shall be clean from all your uncleannesses, and from all your idols I will cleanse you. A new heart I will give you, and a *new spirit* I will put within you. (Ezek 36:25–26)

So we can see how the Qumranites could develop their theology of Spirit-infused water cleansing from the Old Testament texts, but what about this idea of being "born" by water and Spirit? Although the Scrolls never use quite that term, it seems like they were on the verge of the concept. It's clear that members of the community were considered "sons of light," whereas outsiders were "sons of darkness." And at what point did one move from being a "son of darkness" to a "son of light"? It was at that point in the initiation process when the candidates swore the grave oaths and entered the Spirit-infused water for the first time.[15] Arguably, that was their "birth" as "sons of light."

So getting back to Jesus' conversation with Nicodemus: surely Jesus is pushing the theological envelope, if you will, and introducing some new language into Jewish discourse about how to be saved. But the point is, Jesus' teaching isn't so far from concepts that were being discussed and even practiced by the Qumranites and John the Baptist that a presumably well-informed and well-educated individual like Nicodemus couldn't be expected to follow the conversation. If Nicodemus had been reasonably conversant with the theological discussions that were going on in the broader Judaism around him, he shouldn't have been lost by Jesus' discourse. That is why, in light of the Scrolls, Jesus' frustration with him (3:11) is historically plausible, and John 3:1–15 does not need to be considered a fiction written by the early Church.

Moving to John 4, we observe Jesus' conversation with the Samaritan woman at the well. This story, too, revolves around water and its deeper meaning, the gift of the Holy Spirit. When Jesus speaks to the woman about giving her "living water," ultimately he's referring to the Holy Spirit, given through Baptism (1:33). But the Scrolls shed interesting light on this conversation, too.

Obviously, the well where Jesus is sitting is a major focal point of the conversation. It so happens this is Jacob's well. In the Essene literature, "the well" was a metaphor for the law, which gave life to those who interpreted it properly and followed it. Speaking of the founders of their movement, the Damascus Document says:

> He [God] instituted His covenant with Israel forever, revealing to them things hidden. . . . The desires of His will, which Man should carry out and so have life in them, He opened up to them. So they "dug a well," yielding much water. Those who reject this water He will not allow to live. (CD 3:13–14)

As in John 4, here we have the convergence of the ideas of "life" and a "well of water." A later passage clarifies what this "well" was:

> But God called to mind the covenant of the forefathers; and He raised up from Aaron insightful men and from Israel wise men and He taught them and they dug the well: "the well the princes dug, the nobility of the people dug it with a rod" (Num 21:18). *The Well is the Law,* and its "diggers" are the repentant of Israel who went out of the land of Judah and dwelt in the land of Damascus. . . . And the "rod" is the interpreter of the Law of whom Isaiah said, "he brings out a tool for his work" (Isa 54:16). The "nobility of the people" are those who come to "dig the well" by following rules that the Rod made to live by during the whole era of wickedness, and without these rules they shall obtain nothing until the appearance of one who teaches righteousness in the Last Days. (CD 6:2–11)

So the well was a symbol of the law and its correct interpretation and application. But in John 4, Jesus has better water than that from "Jacob's well": the Spirit itself, received through Baptism, which is not only a "washing" but also a "drinking of the Spirit" (1 Cor 12:13). The contrast in John 4 is the same as in John 1: "For the *law* was given through Moses; *grace* and *truth* came through Jesus Christ" (John 1:17). It is the superiority of Jesus' covenant to Moses'.

Skipping ahead in the Gospel of John, we come to the important section John 7–9, all of which takes place on or near the Jewish Feast of Tabernacles. The Feast of Tabernacles was the great Temple feast, when the Jews celebrated God's "tabernacling" (or "dwelling") among them, first in Moses' Tabernacle and then in Solomon's Temple. But Jesus, like the Qumranites, sees that the current Temple is corrupt and will be replaced by a "Temple of Man" (or "Temple of *a* Man"; 4Q174 1:6). Jesus is the new Temple, because he is "the Word [that] became flesh, and *tabernacled* (Gk. *skênôô*) among us" (John 1:14 RSV *alt.*), using the verb from *skênê*, a "tent" or "tabernacle."

The Feast of Tabernacles was observed with ceremonies of light and water, because different Old Testament prophecies promised that one day the Temple would be the source of light and water for the world. The priests erected thirty-foot-high lamp stands in the Temple courts that burned all through the night, and at the climax of the feast they poured out water on the main altar to create the river flowing from the Temple promised by Ezekiel (Ezek 47).[16]

But Jesus is the new "Temple of a Man," so on the last day of the feast, when they poured out the water on the altar to make Ezekiel's river, Jesus stands up and declares, "If anyone thirst, let him come to me; and let him drink who believes in me. As the Scripture has said, 'Out of his heart shall flow rivers of living water'" (7:38 RSV *alt.*).[17] John explains, "Now this he said about the Spirit, which those who believed in him were to receive." It is a reference to the gift of the Spirit through Baptism, which is the "birth" through "water and Spirit" Jesus urged on Nicodemus (3:5).

In the following chapter, Jesus declares, "I am the light of the world; he who follows me will not walk in darkness, but will have the light of life" (8:12). It is not the stone Temple but Jesus the new Temple who will provide the ultimate light.

Then, in chapter 9, the motifs of "water" and "light" come together when Jesus "baptizes"—so to speak—a man blind from birth.

After the Feast of Tabernacles, Jesus runs into a beggar who was born blind. The disciples ask Jesus whose guilt led to this blindness: "Who sinned, this man or his parents, that he was born blind," and Jesus replies, "Neither." Jesus reasserts, "I am the light of the world," and then "he spat on the ground and made clay of the spittle and anointed the man's eyes with the clay, saying to him, 'Go, wash in the pool of Siloam.' So he went and washed and came back seeing" (9:5–7).

Everyone wonders why Jesus spits on the ground and makes clay, and scholars have suggested all kinds of theories to explain it, but here again, the Scrolls have the answer. It is not coincidental that there are at least four passages of the Scrolls that describe a man as "a vessel of clay" kneaded from "dust" and "spittle." The best-known passage is near the end of the *Community Rule* itself:

> Who, indeed, is man among Your glorious works? As what can he, born of a woman, be reckoned before You? Kneaded from dust . . . he is so much spit, mere nipped-off clay. (1QS 11:20–21)

Observe at least four motifs shared in John 9: *birth* from a woman, *kneading* the dust/ground, *spittle,* and *clay.* A very similar passage from elsewhere in the Scrolls adds a fifth motif, *darkness:*

You placed knowledge in my frame of dust in order that I
might praise You. And I was formed of spittle. I was molded
of clay and my formation was in *darkness*. (4Q511, 3–4)

Yet another similar passage adds sixth and seventh shared motifs, both *guilt* and *a cleansing fountain*:

To dust like myself . . . You open a *foun[tain]* to reprove the
vessel of clay of his way, and the *guilt* of one born of a woman
according to his works; that he might open a *fo[untain]* of
Your truth.

Notice that the disciples raised the issue of guilt in John 9:2,
and Jesus sends the man to the Pool of Siloam, which caught the
waters of the famous Gihon Spring, the natural fountain that was
Jerusalem's only source of fresh water.

All these passages from the Scrolls come from hymns probably composed by the Teacher of Righteousness, the founder of
the Qumran community. He wrote many "Hymns of Praise"
(Heb. *Hodayot*) and frequently refers to himself as "a vessel of
clay"[18] or "dust, spit and clay."[19] The images of dust and clay are
clearly references to the story of the creation of Adam in Genesis
2:7: "Then the LORD God kneaded (*yatzar*) the man from the
dust of the ground." The idea of clay comes from the verb used
here, which I have translated "kneaded," which means "to make
something of clay," whose participle is the Hebrew word for "potter": *yôtzêr*. Other Bible verses make this clear: "O LORD . . . we
are the clay, and you are our potter; we are all the work of your
hand" (Isa 64:8, my translation).

But where does the *spit* come from? Well, nothing can be
kneaded from dust; moisture is necessary to make it moldable. So
apparently there was a pious Jewish tradition that God spat on the
dust to make clay to knead the body of Adam, and that tradition

is reflected in all these passages of the Scrolls that speak of man as "mere spit."[20]

So when we take this knowledge back to John 9, it suddenly all makes sense. Jesus spitting on the ground and making clay *is an act of re-creation.* Jesus the Son is re-performing the very acts by which God the Father formed the first man! Jesus is *re-creating* this man, born in darkness, into a "son of the light"! And he is doing it, in part, by having him wash in water. And not just any water, but the Pool of Siloam, which caught the waters of the Gihon Spring, which originally flowed from Eden (Gen 2:13). In this way, the Pool of Siloam is another image of a new creation!

All of John 9 is a catechesis on Baptism. Everyone is like the man born blind: we are born in the darkness of sin. John shares this theology with the Qumranites: everyone is born a "son of darkness" but can become a "son of light" by washing with the Spirit-infused waters. Later Christian theology will call this darkness "original sin." But "original sin" is not a guilt—as Jesus says, "Neither this man nor his parents sinned." Rather, "original sin" is an *absence,* the *absence* of the Holy Spirit, who brings us "light" and "life." Our first parents lost the Holy Spirit when they rebelled against God, but now we may regain it through Baptism. And Baptism is a kind of new creation—as St. Paul will say, "If anyone is in Christ, he is a new creation"! (2 Cor 5:17). So Jesus "re-creates" this man through dust and clay and spittle and a water washing, and the man comes back "enlightened"—filled with light! Truly, Jesus is the "light of the world," and he has brought light into this man's life, so he can be a "son of light."

When the man born blind returns from Siloam seeing, his friends argue about him:

> "Is not this the man who used to sit and beg?" Some said, "It is he"; others said, "No, but he is like him." (John 9:8–9)

When they ask him, the man gives an ambiguous response. He just says, "I AM" (Gk. *ego eimi,* John 9:9).[21]

This is the only place in the Gospel of John where anyone other than Jesus takes the phrase "I AM" on his lips. This is the divine name (Exod 3:14). Usually in John it refers to Jesus' divinity. How can this man use the same phrase? It is the theology of Baptism, which bestows the Spirit, which is divine Life. Therefore, the baptized now shares God's life, and can also say, "I AM."

Many other features of John 9 reflect different aspects of Baptism. That is why, from ancient times to the modern day, John 9 has been used to prepare catechumens (the traditional term for people being instructed in the Christian faith) to receive Baptism. In modern times, the Catholic Church and many other churches read and proclaim John 9 about halfway through Lent, as the Church prepares catechumens for Baptism on Easter. The Scrolls obviously aren't necessary to see the Baptismal imagery, but the similarities of language and image between parts of John 9 and the Scrolls surely bring out the colors of this passage in bold display, and help clarify the curious episode of Jesus spitting and making clay.

We need to move quickly through the rest of John, pointing out the other Baptismal motifs.

In John 11, the raising of Lazarus is an image of Baptism, because in Baptism the spiritually dead person is raised to new life. St. Paul states this explicitly: "you were buried with him in baptism, in which you were also raised with him through faith in the working of God, who raised him from the dead" (Col 2:12).

In John 13, Jesus washes the feet of the disciples, but he refers to their previous Baptism when he says to Peter, "He who has bathed does not need to wash . . . he is clean all over" (13:10). In John 14–16, Jesus discourses about the Holy Spirit, which the Apostles will one day bestow through Baptism (cf. Acts 2:38).

Jesus departs the Upper Room in John 18 to begin his Passion, and Pilate crucifies him in John 19. The climax of John's account of the Crucifixion occurs at John 19:34, when a soldier pierces Jesus' side, and it lets forth a fountain of *blood and water*. What is the meaning of this flow of blood and water?

During festival times in Jerusalem, the priests sacrificed so many lambs in the Temple that they had to use buckets of water to wash the blood down drains in the Temple floor, and a torrent of blood and water gushed out of the side of the Temple Mount into the Kidron Valley below.[22] Ancient Jews would recognize that the flow of blood and water marked the Temple, and Jesus' body was the new Temple (John 2:21), the "Temple of a Man" (4Q174 1:6). This fulfills Jesus' prophecy: "Out of his heart shall flow rivers of living water" (John 7:37–38). In the Bible, the Garden of Eden was the first Temple, and in it were the Tree of Life and the River of Life.[23] Now on Calvary, Jesus' body is the last Temple. The Tree of Life is the cross, the fruit of life is Jesus' body and blood, and the River of Life is the flow of blood and water from his side. In John, blood symbolizes the Eucharist, the necessary meal of Jesus' body and blood: "unless you eat the flesh of the Son of Man and drink his blood, you have no life in you" (6:53). Likewise, water symbolizes Baptism, the necessary washing: "unless one is born from above by water and the Spirit, he cannot see or enter the Kingdom of God" (3:3, 5). For the early Christians, the message was clear: from the Body-Temple of Jesus on the cross flows the river of the sacraments, which convey the Holy Spirit to all who will receive them.

After this quick tour of the Gospel of John, we can see that, arguably, it does read like a document written by someone who spent time as a disciple of John the Baptist and, through him, was influenced by Qumran. From the Baptist, the author imbibed the importance and centrality of this sacred rite. Baptism is either at the forefront or just below the surface all through the Gospel. From the Baptist, too, the author may have picked up the peculiar diction and dualistic thinking that so characterized Qumran and the Essenes generally: "light" versus "darkness," "truth" versus "falsehood," "good" versus "evil."

Furthermore, the Baptist, the Essenes, Jesus, and John the Apostle all shared a critique of the stone Temple in Jerusalem, as defiled ritually or morally or both. All were looking for a replacement with a "Temple of Adam." For the Essenes, this "Temple" was their movement. For the Qumranites, it was their community specifically. But for the Apostle John, it was his Lord, Jesus the Christ—and then by extension the *ekklesia* ("congregation" or "Church") that would eat his "flesh and blood" and so share his Temple-nature.

Although the view that John the Apostle wrote the Gospel of John and was himself a disciple of the Baptist cannot finally be proven, it does fit the available evidence.[24] What can be proven is that the Gospel of John makes its best sense firmly in the world of late Second Temple Judaism, the world before the destruction of the Temple, when at least some readers could have been familiar with the Essene "Thanksgiving Hymns" and the fact that the Temple flowed with blood and water at festival time. Scholars of yesteryear, who made John into a late fiction created from the influence of esoteric forms of Greek Platonism, were very far off the mark.[25] As William Brownlee, one of the first three scholars to lay eyes on the Scrolls, remarks: "If what one is looking for as 'apostolic' is a fresh and independent witness, John has it—and not as fabrications of the imagination stemming from some late period of the Gospel tradition, but as the voice of a living witness from the cultural context of the early decades of Christianity in Palestine!"[26]

The Gospel of John makes sense as the work of the Apostle John, who was a disciple of John the Baptist before following

Jesus. From his formation under the Baptist, John imbibed the importance of this sacred washing, which is a constant theme in his Gospel, as well as some distinctive terminology characteristic of the Qumran community. The Dead Sea Scrolls help us read the Gospel of John in its first-century context and understand some of its otherwise puzzling features.

For Further Reading

Brown, Raymond E. "The Qumran Scrolls and the Johannine Gospel and Epistles." Pages 183–207 in *The Scrolls and the New Testament*. Edited by Krister Stendahl. New York: Harper, 1957.

Brownlee, William H. "Whence the Gospel of John?" Pages 166–194 in *John and the Dead Sea Scrolls*. Edited by James H. Charlesworth. New York: Crossroad, 1990.

Harrington, Hannah K. "Purification in the Fourth Gospel in Light of Qumran." Pages 117–138 in *John, Qumran, and the Dead Sea Scrolls: Sixty Years of Discovery and Debate*. Edited by Mary L. Coloe and Tom Thatcher. Atlanta: Society of Biblical Literature, 2011.

CHAPTER 5

Baptism Today

BAPTISM, AS I MENTIONED BEFORE, IS AN AMAZING WORLD-wide human phenomenon. About one in three of the world's people has been baptized, around 2.2 billion persons. Clearly, many human beings believe that this sacred ritual—popularized by an ex-Essene Jewish prophet-martyr in the first century A.D. and adapted by his cousin, another prophet-martyr—is very important to their spiritual lives and eternal blessedness. But ideas about what actually is going on when a person is baptized vary widely among its practitioners.

We've talked a lot in the previous two chapters about two Johns: the Baptist and the Apostle. Now I want to talk about two more Johns: John, myself, and my onetime best friend Jon (for Jonathan), who grew up with me for some years on a Marine Corps base where both our fathers served as chaplains. Our fathers were close friends, but while both were Protestants, they came from very different theological traditions. My dad was raised in the Dutch Reformed tradition, a movement in the Netherlands that took its inspiration from the French-Swiss Reformer John Calvin. Jon's dad was a Free Methodist, whose movement tried to preserve the spirit of the Anglo-American preachers John (1703–1791) and Charles (1707–1788) Wesley.

When we first met in elementary school, I was baptized but did not receive communion at church, whereas Jon received communion but was not baptized. Our families and our traditions had virtually flip-flopped views of these two sacraments. For the Free Methodists, communion (i.e., Eucharist) could be taken by any believer, but Baptism was reserved for those who had reached an age of discretion and could consciously commit themselves to a life of discipleship to Jesus Christ. For the Dutch Reformed, Baptism was a sign of the covenant, which was extended to children since God works with us as families (Acts 2:39). But communion was reserved for those who had reached adulthood and could make a public "profession of faith" and join the Church as responsible (and voting) members.

Interestingly, neither of us really regarded Baptism as *doing anything* to us. Baptism was rather an external ceremony whereby the person baptized—or his parents, in the case of an infant—professed their faith in Jesus. For this reason, my friend Jon had no qualms about getting baptized more than once. He first got baptized when we were both older elementary students. Years later we met up as teenagers, and he let me know he had been baptized one or more times subsequently, because as he grew in his faith, he suspected he hadn't been sincere in his earlier baptisms. I talked to my dad about this, and he told me privately that "rebaptism just shouldn't be done" because the "Church Fathers were against it." John Calvin, the founder of our movement, read a good bit of the Church Fathers and knew that the early Church had hammered out the theology of Baptism, and the consensus was that no one should be baptized more than once. This was the practice in Christianity up through the Reformation, when some groups broke off and began to rebaptize persons who had experienced a spiritual conversion in their lives (the "Anabaptists," Greek for "Rebaptizers"). Much later, some in the Methodist tradition also adopted this practice.

What did Baptism originally mean, though? Here's where I

think the Scrolls can help us read the New Testament with new eyes.

I am a believing Christian, and I affirm Baptism is from God and is, as the Bible teaches, salvific. But I also believe the form of this ritual had a human history, in which Qumran and the Essenes played a significant role. When we look at what the *Community Rule* says about their own ritual washing, clearly the rite was not merely symbolic; it had spiritual effects, and therefore can be called truly *sacramental*.[1]

For the Essenes, not all washing rituals were the same. There was the standard washing for ritual uncleanliness, which was common to all Jews and took place according to the laws of Moses. But the Essenes also maintained sacred baths filled with a "purer kind of holy water,"[2] according to Josephus, to which no candidate was admitted except after a yearlong probation.

The early columns of the *Community Rule* seem to describe a process of initiation that culminates in washing with the holy waters of purification. There are stern warnings that the candidates must first be truly repentant; otherwise, the washing ritual will be ineffective:

Anyone who refuses to enter the society of God, preferring to continue in his willful heart, shall not be initiated into the Yahad of His truth. . . . He lacks the strength to repent. He is not to be reckoned among the upright. . . . Ceremonies of atonement cannot restore his innocence, neither cultic waters his purity. He cannot be sanctified in oceans and rivers, nor purified by mere ritual bathing. . . . For only through the Spirit of God's true society can there be atonement for a man's ways, all of his iniquities; thus only can he gaze upon the light of life and so be joined to His truth by His Holy Spirit, purified from all iniquity. Through an upright and humble attitude his sin may be covered, and by humbling himself before all

God's laws his flesh can be made clean. *Only thus can he really receive the purifying waters and be purged by the cleansing flow.* (1QS 2:25–3:9; emphasis mine)

We see here a complementarity among three elements: the interior disposition of the candidate, the Spirit-infused community, and the water-washing rite. For the Qumranites, all three must be aligned for the candidate truly to be freed from his sins. If the candidate is not rightly disposed—that is, if he is not repentant—any rituals will be ineffective. Likewise, rituals outside the community will be ineffective, because the Holy Spirit works within the community. Nonetheless, the water ritual within the community is necessary, as the candidate's goodwill and the presence of the community do not transform him unless he washes in the "purifying waters."

These same constitutive elements are present in early Christian teaching on Baptism. For example, in Peter's preaching on the day of Pentecost in Acts 2, the crowds of Jews in Jerusalem are "cut to the heart" and ask,

> "Brethren, what shall we do?" And Peter said to them, "Repent, and be baptized every one of you in the name of Jesus Christ for the forgiveness of your sins; and you shall receive the gift of the Holy Spirit. For the promise is to you and to your children and to all that are far off. . . ." So those who received his word were baptized, and there were added that day about three thousand souls. And they devoted themselves to the apostles' teaching and fellowship, to the breaking of bread and the prayers. (Acts 2:37–42)

Peter insists that repentance must precede Baptism. The Baptism must be performed by representatives of the community—in this case, the Apostles—because in the Book of Acts, the Spirit is poured out only through the Apostles' hands, in their presence, or by their representatives.[3] The Church is the Spirit-infused community. But for all that, the water ritual is essential: "Be baptized . . . and you shall receive the gift of the Holy Spirit" (Acts 2:38).

It is interesting that nowhere in the New Testament is Baptism simply a public profession of one's faith in Jesus. The apostles describe Baptism as something that God does to the believer, not something the believer does for God. St. Paul, for example, who is best known for his teaching on the role of faith in the Christian life, nonetheless has strong things to say about the role of Baptism, too:

> Do you not know that all of us who have been baptized into Christ Jesus were baptized into his death? We were buried therefore with him by baptism into death, so that as Christ was raised from the dead by the glory of the Father, we too might walk in newness of life. (Rom 6:3–4)

St. Paul speaks as though Baptism makes a real spiritual difference for the one who has received it, as he continues his discussion:

> For if we have been united with him in a death like his, we shall certainly be united with him in a resurrection like his. We know that our old self was crucified with him so that the sinful body might be destroyed, and we might no longer be enslaved to sin. For he who has died is freed from sin. . . . So you also must consider yourselves dead to sin and alive to God in Christ Jesus. (Rom 6:5–11)

St. Paul is often associated with the idea of "salvation by faith alone." Certainly faith is important to Paul's argument in Romans, but we do notice that Baptism also plays an important role in uniting a person to Christ's death and enabling him or her to walk in newness of life.

Other teachings of the Apostles and early Church leaders likewise stress the importance of this sacred rite. The conclusion of the Gospel of Mark states it as follows: "He who believes and is baptized will be saved" (Mark 16:16). There we note the combination of the interior disposition ("belief," that is, "faith," Gk. *pistis*) and the external rite (Baptism).

Mark is often thought to represent the preaching of Peter, and the First Letter of Peter likewise stresses the salvific nature of Baptism. Peter brings up the account of the Flood during Noah's lifetime, in which "eight people were saved through water":

> Baptism, which corresponds to this, *now saves you,* not as a removal of dirt from the body but as an appeal to God for a clear conscience, through the resurrection of Jesus Christ. (1 Pet 3:21)

The physical cleansing properties of Baptism are not what is important, Peter teaches—"not as a removal of dirt from the body." Rather, it is the interior effect, because it is "an appeal to God for a clear conscience," that is, an appeal for God to *infuse* a "clear conscience," which in Hebrew would be expressed by the concept of a "clean heart," as David once wrote: "Create in me a clean heart, O God!" (Ps 51:10). Likewise the ancient prophets promised that in the latter days

> I will sprinkle clean water upon you, and you shall be clean from all your uncleannesses. . . . A new heart I will give you, and a new spirit I will put within you. . . . And I will put *my* spirit within you, and cause you to walk in my statutes. (Ezek 36:25–27)

Ezekiel describes here *an act of God* that will cleanse the interior person and infuse the Holy Spirit, all associated with the sprinkling of water. Zechariah similarly promises a fountain that will cleanse not from dirt but from sin:

> On that day there shall be a fountain opened for the house of David and the inhabitants of Jerusalem to cleanse them from sin and uncleanness. (Zech 13:1)

The Qumranites believed this and other prophecies were fulfilled in their own community and its sacred washings. One Qumran liturgical document, while describing how ritual purification should be performed, gives thanks to God for "cleansing his people in the waters of bathing" (4Q414 13:7). The Qumranites and the early Christians associated the water cleansing with the gift of the Spirit, using other prophetic texts like this:

> For I will pour water on the thirsty land, and streams on the dry ground; I will pour my Spirit upon your descendants, and my blessing on your offspring. (Isa 44:3)

To the image of the gift of the Spirit, Jeremiah adds the reality of a new covenant that will transform the inner person:

> Behold, the days are coming, says the LORD, when I will make a new covenant. . . . This is the covenant which I will make with the house of Israel after those days, says the LORD: I will put my law within them, and I will write it upon their hearts. (Jer 31:31, 33)

Although Jeremiah does not mention water or the Spirit, God's act of placing the law within the people and writing it on their hearts certainly refers to a divine act that transforms the "heart" or center of the person, the same reality that Ezekiel describes as "a new heart" and "a new spirit" through the sprinkling of water. These ideas are joined together in one of the Psalms of the Teacher of Righteousness, when he says:

> I know that no one can be righteous apart from you. And I beg your grace by that Spirit which you have placed within me . . . to cleanse me by your Holy Spirit, and to draw me near by your will according to your great mercy (1QH^a 8: 29–30; my translation)

The Teacher can follow God's law—drawing "near by your will"—because he has God's Spirit placed within him.

These were some of the prophetic texts that both the Qumranites and the early Church believed were fulfilled in the sacred washings they performed. In every case, it is a divine act, something that God does to the human person, rather than something primarily done to or for God.[4] In the early Church, Baptism was the usual means for bestowing the Holy Spirit (Acts 2:38; 1 Cor 12:13), and if the Spirit had not been received by Baptism (Acts 8:14–16, 19:1–4), it was considered unusual, and the Apostles had to remedy the situation (8:17, 19:5–6).

The primary reality of Baptism as a divine action explains why the early Church baptized children. This practice is already attested in the New Testament, where entire households—including children—were baptized. For example, the Philippian jailer in Acts 16 is so impressed with Paul and Silas he asks them: "Men, what must I do to be saved?" And they say, "Believe in the Lord Jesus, and you will be saved, you and *your household.*" So "he was baptized at once, *with all his family.* . . . and he rejoiced *with all his household* that he had believed in God" (see Acts 16:30–34).

The early Church could have reasoned that since repentance and faith are necessary for Baptism, children shouldn't be baptized. But that's not the way the early Christians thought. Rather, since Baptism was a divine act necessary for salvation, and they wanted very passionately for their children to share in salvation, they baptized them. Peter had said about the salvation offered through Baptism, "The promise is for you *and for your children*" (Acts 2:39). There was Jewish precedent for this: in the old covenant, entrance to the covenant was through circumcision, which was performed on infants. Baptism was the new circumcision, the "circumcision of the heart" (Deut 30:6) promised by Moses. So St. Paul describes baptism as a "circumcision made without hands" and the "circumcision of Christ":[5]

> In [Christ] also you were circumcised with a *circumcision made without hands,* by putting off the body of flesh in the *circumcision of Christ,* having been buried with him in *Baptism,* through which you were also raised with him through faith in the working of God, who raised him from the dead. (Col 2:11–12)

Infants, since they were innocent of any deliberate sin, could be considered docile to the working of God through Baptism, and their parents could make an act of faith on their behalf, as parents did in the old covenant. So one of the earliest instructions on Christian Baptism outside the New Testament reads:

> Baptize first the children, and if they can speak for themselves let them do so—Otherwise, let their parents or other relatives speak for them. (Hippolytus, *The Apostolic Tradition* 21:16 [A.D. 215])[6]

Likewise the Church Father Origen records:

The Church received from the apostles the tradition of giving baptism even to infants. The apostles, to whom were committed the secrets of the divine sacraments, knew there are in everyone innate strains of sin, which must be washed away through "water and the Spirit" (John 3:5). (*Commentaries on Romans* 5:9 [A.D. 248])[7]

These early Christian testimonies reflect the belief that Baptism is an act of God on the human person. This is part of Christianity's Jewish heritage, because first-century Jews definitely believed that their water washings were not merely symbolic; the washings *did something divine* to them.[8] Yet it is probable that most modern Christians worldwide think of Baptism primarily as an external sign and a public witness of their faith in Jesus Christ: a testimony they give to God, rather than a transformation God works on them. Many think the idea of Baptism as a transformative act of God is a superstition of the Middle Ages, rather than a Jewish idea attested before the birth of Christianity and grounded in the words of the great prophets of Israel. In fact, the Jewishness of Baptism has largely been lost—sadly—and people nowadays see Baptism as a mark of distinction between Christianity and Judaism rather than part of the spiritual heritage that connects the Church with the people of Israel.

The Scrolls help us to see that the New Testament writings are in earnest when they speak of the importance of Baptism as an act by which the Holy Spirit is given to repentant persons. This kind of sacramental realism is not a product of the Middle Ages but reflects Jewish practice of the late Second Temple period, as seen at Qumran.

For Further Reading

Black, Matthew. "Covenant, Initiation, and Baptismal Rites." Pages 91–101 in Black, *The Scrolls and Christian Origins: Studies in the Jewish Background of the New Testament.* Brown Judaic Studies 48. New York: Scribner, 1961.

Johnson, Sherman. "The Dead Sea Manual of Discipline and the Jerusalem Church of Acts." Pages 129–142 in *The Scrolls and the New Testament.* Edited by Krister Stendahl. New York: Harper, 1957.

McKnight, Scott. *It Takes a Church to Baptize: What the Bible Says About Infant Baptism.* Grand Rapids, MI: Brazos Press, 2018.

PART THREE

THE EUCHARIST
AND THE SCROLLS

CHAPTER 6

Did Qumran Have a "Eucharist"?

THROUGHOUT CHRISTIANITY, THERE ARE MANY DIFFERENT ways believers commemorate the last sacred meal of Jesus. In some churches, they pass around brass plates of Wonder bread with crusts removed and cut into little squares, and then large round brass servingware containing dozens of tiny individual cups of grape juice. Everyone sits in the pews, takes their bread and grape juice, and consumes it together on the pastor's cue. Other churches pass a single loaf, and every congregant tears off a piece and dips it themselves in a common cup of grape juice. Still others have everyone file down to the front, where the priest or some other minister hands them a flat round wafer, or places it on their tongue.

Through all this variation, the common elements are always bread and a drink made of grapes—traditionally wine, but increasingly grape juice in America. This practice is almost as universal as Baptism, but the form varies more widely. Even its name is not consistent. Some call it "the Lord's Supper" or "communion," but in "high churches"—Catholic, Orthodox, and some Episcopalian and Lutheran—it is called "the Eucharist." "Eucharist" comes from a Greek word, *eucharistia,* which means "thanksgiving," and it is the oldest attested name for the central ritual meal of Christianity. Justin Martyr, an early Christian writer, describes the practice of early Christians around A.D. 150:

And when the presider has given thanks, and all the people have expressed their assent, those who are called by us deacons give to each of those present to partake of the bread and wine mixed with water over which the thanksgiving was pronounced, and to those who are absent they carry away a portion. And this food is called among us *eucharistia,* of which no one is allowed to partake but the man who believes that the things which we teach are true, and who has been washed with the washing that is for the remission of sins, and unto regeneration, and who is so living as Christ has enjoined.[1]

Almost every Christian is aware that this practice goes back to what Jesus did on the night before he was betrayed, when he took bread, gave thanks, broke it, and gave it to his disciples, saying, "This is my body, given for you. Do this in remembrance of me." And after supper, the cup in the same manner (cf. 1 Cor 11:23–25).

But, as we've already seen, Jesus' actions at the Last Supper did not take place in a cultural vacuum. There were earlier Jewish sacred meals whose meaning and practice he was modifying. The Jewish Passover is the most obvious one. But groups of Jews also shared sacred meals of bread and wine on a more regular basis than the annual Passover, and these meals are also important for understanding what Jesus was doing on the last days before his death. While later rabbinic literature indicates that groups of devout Pharisees gathered for ritual meals,[2] the only such practice for which we have contemporary documentation from the time of Jesus and the Apostles is the common sharing of bread and wine among the Essenes. Josephus writes:

They labor with great diligence till the fifth hour, after which they assemble themselves together again into one place; and when they have clothed themselves in white veils, they then bathe their bodies in cold water. And after this purification is over, they every one meet together in an apartment of their own, into which it is not permitted to any of another sect to enter; while they go, after a pure manner, into the dining room; as into a certain holy temple, and quietly set themselves down; upon which the baker lays them loaves in order; the cook also brings a single plate of one sort of food, and sets it before every one of them; but a priest says grace before meat; and it is unlawful for anyone to taste of the food before grace be said. The same priest, when he has dined, says grace again after meat; and when they begin, and when they end, they praise God, as he that bestows their food upon them; after which they lay aside their [white] garments, and betake themselves to their labors again till the evening; then they return home to supper, after the same manner. (*War* 2:129 [2.8.5.1])

It is clear from Josephus's description that, while this meal did satisfy physical needs, it was much more than merely a shared lunch. Several elements mark this out as an act of liturgical worship. First, they dress in a priestly fashion, in "white veils," which we may safely identify with the white linen fragments recovered from Qumran,[3] since white linen was associated with the Israelite priesthood (Lev 16:4, 23, 32). They then bathe, which likewise was a ritual requirement for the Israelite priests to enter the sanctuary to perform any act of worship (Exod 30:20; Lev 8:6). Qumran was equipped with enough ritual baths to accommodate scores of men bathing in a relatively short amount of time. Third, after the bath they enter a sacred space—Josephus notes no one else was permitted to enter, and it was "like a holy temple." This agrees with the Essenes' internal documents that, as we have seen, describe the community as a "Holy of Holies for Aaron" and a "Temple of Adam." There is also evidence that the Qumranites maintained their own altar and performed their own sacrifices, consuming the meat at these ritual meals (the "single plate of one sort of food").[4] Fourth, Josephus's comment that the baker "lays them loaves in order" seems intentionally to recall the words of Exodus 40:23, where Moses "set the loaves in order before the Lord" on the table of the Bread of the Presence. Fifth, Josephus's insistence that the prayer of the priest must precede any consumption of the food—in fact, it is "unlawful . . . to taste of the food" before the priest has said grace—underscores the fact that this is no ordinary meal but also an act of worship. And last but certainly not least, what marks this as a liturgical event is the fact that the meal is preceded and concluded by an act of worship—they "praise God," Josephus says, which almost certainly refers to the chanting or singing of psalms or hymns. These were probably the "Thanksgiving Hymns," or *Hodayot,* composed by the Teacher of Righteousness. Strikingly, each of these hymns begins with the same statement: "I give thanks to you, my Lord," which in Greek would be *eucharistô soi, kyrie mou.*[5]

There is fairly good correlation between Josephus's description of the Essene meal practice and the internal documents of the Essenes recovered from Qumran. The *Community Rule* describes the communal life of the members of the *yahad* ("community"), including the following instructions:

In this way shall they behave in all their places of residence. . . . They shall eat together, together they shall bless [i.e., pray] and together they shall take counsel. In every place where there are ten men of the Community council, there should not be missing amongst them a priest. And every one shall sit according to his rank before him. . . . And when they prepare the table to dine or the new wine for drinking, the priest shall stretch out his hand as the first to bless the first fruits of the bread and the new wine. And in the place in which the Ten assemble there should not be missing a man to interpret the law day and night, always, one relieving another. And "the Many" [Heb.

ha-rabbim] shall be on watch together for a third of each night of the year in order to read the book, explain the regulation, and bless [i.e., pray] together. (1QS 7:1–8)[6]

Two obvious points of connection between Josephus's account and this passage of the *Community Rule* are the emphasis on the meal taking place in order—men sitting by rank, the baker laying the loaves "in order"—and the role of the priest to bless the food before anyone else touches it.

Certain aspects of the Qumran sacred meal remind us of the Gospel accounts of the Last Supper. First, there is the exclusive nature of who was invited—"an apartment of their own, into which it is not permitted to any of another sect to enter it." While Jesus often shared table with a wide variety of persons—"tax collectors and sinners"—when it comes to the Last Supper, he has Peter and John prepare an "apartment of their own" (Luke 22:7–13), and only the Twelve are invited for the meal (Mark 14:17; Luke 22:14).

Second, there is the washing before the meal. John places great emphasis on this act (John 13:1–17). Jesus washes the feet of all the disciples, which recalls the requirement that the priests wash their feet before entering the sanctuary (Exod 30:19–21). Peter protests that he needs a more thorough washing, but Jesus insists that the Apostles have already had a "bath," which probably refers to their baptisms (John 13:9–10).

Third, there is the prayer before and after the food. Jesus takes on the role of the priest in the Essene meal ritual, blessing the food at the beginning and end of the supper (Luke 22:17, 20). The Apostles would have perceived Jesus' "blessing" or "giving thanks" over the meal as a priestly act.

Fourth, the *Community Rule* especially emphasizes a blessing over both the bread and the wine, and the Gospels likewise record distinct blessings over each at the Last Supper (Luke 22:17, 19).

Fifth, the argument among the Apostles over who was the greatest as recorded by Luke (Luke 22:24) suddenly makes more sense in light of the need for "everyone to sit according to rank," something on which the *Community Rule* places a great deal of emphasis. The Apostles were arguing over their relative ranks and thus who should sit where at the Last Supper.

Sixth, Jesus utters strange words over the cup at the Last Supper, which have puzzled Christians for centuries: "This is my blood of the covenant, which is poured out *for Many*." What does Jesus mean, "for Many"? Shouldn't he have said, "for everyone"? But the Lord's words become explicable in light of the Jewish practice of referring to the members of a community as "the Many"—Hebrew *ha-rabbim,* attested in the *Community Rule,* elsewhere in the Scrolls, and also in latter rabbinic literature.[7] In its Jewish context, "for Many" means "for the members of the community," in other words, for Jesus' community, known elsewhere as the *ekklesia* or "church" (Matt 16:18, 18:17; Acts 5:11 etc.).

Seventh, there is the singing of a thanksgiving hymn. Josephus mentions the Essenes "praising God" at the beginning and end of the meal, probably singing one of the *Hodayot,* or "Thanksgiving Hymns" (1QH[a]), which all begin "I give thanks to you, my Lord," paralleling the theme of "thanksgiving" (Gk. *eucharistia*) found in the Gospel accounts of the Last Supper (Matt 26:27; Mark 14:23; Luke 22:17, 19; cf. John 6:11, 23). Jesus and the apostles also sing a hymn of thanksgiving at the end of the Last Supper (Matt 26:30; Mark 14:26).

Finally, it is intriguing that the description of the common meal in the *Community Rule* is followed almost immediately by a description of staying up for a "third of the night" to meditate on Scripture and pray together. One cannot help but think of the departure of the Apostles from the Upper Room to pray together in Gethsemane. Luke says, "And he came out, and went, *as was his custom,* to the Mount of Olives" (22:39), making it sound as if Jesus habitually ate supper in Jerusalem or nearby, then brought his disciples to this garden on the slopes of the Mount of Olives for a prayer vigil into the night.

So there are many provocative parallels between the sacred meal of the Qumran Essenes and the accounts of the Last Supper, but many of the correlations we have mentioned can also be found more generally in Jewish practice or among other Jewish sects.[8] Therefore, we are not, at this point, arguing that Jesus modeled the Last Supper *directly* on Essene practice, but we are allowing the Dead Sea Scrolls, as the only Jewish documents contemporary with the ministry of Jesus, to help us understand his words and gestures as if we were Jews living in his day.

But to return to the meal of the Essenes: we have seen that it was no meal of mere physical necessity but in every way was structured as an act of priestly, liturgical worship. But what was the *meaning* of this meal to the Essenes? Here, we have to engage in some scholarly reconstruction, because there is no text from Josephus or within the Dead Sea Scrolls that explicitly unpacks the meaning of their meal ritual. However, applying some logic and common sense to a careful reading of their documents, we can reconstruct several aspects of what this communal, holy meal signified to them.

The first thing we should note is that all outsiders and even those in the process of initiation for the community were excluded from the holy meal. Josephus says initiates could participate in the baptism with the "purer waters" after a one-year process, but participation in the "pure food of the Many" was not allowed until one or two more years of probation had passed, "and before he is allowed to touch their common food, he is obliged to take tremendous oaths" (*War* 2:138–139). The content of these oaths appears to be preserved in the early columns of the *Community Rule.* The partaking in this sacred communal meal, therefore, *signified* and *actualized* the participation of each member in the inmost circle of the "new covenant community"—for that is what Qumran believed itself to be. To put it bluntly: partaking of the meal meant full initiation into the covenant. Conversely, sin against the covenant community resulted in exclusion from the meal: "No man belonging to the Covenant of the Yahad who flagrantly deviates from any commandment is to touch the pure food of the holy men" (1QS 8:16–17). Thus, eating of the pure food of the community signified and made real the fact that one was in good standing in the covenant.

Another clue to the meaning of the sacred meal is found in an appendix to the first copy of the *Community Rule* discovered in Cave 1. This document is titled "The Rule for the Whole Congregation of Israel in the Latter Days"—which scholars shorten to "The Rule of the Congregation"—and it describes how the Qumranites envisioned the whole nation of Israel being governed in the last days, when the Messiah arrived:

The procedure for the meeting of the men of reputation when they are called to the banquet held by the party of the Yahad, when God has fathered the Messiah (or when the Messiah has been revealed) among them: the Priest, as head of the entire congregation of Israel, shall enter first, trailed by all his brothers, the Sons of Aaron, those priests appointed to the banquet of the men of reputation. They are to sit before him by rank. Then the Messiah of Israel may enter, and the heads of the thousands of Israel are to sit before him by rank, as determined by each man's commission in their camps and campaigns. Last, all the heads of the congregation's clans, together with their wise and knowledgeable men, shall sit before them by rank. When they gather at the communal table, having set out bread and wine so the communal table is set for eating and the wine (poured) for drinking, none may reach for the first portion of the bread or the wine before the Priest. For he shall bless the first portion of the bread and the wine, reaching for the bread first. Afterward the Messiah of Israel shall reach for the bread. Finally, each member of the whole congregation of the Yahad shall give a blessing, in descending order of rank. This procedure shall govern every meal, provided at least ten men are gathered together. (1QS^a 2:11–22)

It is interesting that the Qumran community would take the time to describe in detail how the procedure—we might even say "liturgy"—of their sacred meal would be observed in the time of the Messiah. Actually, we should say "Messiahs," because, as we observed in chapter 2, they expected two: a priestly "Messiah of Aaron" and a royal "Messiah of Israel" (a descendant of David). Therefore, there is good reason to suppose the "Priest" mentioned here who is "head of the entire congregation of Israel" is the Messiah of Aaron. In any event, it is fascinating that the Qumranites imagined that their sacred meal of bread and wine would continue in the messianic age, only they would celebrate with the Messiahs and with all the "men of reputation" (literally, "men of name"). It reminds us of Jesus' words in the Gospels:

There you will weep and gnash your teeth, when you see Abraham and Isaac and Jacob and all the prophets in the kingdom of God and you yourselves thrust out. And men will come from east and west, and from north and south, and sit at table in the kingdom of God. And behold, some are last who will be first, and some are first who will be last. (Luke 13:28–30)

"Abraham, Isaac, Jacob, and all the prophets" are among the "famous men," the "men of name," who will be at the messianic banquet. But the seating order will be surprising, when people discover what God (or the Messiah) considers each man's *real* rank to be: "Some are last who will be first, and some are first who will be last."

Getting back to the Qumran description of the sacred meal in the Rule of the Congregation, it is significant that they envisioned the meal ritual proceeding essentially in the same fashion in the end-times, only in the presence of the Messiah(s) and all the famous men of Israel. This sheds light on the meaning of their daily meal ritual. Each time they gathered in their dining room for the sacred meal of bread and wine, they were performing a ritual that one day they would celebrate in the presence of the Messiah himself. We can say, then, that the daily "thanksgiving meal" of the Qumranites was an *anticipation* of the messianic banquet when the "kingdom of God" would be established.[9]

This idea of performing rituals in *anticipation* or in *expectation* of an event is a bit foreign to us modern, secularized people, but it was a regular part of the religious life of ancient Judaism. Many, perhaps most, of the sacred rites of Judaism had an anticipatory character. For example, on the last and greatest day of the Feast of Tabernacles, the priests would walk down from the Temple to the Pool of Siloam and fill a golden pitcher of water, then take it back up to the Temple and pour the water on the main altar, creating an artificial river flowing from the altar.[10] This was in anticipation of the fulfillment of Ezekiel 47, the prophet's famous vision of a river of life flowing from the heart of the Temple. This whole ritual and its mysticism forms the backdrop of John 7–9, as we saw in the previous chapter. So expectation of the end-times, or "eschatological anticipation," was a common feature of Jewish religion.

We see this "eschatological anticipation" also in the rituals Jesus leaves for his disciples (the nucleus of the Church) to perform. St. Paul explains the anticipatory nature of the Eucharist, or Lord's Supper: "For as often as you eat this bread and drink the cup, you proclaim the Lord's death until he comes" (1 Cor 11:26).

The Qumran Rule of the Congregation sheds light on the

meaning of the Last Supper, and how Jesus' words and actions would have been perceived by the disciples. The Qumranites foresaw a banquet of bread and wine to which all the leaders of Israel would be gathered, presided over by the chief priest, or the Messiah of Aaron, with the participation of the royal Messiah of Israel.

Now, everyone acknowledges that Jesus chose twelve Apostles intentionally to suggest the reconstitution of the twelve-tribe nation of Israel.[11] The Twelve were a kind of "sacrament" of the new Israel. In the Upper Room, Jesus gathers together this nucleus of the New Israel and celebrates with them a banquet of bread and wine, taking himself the role of the priestly Messiah, by reaching out his hand first to bless the bread and the new wine. There is no missing the symbolism of what Jesus is doing. We will take a closer look at Luke's account of the Last Supper—the longest—in chapter 8.

We are now in a position to answer the initial question of this chapter. Did the Essenes at Qumran have a "Eucharist"? Obviously, they did not in the full Christian sense, because the early Church believed the Eucharistic bread and wine were actually transformed into the body and blood of the Messiah, Jesus of Nazareth. And we do not find in Josephus's descriptions or the internal documents of Qumran any hint of the Messiah giving his body and blood to be consumed.

However, with the proper qualifications, we can say that Qumran did celebrate a "Eucharist"—if we understand that in a more general sense—because they practiced a daily meal of bread and wine that was preceded by and concluded with hymns of thanksgiving (Gk. *eucharistia*), which both signified and actualized their full initiation into the "new covenant," and anticipated the banquet they would one day celebrate in the presence of the Messiah and all the famous men of Israel. Yes, the meal instituted by Jesus is even more than all that, but it certainly is also everything that the Qumran "thanksgiving meal" represented.

The Essenes truly had a kind of "eucharist," that is, a sacred meal of bread and wine, presided over by a priest, celebrated daily in thanksgiving to God and in anticipation of the coming of the Messiah. This Essene practice sheds considerable light on the Gospel narratives about the Last Supper, and the early Christian celebration of the Eucharist.

For Further Reading

Black, Matthew. "Qumran Baptismal Rites and Sacred Meal." Pages 99–117 in Black, *The Scrolls and Christian Origins: Studies in the Jewish Background of the New Testament.* Brown Judaic Studies 48. New York: Scribner, 1961, esp. pp. 102–117.

Daniélou, Jean. "Jesus and the Zadok Priests." Pages 25–36 in Daniélou, *The Dead Sea Scrolls and Primitive Christianity.* Translated by Salvator Attanasio. Baltimore: Helicon Press, 1958.

Smith, Dennis E. "Meals." In *Encyclopedia of the Dead Sea Scrolls,* 1:530–532. Edited by Lawrence H. Schiffman and James C. VanderKam. Oxford: Oxford University Press, 2000.

CHAPTER 7

When Was the Last Supper?

ATHEIST BIBLICAL SCHOLARSHIP IS A RELATIVELY RECENT PHE-
nomenon in Western civilization. It may seem like an oxymoron,
but if you think about it, even atheists need scholars who know
how to handle the Bible and defeat the claims it makes. They need
to be able to offer nonsupernatural explanations for all the different kinds of events and revelations that the Bible records.

The current favorite son of this movement is a scholar by the
name of Bart Ehrman. Ehrman grew up in a conservative Christian environment and went to Moody Bible Institute, a bastion of
traditional American Protestantism, whose approach to the Bible
is a strong but inflexible combination of three convictions: the
"Bible Alone" (*sola scriptura*) as the source for faith and life; the
divine inspiration of the words of Scripture; and a literalistic approach to interpretation. Ehrman was an excellent student and
graduated from Moody to go on for a doctorate in Scripture at a
major university. There, while studying the ancient handwritten
copies of Scripture that we use for modern translations, Ehrman
encountered the messy side of biblical studies, like the fact that
ancient scribes made errors and sometimes intentional changes to
the texts. How could one trust the Bible if scribes sometimes
made mistakes with its very words? Ehrman's brittle approach to

Scripture shattered under the pressure, and he gave up on the faith altogether.

I run into Ehrman periodically at the annual national convention of Bible scholars. Sporting an ear stud, dark T-shirt, and sport coat, he's definitely photogenic and resembles more a Hollywood celeb about to go on a talk show than your typical stuffy academics in tweeds or sweater vests. Since divesting himself of faith, he's made a name for himself—and doubtless a good bit of profit, too—writing popular books that undermine Christian faith in the Bible by pointing out apparent errors and inconsistencies. One of Ehrman's favorite examples is the disagreement between the Gospels over the dating of the Last Supper and Crucifixion.[1] Many readers may not even be aware of this problem, so let me take a moment to explain it.

When we read the various Gospel accounts of Passion Week, a curious discrepancy starts to show up between Matthew, Mark, and Luke (the "Synoptic Gospels") on the one hand, and John on the other. Mark, for example, dates Mary's famous anointing of Jesus at Bethany to "two days before the Passover" (Mark 14:1–3), whereas John seems to date the same event to "six days before the Passover" (John 12:1–3). Then, Mark states that "on the first day of Unleavened Bread, when they sacrifice the Passover Lamb," (Mark 14:12), Jesus instructed Peter and John (Luke 22:8) to go into Jerusalem and prepare for the Twelve to "eat the Passover," which they do that very evening (Mark 14:17). That clearly makes the Last Supper a Passover celebration. But *John* describes the Last Supper as taking place "before the Feast of the Passover" (John 13:1), so it *can't* be a Passover. Furthermore, John notes that, during the Passion, the Jewish authorities do not want to be defiled by entering Pilate's palace, since they want to "eat the Passover" (18:28), which implies that Good Friday was the day *before* the Passover meal. Finally, John remarks that Jesus' Crucifixion takes place on "the day of Preparation of the Passover" (19:14), which again seems to imply the day *before* the holy festival. So what is going on here? Why do Matthew, Mark, and Luke all insist that the Last Supper was on the Passover, whereas John seems to insist Jesus was crucified on the day before the Passover? Can't the Gospel authors get their story straight? Or is one or more of them confused or, worse—lying?

A closer look at the details of the different Gospel accounts, however, begins to suggest a way to unravel this mystery. Let's observe some curious facts that most readers and commentators overlook or ignore because their significance is lost on those who have not studied the Dead Sea Scrolls.

For example, Luke relates that Jesus told Peter and John, "Behold, when you have entered the city, *a man carrying a jar of water will meet you;* follow him into the house which he enters, and tell the householder, 'The Teacher says to you, Where is the guest room, where I am to eat the Passover with my disciples?' " (Luke 22:10–11; emphasis mine). What is the significance of a man carrying a jar of water? Most readers assume it's just a random fact or some curious example of Jesus' divine foreknowledge of events. But those familiar with ancient Near Eastern culture immediately recognize: carrying jars of water was *women's work.*[2] The Bible itself gives numerous examples illustrating how gender-specific this task was.[3] Men didn't fetch water, and when they needed a drink, they typically had to ask a woman. If men carried water at all, like on long journeys, they used leather flasks, not jars.[4] Servants might be sent to fetch water, but Jesus does not say "a *servant*" (Gk. *doulos*) but "a *man*" (Gk. *anthrôpos*), suggesting a free man carrying water—and one could tell by the way a person was dressed whether he was slave or free.[5]

So why would a free man in Jerusalem be carrying a jar of water? It so happens that we know of one branch of Jews who lived in communities with neither *women* nor *servants,* so their men had to do tasks usually performed by other groups. And that branch or sect was, of course, the Essenes. There was a community of Essenes who lived in Jerusalem. There were enough of them that one of the several gates in Jerusalem's defensive wall was dedicated for their use and simply called "the Essene gate."[6] This gate had been excavated by archeologists, including Bargil Pixner, a Benedictine archeologist and Bible scholar, and nearby the gate they also discovered ritual baths and a latrine that would have allowed Essene Jerusalemites to fulfill the strict requirements they maintained for living in the Holy City: one could not relieve oneself within the city limits, and anyone with a bodily emission had to leave immediately and wash.[7] Furthermore, for all intents and purposes, those Essenes who lived in Jerusalem had to be celibate, because they absolutely forbade marital relations within the city that contained the Holy Temple.[8] The Essenes of Jerusalem, then, would have consisted mostly or exclusively of celibate men, and Philo emphasizes that they did not hold slaves but served each other by performing menial tasks for one another.[9] This all leads us to strongly suspect that the man carrying "a jar of water"— usually a feminine or servile task—was an Essene, and the house to which he led Peter and John was a building within the Essene area (or "quarter") of Jerusalem.

There is more, however. Later in Mark's account of the Last Supper, we learn that Jesus went out to the Garden of Gethsemane, where he was arrested. The disciples fled, and Mark records that following them was a young man "with nothing but a linen cloth about his body; and they seized him, but he left the linen cloth and ran away naked" (Mark 14:51–52). What is the significance of being clothed with a single linen garment? We know from archeology that linen was an uncommon fabric in Judea at this time, making up only about 30 percent of all clothing.[10] It was uncommon because it was highly valued and expensive: the flax from which linen was made grew only in Galilee, and it had to be imported to Judea at a high price. Wool, by contrast, was cheap and readily available, and made up about 70 percent of all clothing.[11] So this young man is a bit of a self-contradiction. On the one hand, linen is a sign of wealth and luxury; on the other, wearing but a single garment was a sign of poverty or slavery. It would be like wearing a pair of Armani dress pants—but nothing else. This odd combination of luxury and poverty is only attested among the Essenes. All the remains of clothing found at Qumran were linen.[12] Josephus also tells us that the Essenes wore only a single garment, and would continue to wear it until it was completely worn out: "Nor do they allow of the change of garments, or of shoes, till they be first entirely torn to pieces or worn out by time" (*War* 2:126).

Who was this young man dressed like an Essene? A very old Christian tradition identifies him as none other than John Mark, the author of the Gospel.[13] Just like the painter who brushes in a little portrait of himself, looking at the viewer, in the corner of his masterpiece, so John Mark writes in a little portrait of himself in Mark 14:51–52. We later learn that John Mark's mother owned the house that served as the center of operations for the Apostles and the early Church (Acts 12:12), apparently the same house where the Apostles gathered in the "upper room" before Pentecost (Acts 1:13) and, even before that, for the Last Supper (Luke 22:12). If each link in this chain of connections holds, one could conclude that John Mark had Essene ties, and it was his family's property that hosted Jesus' last Passover.[14] This all would seem to indicate that Jesus celebrated the Last Supper in the Essene neighborhood of Jerusalem.

How do we know there was a neighborhood or "quarter" rather than Essenes scattered throughout the city? Because their stringent laws of ritual cleanliness—their *kosher* regulations, if you will—would have required them to stick together and stay apart from the rest of the population.

What does this have to do with the controversy over the date of the Last Supper? Quite a bit, as it turns out. It just so happens that, in the process of studying the Dead Sea Scrolls, it became apparent that the Qumran community (and the Essenes generally) followed a different liturgical calendar from that observed by the Pharisees, who dictated the regulations of the Jerusalem Temple.[15] The Pharisees followed a lunar-solar calendar consisting of twelve lunar months totaling 354 days, and every three years it was necessary to add a thirteenth month to catch up to the true solar year. The Essenes, however, followed a solar calendar of exactly 364 days, which was actually quite old and traditional in Israelite religion, and had probably been in use by all the Jews up until the time when the Maccabean kings took over the high priesthood about 150 B.C.[16] The Maccabees favored the Pharisees, who also espoused a lunar-solar calendar, which the Maccabees then implemented at the Jerusalem Temple. Many Jews of a more traditional and religious bent, however, were loyal to the older calendar, and popular works like the *Book of Jubilees* and *1 Enoch* defended and advocated it. These works were translated into Greek and read widely by Jews throughout the Roman Empire, and later by the early Christians. Many copies of both have been found among the Dead Sea Scrolls.[17] It is certain that the Qumranites considered *Jubilees* to be a "biblical" book, and all their literature reflects the implementation of its 364-day liturgical calendar. It is not unusual in the Scrolls to run into remarks like these:

That day Noah went out from the ark, at the end of an exact year, *three hundred and sixty-four days.* (4Q252 2:2–3; emphasis mine)

On the twenty-eighth of the month is a Sabbath. The month continues with the day after the Sabbath (Sunday), the second day, and an addition of the third day. The year is complete: three hundred sixty-four days. (4Q394 1:1)

The great advantage of such a calendar is that it comprises exactly fifty-two weeks with no remainder, and thus all the holy days and festivals fall on the same day of the week every year. Passover, for example, always fell on a Wednesday, meaning that the meal itself fell on Tuesday night, since the day was reckoned from sunset to sunset (cf. Gen 1:5). This calendar would fall behind the true solar year by a little more than a day per year, so those who used it must have inserted an entire week every several years. We don't know their exact schedule of *intercalation* (the adjustment of one's calendar by adding days), but they must have had one, as they certainly did use this calendar, and kept it up with the natural seasons.[18]

Thus, we can be absolutely confident of the fact that there were *at least* two liturgical calendars in operation among Jews during the lifetime of Christ: the Pharisaic lunar-solar calendar observed in the Temple, and a 364-day solar calendar followed by other Jews, including the Essenes. There may have been others: the Samaritans surely followed their own calendar, and other sects of Jews may have had calendrical variations. So, the reality of Judaism in the time of Jesus is similar to the reality of Christianity today, with multiple liturgical calendars (Catholic, Orthodox, and lesser-known rites) placing feast days (e.g., Easter) on different days.

Could this explain the discrepancy in the date of Passover in the Gospels? Many scholars think so. Back in the 1960s, the French biblical scholar Annie Jaubert published a work known in English simply as *The Date of the Last Supper*, in which she laid out the case that Matthew, Mark, and Luke date Passion Week according to the old solar calendar, in which Passover fell on Tuesday evening, but John dates events according to the lunar-solar Temple calendar, in which Passover fell on a Saturday (Sabbath) in the year of Jesus' death.[19] What evidence is there that this may be true?

We've already noted that the man carrying a jar of water and the young man clothed in a linen garment are both strongly suggestive of an Essene connection with Jesus' celebration of the Last Supper. But there are additional factors. Both Mark and Luke record Jesus telling Peter and John, "Ask the householder (*oikodespotes*, "lord of the house"), Where is the guest room (*kataluma*) where I am to eat the Passover with my disciples?" Now, the Essenes were renowned for their hospitality, not only among one another but also toward outsiders. Josephus remarks:

> They have no certain city but many of them dwell in every city; and if any of their sect come from other places, what they have lies open for them, just as if it were their own; and they go into such as they never knew before, as if they had been ever so long acquainted with them. For which reason they carry nothing with them when they travel into remote parts, though still they take their weapons with them, for fear of thieves. Accordingly there is, *in every city where they live, one appointed particularly to take care of strangers,* and to provide garments and other necessaries for them. (*War* 2:124–125)

Josephus remarks that *"many"* of them "dwell in *every* city," and surely Jerusalem, the chief city, would be no exception—thus they had their own "Essene" gate (*War* 5:145). Furthermore, it seems quite possible that the "lord of the house" to whom Jesus directs Peter and John was one of these officials appointed "to take care of strangers."[20] The word translated "guest room" in the Gospels is *kataluma*, a rare Greek word used only for the Upper Room and for the "inn" in Bethlehem that had no room for Mary and Joseph (Luke 2:7). It refers to a space set aside for guests, "a place of lying down." The Essenes apparently maintained these guesthouses or guest rooms in all their settlements.[21] The Damascus Document, one of the constitutional documents of the Essene movement, stipulated that each local community had to give alms to support a communal house where the poor and needy were cared for:

> This is the rule of the Many for meeting all their needs: a wage of two days every month at least shall be given to the Overseer. Then the judges will give some of it for their wounded, with some of it they will support the poor and needy, and the elder bent with age, the man with a skin disease, whoever is taken captive by a foreign nation, the girl without a redeemer, the boy without an advocate; and for whatever is common business, so that *the communal house* [Hebrew *beth ha-hever*] should not be cut off. (CD 14:12-17; emphasis mine)

This "communal house," or more literally "house of the association," appears to refer to a building maintained by the local Essene community where charitable care could be dispensed. Could such a "communal house," owned or operated by the family of John Mark, be where Jesus sought hospitality during Passion Week?

Is there a reason Jesus, though clearly not an Essene himself, might lodge with the Essenes in Jerusalem? It's not hard to figure out why. The Gospels make clear that *both* the Sadducees *and* the Pharisees were plotting to kill him, and he knew it![22] Therefore, staying in any part of Jerusalem that was controlled by or sympathetic to these two groups was dangerous. The Essenes, however, were pacifistic[23] and are never recorded in the Gospels as coming into open conflict with Jesus. Moreover, there seem to have been ties of personal contact and common sympathies between Jesus' entourage and the Essenes, and both were adamantly opposed to the prevailing regime of the Sadducees and Pharisees. It is not a coincidence, for example, that the Gospels record Jesus defeating the Pharisees and Sadducees in public debate during Passion Week (Matt 22:23–46). Likewise, the Qumran Essenes mocked both these groups with derogatory names, calling the Pharisees, for example, the "seekers after smooth things"—implying they sought the easy way out of religious obligations.[24] There is an old saying: "the enemy of my enemy is my friend"—and that may apply to Jesus and the Essenes. Although they disagreed over ritual purity, they shared much in common in their critique of the two dominant Jewish sects. The Sadducees and Pharisees also cooperated in control of the Temple, and both Jesus and the Essenes strongly objected to the way the Temple was being run, as can be seen from the Temple-cleansing accounts in the Gospels and certain texts of the Dead Sea Scrolls (e.g., 4QMMT).

We can now bring archeology into the picture. The traditional site of the "Cenacle" or Upper Room in Jerusalem has a strong claim to authenticity, since historical records and archeological data trace it back to a Jewish-Christian synagogue built on the site of the Upper Room not long after the destruction of Jerusalem in A.D. 70.[25] Moreover, this traditional site is close to the ancient Essene gate, which has also been excavated by archeologists.[26] It seems likely, then, that the Upper Room was in the part of Jerusalem used by Essenes. As noted earlier, archeologists who had excavated the Essene gate found a short distance outside of it a latrine and ritual baths that would have suited Essene requirements for ritual purity for those living in the city.[27] Distinctive "Essene" graves like those in the cemetery of Qumran have been found nearby.[28] Also, a path leading out of the Essene gate can be reconstructed all the way down to the Dead Sea, terminating at Qumran.[29] All of this circumstantial evidence supports the hypothesis that the Essenes lived in the area near the Upper Room, and thus it is more likely that Jesus celebrated the Passover in or near their community and according to their calendar.[30]

There is some overlooked textual support for this hypothesis in the Gospel of John. John has a curious habit of describing the various religious festivals in Israel and always clarifying that they are "of the Jews":

> The Passover *of the Jews* was at hand, and Jesus went up to Jerusalem. (John 2:13)

> After this there was a feast *of the Jews,* and Jesus went up to Jerusalem. (5:1)

> Now the Passover, the feast *of the Jews,* was at hand. (6:4)

> Now the Passover *of the Jews* was at hand, and many went up from the country to Jerusalem before the Passover, to purify themselves. (11:55)

Let's think about this expression "the Passover of the Jews" in John 11:55. At first glance, it seems redundant: "Passover of the Jews"? What other kind of Passover was there? It's like saying "the Fourth of July of the Americans." Who else celebrates the Fourth of July?

So what does John mean by "the Passover of the Jews"? First of all, this is not a good translation. John's Greek term *ioudaios* is better rendered by "Judeans" than by the modern word "Jews," for reasons I mentioned in chapter 4. Second, the term is *not* redundant. There was *not* just one Passover. The "Passover of the Judeans" would refer to the Passover celebrated by the Temple-state of Judea, run by Herod and the alliance of Pharisees and Sadducees. But there were other Passovers as well. In the time of Jesus, the Samaritans celebrated Passover according to their own calendar and at their own temple on Mt. Gerizim, to the north of Jerusalem, and still do to this day.[31] There were a lot more Samaritans at that time than we realize, and like the Judeans, they had communities and synagogues in major cities throughout the Roman

Empire, except they always self-identified as "Israelites," not as "Judeans."[32] And there was also the Essene Passover, and like the Samaritans, the Essenes considered themselves "Israelites" rather than "Judeans."[33]

So, when John says things like "the Passover of the Judeans was at hand," it is not a throwaway line or a redundancy. It means he is dating the event according to the liturgical calendar used by the Judeans and the Jerusalem Temple, as opposed to the calendar of the Samaritans, the Essenes, or others. It seems that, according to the Temple calendar, Passover fell on a Saturday (a Sabbath) on the week of Jesus' Passion, and so the Lord celebrated the Last Supper well before the Judean feast began (John 13:1) and he was crucified on the day directly before it (John 19:14), which explains the urgency of the Judeans to remove the bodies before the beginning of the holy day (John 19:31).[34]

The Last Supper itself, however, would have been celebrated according to the old solar calendar used by the Essenes and others, on Tuesday evening earlier in the week. The difference between the Tuesday evening Passover of the solar calendar and the Saturday Passover of the Judean calendar nicely explains the four-day gap between Mark's and John's datings of the anointing at Bethany as "two days" and "six days" before the Passover, respectively (Mark 14:1; John 12:1). A Tuesday evening Last Supper would also explain the otherwise inexplicable fact that the early Church observed a fast on Wednesdays to commemorate the arrest of the Lord on that day. Since no one could conclude from the Gospels that the Lord's arrest was on Wednesday, this practice must have been based on independent tradition.[35] Furthermore, two early Church Fathers, Epiphanius of Salamis and Victorinus of Pettau, relate a tradition that the Last Supper was on a Tuesday.[36] The testimony of Epiphanius is particularly important, since he seems to have been born into a Jewish-Christian family from the Holy

Land, and he was in touch with Jewish-Christian traditions from Jerusalem going back to the first century C.E.[37]

One of the strongest reasons for holding this calendrical explanation for the "discrepancy" between John and the Synoptics on the dating of the Last Supper is that it would allow enough time for all the trials and other events that the Gospels say took place between the arrest and Crucifixion of Jesus. Using John, the most detailed account, as our chronological framework, these events would include

1. A hearing before Annas, the High Priest emeritus (John 18:13–24)

2. A hearing before Caiaphas, the sitting High Priest (John 18:24–28; Matt 26:57–68; Mark 14:53–72; Luke 22:54–62)

3. A trial before the entire Sanhedrin (the full Jewish council) (Matt 27:1–2; Mark 15:1; Luke 22:66–71)

4. An initial hearing before Pontius Pilate (John 18:28–32; Matt 27:11–14; Mark 15:2–5; Luke 23:1–2)

5. A private interrogation before Pilate (John 18:33–38; cf. Luke 23:3)

6. A *lengthy* interrogation before King Herod (Luke 23:8–12)

7. A public hearing in which Pilate tries to exchange Jesus for Barabbas (John 18:38–40; Mark 15:6–11?; Luke 23:13–19)

8.   The scourging and mockery of Jesus (John 19:1–3; Matt 27:27–31; Mark 15:16–20)

9.   A public exposure of Jesus to the crowds after his scourging (John 19:4–7)

10.   Another private interrogation before Pilate (John 19:9–11)

11.   Negotiations between Pilate and the Jewish authorities in which Pilate tries to get Jesus released (John 19:12–13)

12.   The final "showdown," when Pilate sits on the judgment seat, attempts to release Jesus, but ultimately capitulates to the crowd and hands Jesus over for execution (John 19:12–16; Matt 27:15–26; Mark 15:6–15 [or 12–15?]; Luke 23:22–25)

None of the Gospels records all of these events in sequence, so it is clear that each author is exercising some literary freedom and relating the events of the Passion selectively. The Gospel authors could not relate everything Jesus said and did (John 21:25), so they chose the events that best illustrated the truths about Jesus they were trying to communicate, and omitted others. For example, there are no obvious time breaks in Mark's narration of Jesus' Passion: nonetheless, in between events that he records, we must allow time for encounters he omits, like the hearings before Annas and Herod, and the multiple interrogations before Pilate. It is also virtually impossible that all these hearings, trials, and negotiations took place within only twelve hours between midnight Thursday and noon Friday—and on the Passover, too! Some scholarly reconstructions would have us believe that—*on the very day of the Judean Passover,* the Judean religious authorities assembled as a legal court multiple times, underwent serious negotiations with the Roman governor and the Jewish king, gathered and instigated a mob, and had Jesus crucified, all within *half a day,* despite the fact that they had previously resolved *not* to arrest him on the feast (Mark 14:2) and that night trials and trials on feast days were *forbidden* in Jewish law (*Mishnah Sanhedrin* 4:1). Then, strangely, it *doesn't* bother these scholars that Jesus is hanging on a cross during Passover—the holiest day of the year next to Yom Kippur—but they *do* want to rush to get him off the cross for the Sabbath the following day (John 19:31)! All of this does not seem very plausible.[38]

Rather, one could propose the following scenario: the Jerusalem authorities plotted to get rid of Jesus prior to the weeklong festival of Passover and Unleavened Bread in Jerusalem. They had him arrested on Tuesday night before the Passover on Saturday, thinking they had plenty of time for a trial on Wednesday and execution on Thursday. But the legal process did not go smoothly, especially when Pilate became sympathetic to Jesus and started to impede the proceedings, and so they ended up having to rush to get him executed prior to the start of the Passover Feast at sundown on Friday.

Jesus, however, had observed Passover according to the old liturgical calendar, along with the Essenes, who had sympathies with Jesus and his disciples because of personal ties and a common opposition to the ruling parties. In this way, providentially, Jesus both gave himself sacramentally in the Upper Room on Passover and gave himself physically on the cross on Passover—each by a different calendar.

It's true that this explanation of the Last Supper cannot be proven, but it does make sense of a great deal of data that otherwise seems like random "noise": the man carrying the jar of water, the young man wearing a single linen garment, the site of the

Upper Room near the ancient Essene gate, the curious four-day discrepancy of Mark 14:1 and John 12:1, John's phrase "Passover of the Judeans," the too many trials for the wee hours of Friday morning, and the otherwise inexplicable ancient references to a Tuesday night Last Supper and arrest on Wednesday.

Oftentimes the best proof of a theory is its explanatory power, and when in scholarship one can advance a single theory that suddenly unites and makes sense of a lot of data that otherwise seemed unrelated and inexplicable, it's often an indication that one has hit upon the truth.

In any event, the calendrical hypothesis is a plausible solution to the apparent disagreement between the Gospels concerning when Passover fell during Passion Week, and it respects what all the Gospels have to say on the matter without dismissing any of them as fictitious or unhistorical. Moreover, it's based on solid scholarship in archeology, the Dead Sea Scrolls, Second Temple Judaism, and Gospel studies. So if I were Bart Ehrman, I wouldn't use this as a leading example that the Gospels disagree with one another and therefore can't be trusted. Rather, I would point out that attention to the details of the Gospel accounts leads us into a fascinating religious and cultural "backstory" of Passion Week.

The Dead Sea Scrolls may help solve the discrepancy that the first three Gospels portray Jesus celebrating the Last Supper on Passover, yet John describes him as crucified the day before that holy feast. The Scrolls show us that the Essenes followed an older liturgical calendar, in which Passover fell on a Tuesday evening. Matthew, Mark, and Luke seem to be dating the events of Passion Week by this older calendar, whereas John dates by the newer Judean Temple calendar. Curious features of the Gospel accounts, as well as archeological data and ancient patristic traditions, would be explained if Jesus celebrated the Last Supper in the Essene neighborhood of Jerusalem, according to the calendar they used.

For Further Reading

Jaubert, Annie. *The Date of the Last Supper.* New York: Alba House, 1965.

Pixner, Bargil. *Paths of the Messiah and the Sites of the Early Church from Galilee to Jerusalem.* Edited by Rainer Riesner. Translated by Keith Myrick et al. San Francisco: Ignatius Press, 2010. Especially chaps. 15, 18, 19, 25, and 26.

Saulnier, Stéphane. *Calendrical Variations in Second Temple Judaism: New Perspectives on the "Date of the Last Supper" Debate.* Supplements to the *Journal for the Study of Judaism* 159. Leiden: Brill, 2012.

CHAPTER 8

Putting It All Together: Reading the Last Supper in Light of the Scrolls

WHEN I WAS IN JUNIOR HIGH SCHOOL, MY FAMILY ATTENDED a Conservative Baptist church in Connecticut, where—since I was a bookish sort of boy—I got a volunteer position as assistant church librarian. I would open up the church library on Sunday evenings during the social hour after the service and check out books to people. This gave me access to a lot of good literature, and I was a voracious reader. One book I picked up on these Sunday evenings was *The Gospel Blimp and Other Stories* by Joseph Bayly. It was a collection of modern parables gently poking fun at American church life in the late twentieth century. One story was called "How Shall We Remember John?"[1] The premise was, a certain family lost one of their sons and brothers, John, to an accident. They pondered how to keep his memory alive, and hit upon the idea of eating his favorite food, oatmeal, for breakfast. So they would eat oatmeal for breakfast every morning to remember John. But in time, they began to ritualize the meal, eating it in little silver bowls with fancy spoons. Then they moved to once a week, then once a month, then once every three months. The narrator concludes by wishing that they had never gotten away from remembering John at every breakfast.

The message of Bayly's parable was clear: all Jesus intended by the Last Supper was for us to have a meal to remember him. But then the Church got involved over the centuries, and corrupted this ordinary meal into a liturgical ceremony we call the Eucharist. And so what modern Christians need to do is just go back to the simple old family meal where we got together and remembered Jesus.

Bayly's reading of the Last Supper and Church history makes perfect sense through the eyes of a good American Christian at the end of the twentieth century. But it has almost nothing to do with the actual Last Supper, which was celebrated by first-century Jews in Israel.

When we allow the Dead Sea Scrolls to take us back to the mind-set of the Israelites living at the time of Jesus, then Jesus' words and actions at the Last Supper convey a great deal more than just a "meal to remember John."

We will use Luke's account of the Last Supper as our basis, since it is the most detailed. Luke's Gospel is often thought to have been written to educated Greeks and Romans, and many think Luke was a Gentile—the only one to write any book of the New Testament. Nonetheless, I've discovered through studying and teaching this Gospel that Luke is every bit as familiar with the Old Testament and Jewish traditions as the other New Testament writers. He even has several unique parallels to the Dead Sea Scrolls that are not found elsewhere—as we saw in chapter 4.

Luke begins his Last Supper narrative by saying, "Then came the Day of Unleavened Bread, on which it was necessary to sacrifice the Passover lamb" (Luke 22:7). In the Old Testament, the Passover was followed by a weeklong Festival of Unleavened Bread. But by the time of Jesus, these two festivals were fused and both called Passover, as Luke says earlier: "The Feast of Unleavened Bread . . . which is called Passover" (Luke 22:1).

If we are correct, this would have been Tuesday of Passion Week, the start of the Passover by the old calendar. Some take the statement "on which it was necessary to sacrifice the Passover lamb" as indicating that Jesus' disciples actually sacrificed a lamb for the meal at the Temple on this day, and so this had to be the Passover by the Temple calendar.[2] But this is overreading Luke 22:7 and the parallel in Mark 14:12 ("when they would sacrifice the Passover"), both of which mean only that this was the day when law and custom dictated that the lamb should be sacrificed.[3] Whether Jesus and his disciples actually sacrificed a lamb is an open question. The Essenes, and probably other Jews as well, did not participate in the Temple sacrifices because they regarded the Temple as defiled for a variety of reasons.[4] Jesus, likewise, rebukes the Temple leadership by "cleansing" the Temple, and we never see him offering sacrifice there. Some have reasoned, therefore, that the Essenes celebrated Passover without a lamb, since the only place of sacrifice was the Temple, and it was unavailable due to defilement. And perhaps Jesus did likewise. However, recently archeologists have found evidence that the Essenes at Qumran offered their own sacrifices at their own altar.[5] Perhaps the Essenes had altars elsewhere as well, and did celebrate the Passover with a lamb. At this point it's difficult to say one way or the other.

Yet to many theologians, a lamb at the Last Supper seems redundant, since Jesus himself was "the Lamb of God who takes away the sin of the world" (John 1:29), and he knew he was going to give his own "body" and "blood" as the "lamb meat" for this Passover. So, in the absence of any clear description of a lamb being at this meal, it's plausible Jesus celebrated without one and provided Himself as the Lamb, as Genesis 22:8 says: "God will provide Himself the lamb."

Luke continues his description, saying that Jesus sent Peter and John to find a man "carrying a jar of water" who would take them to a "guest room" consisting of a "large upper room." As we saw in the previous chapter, there is reason to believe that the man was a celibate Essene who led them to one of the communal houses run by the movement, and that the house became the center of the Church in Jerusalem, still venerated to this day as the site of the Last Supper.

Luke remarks, "And when the hour came, he sat at table, and the apostles with him" (Luke 22:14). John inserts at this point the account of the foot washing (John 13:1–20). From the Scrolls and Josephus, we know that ritual washing before a sacred meal was an important practice of the Essenes' piety: they washed and dressed in white before every sacred meal. In Christianity, the washing and dressing in white was reconfigured to a once-in-a-lifetime experience of Baptism.

We know that the Essene concern for ritual cleansing was, of course, shared with Judaism more broadly, because John remarks that many Judeans got to Jerusalem well before the Passover to purify themselves (John 11:55), probably referring to ritual washing in the *miqva'ot* of the city. Jesus' washing of the disciples' feet was a smaller-scale ritual cleansing, presuming that they had already performed a fuller ceremony (John 13:10). It carried with it some priestly connotations, because priests had to wash their hands and feet before entering the sanctuary to perform sacrifice (Exod 30:19–21), and Jesus was, in fact, leading the disciples into a kind of sanctuary to show them how to perform a new sacrifice for a new covenant. Josephus says the Essenes went "into the dining room; as into a certain holy temple" (*War* 2:130), and on the night of the Last Supper, Jesus was likewise transforming the Upper Room into a "certain holy temple."

Usually a slave performed the washing of guests' feet, but there were no slaves present. The Essenes held no slaves, but performed for each other whatever menial acts of service were usually relegated to slaves.[6] Although Jesus was not an Essene, he shared a similar egalitarian ethic and used the foot-washing episode to teach, among other things, that the community he was founding was one in which the leaders would need to set the example of humility and service: "I have given you an example, that you also should do as I have done to you" (John 13:15).

Luke makes clear that Jesus presides at the Last Supper, being the first to reach for the cup, and the first to reach for the bread (22:17, 19). Over both he "gives thanks" (Gk. *eucharisteo*), which is synonymous with "blesses," that is, to consecrate the food by offering it to God in a prayer of thanksgiving.[7] From Qumran, we recognize this as a priestly act, for the priest was to preside in blessing the bread and wine of the eschatological meal with the Messiah. In the Upper Room, Jesus is both priest and king, the Son of David, who also was both (Ps 110:4).

Jesus stresses the kingly or royal dimension of what he is doing by repeatedly referring to the soon-coming kingdom of God. He says, "I shall not eat it (again) until the kingdom of God comes," and "from now on I shall not drink of the fruit of the vine (i.e., wine) until the kingdom of God comes" (Luke 22:16, 18). Since wine was a regular part of one's main daily meal, Jesus' words imply that the kingdom of God is about to arrive: before he partakes of his next daily meal, it will already be here. The Essenes celebrated their daily meal of bread and wine in anticipation of the day when the royal "Messiah of Israel" would recline at table and share it with them, after all things were safely under his rule. Jesus is saying that expectation is about to be fulfilled; the Apostles are right on the cusp of it.

Over the bread, Jesus says, "This is my body which is given for you. Do this in *remembrance* of me." But this is no "favorite meal to remember John." In the Temple they celebrated a "Remembrance" or "Memorial" offering, which usually was a portion of bread offered with the animal sacrifice (Lev 24:7). In fact, according to tradition, David wrote two psalms for this sacrifice (Pss 38 and 70), and the heading of the Greek version of these psalms reads *eis anamnêsin,* which modern English translations render "for the memorial sacrifice." Yet this is the same phrase that Jesus employs at the Last Supper. In fact, we can translate Jesus' words as follows: "Do this as my memorial offering."[8] Jesus' words call to mind the Temple offerings and the ceremonies that renewed God's covenant with Israel, because the idea of "remembrance" was associated with the covenant for ancient Israelites.[9] In the Hebrew language, one "remembers" his covenant, which means "to call to mind and then act upon the obligations one has because one is in a covenant relationship."[10] So we read in Zechariah's Benedictus that God has now acted "to *remember* his holy covenant, the oath he swore to our father Abraham" (Luke 1:72–73). The "memorial" or "remembrance" offering in the Temple served to prompt God to "remember" the covenant that he had made between Himself and His people, and send them blessing.[11] Jesus' words call to mind this Temple offering: Jesus is performing a liturgical, covenantal act in this meal.

Over the wine, Jesus says, "This cup which is poured out for you is the *new covenant in my blood*." A covenant is "the extension of kinship by oath," in other words, a family relationship formed by swearing an oath.[12] The old covenant was the covenant of Moses, which had been broken repeatedly, but Jeremiah had promised a new covenant one day:

The days are coming, says the LORD God, when I will make a *new covenant* with the House of Israel and the House of Judah. (Jer 31:31)

"Israel" and "Judah" meant the northern ten tribes *and* the southern two tribes together: all twelve tribes, not just the "Judeans" (Gk. *ioudiaoi*). This "new covenant" would not be like Moses' broken covenant: "not like the covenant which I made with them when I took them by the hand to lead them out of Egypt—my covenant which they broke" (Jer 31:32). It would involve God's supernatural transformation of Israel's hearts: "I will put my law within them, and I will write it upon their hearts. . . . They shall all know me . . . for I will forgive their iniquity." (Jer 31:33–34).

The Essenes thought the "new covenant" had already arrived with them. The Damascus Document speaks repeatedly of the "new covenant" (Heb. *berith ha-hadashah*) that was made "in the land of Damascus."[13] Scholars think either the group literally moved to Damascus at one point and established the covenant there or "Damascus" is a code name for Qumran or another location.[14] In any event, the Essenes were convinced that they were already part of the "new covenant community" that God was establishing at the end of time. The common meal of bread and wine they shared daily was a sign and expression of the fact that each member had been fully initiated into this new covenant.[15]

Jesus and other Jews, however, were not convinced that the Essenes were the final answer. Jesus at the Last Supper claims, to the contrary, that *he* is establishing the new covenant on Zion. The Twelve Apostles represent twelve new patriarchs of the Twelve Tribes of Israel. Mystically, the Twelve Apostles are the nucleus of the new Israel that Jesus is forming through a new covenant established by this ritual meal.[16]

Jesus' words recorded in Matthew and Mark more closely recall Moses' covenant with the Twelve Tribes at Sinai, when Jesus says over the cup, "this is my blood of the covenant"—using the phrase "blood of the covenant" that Moses used for the blood sacrifices which consecrated the covenant between God and Israel at Sinai.[17] The implication is: *What I am doing here with you Twelve Apostles on Zion is as momentous as what Moses did with the Twelve Tribes at Sinai.*

Jesus also speaks of his blood being "poured out for Many."[18] As we mentioned in chapter 6, the Dead Sea Scrolls illuminate this expression. The Hebrew term "Many" was the typical way to refer to the community as a whole.[19] The disciples are the nucleus of that community, and so Luke records Jesus' words in that sense: "poured out for you all" (Luke 22:20), that is, the Apostles.

After Jesus gives his body and blood to the Apostles, a dispute breaks out among them concerning who is the greatest (Luke 22:24). As we noted in chapter 6, in the sacred meals of the Essenes and other Jewish societies, it was important that everyone be seated in order of their rank within the society.[20] It wasn't *just* that the Apostles were excessively vain—although they were vain to some extent. Jesus urges them not to be so concerned about their ranking:

> The kings of the Gentiles exercise lordship over them; and those in authority over them are called benefactors. But not so with you; rather let the greatest among you become as the youngest, and the leader as one who serves. For which is the greater, one who sits at table, or one who serves? Is it not the one who sits at table? But I am among you as one who serves. (Luke 22:25–27)

This ideal of mutual service is one that the Essenes also practiced, despite their concern about proper rank in ritual proceedings. Philo records about them that

> they repudiate and keep aloof from everything which can possibly afford any inducement to covetousness; and there is not a single slave among them, but they are all free, aiding one another with a reciprocal interchange of good offices; and they condemn masters, not only as unjust, inasmuch as they corrupt the very principle of equality, but likewise as impious, because they destroy the ordinances of nature, which generated them all equally. . . . But in their view this natural relationship of all men to one another has been thrown into

disorder by designing covetousness, continually wishing to surpass others in good fortune, and which has therefore engendered alienation instead of affection, and hatred instead of friendship.[21]

One can see the similarity in spirit with Jesus' teachings about servant-leadership at the Last Supper. One might easily object that this fraternal spirit that Philo attributes to the Essenes seems at odds with some of their internal writings in the Scrolls that place such a heavy emphasis on the hierarchical structure of the community. Yet for all their emphasis on the hierarchy within the community, the Scrolls also stress a fraternal and egalitarian spirit among its members: humility and brotherly love one toward another are strongly emphasized, as well as the right of every member of the community to speak in a deliberative session, and the need for the Overseer to consult the opinion of every member of the community on important decisions.[22]

After Jesus stresses the need for servant-leadership, he commends the disciples for their loyalty:

> You are those who have continued with me in my trials; and I *covenant* to you, as my Father *covenanted* to me, a kingdom, that you may eat and drink at my table in my kingdom, and sit on thrones judging the Twelve Tribes of Israel. (Luke 22:28–30, RSV *alt.*)

In many ways this is the climax of Luke's account of the Last Supper, as Jesus bestows upon the Apostles the kingdom given him by his Father. The verb used for bestowing the kingdom is usually translated "appoint" or something similar in English, but it is the usual Greek word (*diatithêmi*) for covenant-making in the Old Testament.[23] There was only one kingdom in the Old Testament established by, and associated with, a covenant—and that was the Kingdom of David.[24] Of course, Luke is at pains to demonstrate that Jesus is the Son of David (Luke 2:4–7, 3:31).

It is this kingdom that Jesus is giving to the Apostles, as part of a new covenant that he has established with them through participation in this meal. Jesus the Son of David is establishing the Apostles as his twelve royal officers, just as Solomon Son of David had twelve officers over his kingdom (1 Kings 4:7). He has just fed them with the free supper promised by Isaiah that would establish with the supper guests the covenant of David (Isa 55:1–3). The privilege of receiving the kingdom is first of all that they will be able to "eat and drink at my table in my kingdom" (Luke 22:30a). This is the end-times banquet for the officers of Israel with the royal Messiah, which the Essenes foresaw so vividly and specified instructions for in the Rule of the Congregation. But the Apostles would also "sit on thrones judging the Twelve Tribes of Israel" (Luke 22:30b). This recalls the image of the Messiah of Israel sitting down at the banquet with the high officers of the kingdom, the "heads of the thousands of Israel," as the Rule of the Congregation says, which in turn may reach back to the image of the officers Solomon placed over the Twelve Tribes in 1 Kings 4:7.[25] What is absolutely clear is that Jesus asserts he is reestablishing the Davidic kingdom of Israel at this supper, and establishing the Twelve Apostles as the viceroys or princes of that kingdom.

To sum up, when we see the Last Supper through the lens of Qumran and the sacred meal tradition of the Essenes, whole new dimensions of this event surface. We see in Jesus' leadership in the meal and blessing of the bread and wine a distinct priestly role, but also an unmistakably royal role evoked by his "covenanting" of his kingdom to the Apostles. No casual meal, the Last Supper unfolds according to Jewish sacred meal traditions ultimately connected to the Temple and the priesthood. Most of all, this is a *covenant meal* that symbolized and actualized each diner's participation in the *new covenant*, just as partaking in the Passover joined every Israelite to the Covenant of Moses, and partaking in the Essene meal joined every Essene to their "new covenant of Damascus." The command "do this in remembrance of me" suggested this meal was to be repeated by the Apostles as a kind of "memorial" offering intended to "remember"—that is, call to mind and renew—the covenant that communicated forgiveness of sins to the "Many," the whole community formed and joined together by this covenant.

Now, many of the similarities and connections are not entirely unique to the Essenes, but the Dead Sea Scrolls provide us the attestation of these concepts and practices that is closest in time and place to the ministry of Jesus of Nazareth. In light of the Scrolls, we have certainly seen enough to conclude that the Last Supper was far, far more than just a "meal to remember John."

Finally, it is fascinating to see how the themes, motifs, and practices we have identified continue into the life of the early Church, and I would like to conclude this section with the oldest description of the Christian Lord's Supper/Eucharist that we have, from only sixty years after the death of the Apostle John, the last surviving participant of Jesus' Last Supper. This description was written by the Church Father Justin Martyr (A.D. 100–165), who was trying to explain to educated Greeks and Romans the nature of the weekly meal celebrated by Christians:

> But we, after we have thus washed [i.e., baptized] him who has been convinced and has assented to our teaching, bring him to the place where those who are called brethren are assembled. . . . There is then brought to the president of the brethren bread and a cup of wine mixed with water; and he taking them, gives praise and glory to the Father of the universe, through the name of the Son and of the Holy Ghost, and offers thanks (Gk. *eucharisteo*) at considerable length for our being counted worthy to receive these things at His hands.

And when he has concluded the prayers and thanksgivings, all the people present express their assent by saying Amen. . . . Those who are called by us deacons give to each of those present to partake of the bread and wine mixed with water over which the thanksgiving (Gk. *eucharistêsis*) was pronounced, and to those who are absent they carry away a portion. And this food is called among us "the Eucharist," of which no one is allowed to partake but the man who believes that the things which we teach are true, and who has been washed with the washing that is for the remission of sins, and unto regeneration, and who is so living as Christ has enjoined. For not as common bread and common drink do we receive these; but in like manner as Jesus Christ our Saviour, having been made flesh by the Word of God, had both flesh and blood for our salvation, so likewise have we been taught that the food which is blessed by the prayer of His word, and from which our blood and flesh by transmutation are nourished, is the flesh and blood of that Jesus who was made flesh. For the apostles, in the memoirs composed by them, which are called Gospels, have thus delivered unto us what was enjoined upon them; that Jesus took bread, and when He had given thanks, said, "This do ye in remembrance of Me, this is My body;" and that, after the same manner, having taken the cup and given thanks, He said, "This is My blood;" and gave it to them alone.[26]

The Dead Sea Scrolls help us flesh out the Jewish sacred meal practices of the first century, and in this light, the accounts of Jesus' Last Supper in the Gospels take on vibrant color. Jesus acts like a messianic priest and king in the Upper Room, forming a covenant with the Apostles that confers on them the status of princes of the Davidic covenant. This meal is a liturgical act with connections to the Jewish priesthood and Temple, and it is meant to be repeated until Jesus the Messiah returns.

For Further Reading

Hahn, Scott. *The Fourth Cup: Unveiling the Mystery of the Last Supper and the Cross.* New York: Image, 2018.

Pitre, Brant. *Jesus and the Jewish Roots of the Eucharist: Unlocking the Secrets of the Last Supper.* New York: Image, 2011.

Van Der Ploeg, J. "The Meals of the Essenes." *Journal of Semitic Studies* 2, no. 2 (1957): 163–175.

PART FOUR

MATRIMONY, CELIBACY, AND THE SCROLLS

CHAPTER 9

Celibacy in the Scrolls

IN 2003, DAN BROWN, THE AUTHOR OF SEVERAL *NEW YORK Times* bestsellers, caused quite a stir with his book *The Da Vinci Code*, in which he argued (among other things) that Jesus was actually married to Mary Magdalene.[1] One of the arguments Brown used to support this otherwise fairly absurd hypothesis was that Jesus *had* to be married, because Jews don't practice celibacy and place a high value on procreation. A good Jew takes God's blessing to "be fruitful and multiply" (Gen 1:22) as the first *mitzvah* (commandment) in the Torah, and therefore he has a moral obligation to find a wife and raise children for the glory of God and the people of Israel. Rabbis, especially, had to set the example, so Jesus the Rabbi must have been married, and Mary Magdalene was his wife.

I didn't care for *The Da Vinci Code*, but I can't blame Dan Brown too much; for most of my life I made the same basic mistake he makes: assuming modern Judaism is identical to ancient Judaism. For example, growing up a devout Protestant, I read the Bible daily in my teen years, but I can remember being quite confused by Jesus' teaching on marriage and celibacy in Matthew 19:

> He said to them, "Whoever divorces his wife, except for unchastity, and marries another, commits adultery; and he who

marries a divorced woman, commits adultery." The disciples said to him, "If such is the case of a man with his wife, it is not expedient to marry." But he said to them, "Not all men can receive this precept, but only those to whom it is given. *For there are eunuchs who have been so from birth, and there are eunuchs who have been made eunuchs by men, and there are eunuchs who have made themselves eunuchs for the sake of the kingdom of heaven.* He who is able to receive this, let him receive it." (19:8–12; emphasis mine)

I understood well enough that "eunuchs who have been so from birth" must mean men born with a condition that prevented them from having children, and I also knew what "eunuchs who have been made eunuchs by men" meant: it was common practice for kings in the ancient Near East to employ eunuchs to watch over the royal harems as well as serve in other offices in the palace, so much so that in some ancient languages the words for "eunuch" and "royal officer" are the same.[2] But what puzzled me was the phrase "eunuchs who have made themselves eunuchs for the sake of the kingdom of heaven." I knew that had to refer to men who voluntarily accepted celibacy for religious reasons, but who was doing this in Jesus' day? Celibacy was a Christian practice—so I thought—that developed much later, when the Pope in the Middle Ages forced all the clergy in the Catholic Church to become celibate so their sons wouldn't inherit their land and the Pope could take it all for himself.[3]

But getting back to Jesus' words, he says not "There *will be* men who *will make* themselves eunuchs for the sake of the kingdom" but "there *are* eunuchs who *have made* themselves eunuchs for the sake of the kingdom of heaven." So clearly, Jesus is speaking about celibate men of his own day, who are celibate for "the kingdom of heaven." This I found confusing as well, because this idea of "the kingdom of heaven" was unique to Jesus' preaching (I thought). Since Jesus had only recently come on the scene and begun preaching about the "kingdom of heaven," how could there *already be* men who had made themselves eunuchs for its sake?

A scholar would say that both Dan Brown and I were confused, because we were failing to distinguish *rabbinic Judaism* from the *religion of ancient Israel.* This is a mistake I was firmly warned against by my Judaism professor in graduate school.

This requires some explanation: the religious system that we call Judaism, or more accurately, rabbinic Judaism, is largely a postbiblical development, that is to say, it evolved after the books that make up the Old Testament (a.k.a. the Hebrew Bible) had been written. And there are dramatic differences between the way ancient Israelites practiced their religion and the way modern Jews practice theirs.

For example, the religion of ancient Israelites—as reflected in the Bible—revolved around the Temple and the priesthood. There were three major annual feasts for which the Israelite would go on pilgrimage up to the Temple to offer animals in sacrifice, with the assistance of the priests. In addition, when an Israelite committed a grave sin—or conversely, experienced a great blessing—he would travel to the Temple to offer an animal in sacrifice for either atonement or thanksgiving, respectively. Temple, priesthood, animal sacrifice—these were central to the ancient Israelite.

By contrast, the life of the modern Jew revolves around the synagogue, the rabbi, the study of Torah, and prayer. The Old Testament does not mention synagogues or rabbis. A synagogue is not a Temple, and no sacrifices are performed there. It is not even primarily a place of worship. The term "synagogue" is Greek for "coming together," and synagogues developed in the Hellenistic period (c. 300–100 B.C.), when Jews were scattered around the Mediterranean too far to travel to the Temple. So to maintain their faith, they established common houses to gather together for prayer and the study of the Scriptures. The teachers of the Scriptures became known as "rabbis," and so began the tradition of the synagogue as a house of study and prayer, and it continues to this day.

In the lifetime of Jesus, both systems—the rabbi-synagogue and the priest-Temple—were operational. Jews in the land of Israel prayed weekly or daily in the synagogue, but then also made pilgrimage to offer animal sacrifice in the Temple according to the law of Moses. But in A.D. 70, the Romans destroyed the Temple in Jerusalem, and the priesthood was dispersed. That left only the rabbi-synagogue system, which developed further in order to adapt the law of Moses for observance when its central focus—the sanctuary or Temple—was no longer in existence. The body of law that developed from this process was collected in various documents, like the Mishnah (c. A.D. 200) and the Talmud (c. A.D. 600). One of the differences that developed was the system of *kosher* food. While the law of Moses prohibits many kinds of food, the system of *kosher* is considerably more complex. Moses forbade the boiling of a young goat in its mother's milk (Exod 23:19, 34:26; Deut 14:21), which was a Canaanite magic ritual. Rabbis in late antiquity took this to imply a general prohibition against mixing milk products with meat products, which in turn required a whole classification system of foods into "meaty" (*fleishig*), "milky" (*milchig*), or "neutral" (*pareve*), and the development of a culinary system that kept them separate. That whole system is far more complex than the relatively simple lists of prohibited foods in the law of Moses. Thus, to talk about Moses and the Israelites "keeping kosher" in the desert would be an *anachronism*—that is, something out of proper sequence in historical time.

Another anachronism is the idea that ancient Israelites were opposed to celibacy. Although modern rabbinic Judaism strongly encourages every Jewish man to raise children, the same compulsion was not felt in antiquity. Celibacy actually was practiced already by the ancient Israelite prophets. Elijah and Elisha, for example, gave up regular family life in order to serve their divine calling.[4] Likewise, God commanded Jeremiah to remain single as a witness to his contemporaries (Jer 16:1–4), and Ezekiel was told to remain a widower (Ezek 24:15–24) for the same reason. Other prophets were also celibate, as was the last and greatest of them, John the Baptist. In the New Testament, Jesus, John the Apostle, and Paul were all celibate, and others as well.

Why be celibate? One reason was as a sign of the impending judgment of God. Sometimes the prophet remained single as a sign that now was not the time to raise a family, because God was bringing an awful punishment on the people.[5] But there was also the practical reason that the demanding lifestyle of a prophet was incompatible with both the responsibilities and the pleasures of family life. So there was a certain tradition of prophetic celibacy.

For the priests, too, there was a kind of periodic celibacy. According to the law of Moses, marital relations rendered one unclean for at least a day, and so a priest on continuous duty in the sanctuary could not engage in relations with his wife.[6] Priests thus had to remain "celibate" for stretches of time when they were on duty at the Temple, and the opportunity to conceive a child was limited to those times when they were "off duty," so to speak—that is, they had a stretch of days when they were not required to serve.

Now, as we have seen, the Essenes regarded themselves as the heirs of both the prophets and the priesthood, and their practice of celibacy was one of the most notable features of their religious lifestyle. All the classical scholars that describe the Essenes—Josephus, Philo, Pliny, and some less important writers—remark on their celibacy:

These Essenes reject pleasures as an evil, but esteem continence. . . . They neglect wedlock, but choose out other persons' children . . . and form them according to their own
manners. (Josephus)[7]

They repudiate marriage; and at the same time they practice
continence in an eminent degree; for no one of the Essenes
ever marries a wife. (Philo)[8]

The solitary tribe of the Essenes which is remarkable beyond
all the other tribes of the whole world as it has no women and
has renounced all sexual desire. (Pliny)[9]

It is a remarkable convergence that not one but three ancient
scholars would record that the Essenes were celibate. Moreover,
their testimony to this practice is not limited to an isolated comment, but all three also go on to describe the kind of communal
life the Essenes lived, without ever mentioning women or children as being present among them—and indeed, the austere Essene lifestyle the classical authors describe leaves no room at all for
raising one's own family. The Essenes lived an ascetical life with
meals, possessions, and finances in common—and whether then
or now, one cannot raise a family in circumstances like that.

Many scholars have argued that the Essenes weren't really celibate, and the idea that they were arose from some other reason.

Some argue, for example, that all the classical authors were
wrong about the Essenes because they were affected by a suppos-
edly "pro-celibacy" worldview of antiquity.[10] However, there is no
evidence that Josephus, Philo, or Pliny was pro-celibacy. None of
them were themselves celibate, and with one exception, they do
not claim in their writings that any other groups besides the Essenes were celibate.[11] Greco-Roman culture did not encourage or

promote celibacy. True, the ancient authors were impressed by the Essenes' self-control, but not so much that they wanted to adopt the lifestyle for themselves!

Some argue that the idea the Essenes were celibate largely arose because certain Catholic priests like Fr. Roland De Vaux played a leading role in the initial discovery of the Scrolls, and popularized the notion. But many, many scholars of a wide variety of religious and ethnic backgrounds—including Israeli scholars of such eminence as Yigael Yadin, Elisha Qimron, and Magen Broshi—have been convinced the Qumran Essenes were celibate.[12]

Others insist that it is only the external testimony of the classical authors that suggests the Qumran site was inhabited by celibate men. If we just went on the basis of the archeological remains and Dead Sea Scrolls themselves, the argument goes, we would never get the idea that the Qumran Essenes were celibate. However, that argument does not hold water either. Both the Scrolls and the archeology suggest a celibate male community lived at Qumran. Archeologically, we find at Qumran almost no feminine-gendered objects—things like jewelry, certain kinds of combs, hand mirrors, or spindles, which are found at other Jewish sites from the period and are reliable indicators of the presence of women.[13] Furthermore, although some female skeletons have been found in the cemetery, further investigation has shown that these burials were probably not from the period when the Qumran community was occupied. There is not a single undisputed female or child skeleton among the more than thirty skeletons exhumed from the main cemetery, which consists of nearly one thousand north-south-oriented shaft graves.[14] We should recall that in most ancient cemeteries, adult men make up less than 25 percent of the remains. Moreover, these shaft graves themselves seem to indicate the rejection of family life, because each one contains but a single skeleton, contrary to Jewish burial practice of the time, in which all members of a nuclear or even extended family were interred in a common cave or tomb.

The point is, even without the external historical witness, the absence of women and children from the *Community Rule* and their nearly complete absence from the archeological record at Qumran during its occupation period would appear suspicious. It would suggest that whoever lived here rejected the normal form of Jewish family life.

The next obvious question is, Why were the Essenes practicing celibacy? And although they never explicitly provide a rationale in their internal documents, it is not even a challenge to figure out the reason: marital relations rendered one unclean, and the Qumranites never wanted to be unclean! They aspired to "perfect holiness"—and cleanliness, while not the *same* as holiness, was a *prerequisite* for holiness.[15]

For example, we've looked in chapter 1 at this famous passage from the Damascus Document:

> In short, for all who conduct their lives by these laws, in *perfect holiness* (Heb. *tamîm qôdesh*), according to all the instructions, God's covenant stands firm to give them life for thousands of generations. [space] *But* if they live in camps according to the rule of the land and marry women and beget children, then let them live in accordance with the Law. (CD 7:4–7; emphasis mine)

This passage contrasts two different lifestyles: the life of "perfect holiness" and the life of "living in camps," where they "marry and beget children." The unavoidable implication, then, is that the life of "perfect holiness" means giving up on marriage and children.[16] Such persons need some encouragement, because they lack the natural consolation of seeing their own offspring carry on their legacy. So the Damascus Document provides that encouragement: "God's covenant stands firm to give them life for thousands of generations."

The other group, the one that marries and raises children, must certainly be the "other order of Essenes" that Josephus alone mentions—an order that lives regular family life:

> Moreover, there is another order of Essenes, who agree with the rest as to their way of living, and customs, and laws, but differ from them in the point of marriage, as thinking that by not marrying they cut off the principal part of the human life. (*War* 2:160)

What percentage of the Essene movement belonged to the marrying branch is an open question. From the fact that the ancient authors describe the celibate Essenes almost exclusively, it would seem that the marrying Essenes were not characteristic of the movement as a whole.

The majority of the movement was attracted to the idea of "perfect holiness," which means not celibacy per se but a lifestyle in which one never becomes unclean—at least not voluntarily—and thus would *include* celibacy but not be *defined* by celibacy.

Interwoven with their desire to live "perfect holiness" was the Qumranites' self-conception as a priesthood and a Temple. Referring to the *Yahad* of Qumran, the *Community Rule* states:

> They will be "the tested wall, the precious cornerstone" (Isa 28:16) whose foundations shall neither be shaken nor swayed, a fortress, a *Holy of Holies for Aaron,* all of them knowing the Covenant of Justice and thereby offering a sweet savor. They shall be *a blameless and true House* in Israel, upholding the covenant of eternal statutes. (1QS 8:7–10)

"House of God" is the Hebrew idiom for the Temple,[17] and the description *"blameless and true House"* is temple-language. The Qumran community regarded themselves as the dwelling place of the Spirit of God, not merely a temple but truly a "Holy of Holies for Aaron," that is, the most holy part of the Temple, where atonement could be made for all the people.[18]

However, nothing unclean could enter the Temple, and it was unthinkable that anyone would engage in marital relations in the Temple, because such an act rendered the persons and their environment unclean. Therefore, the Essenes forbade relations not only in the Temple but indeed in the entire city of Jerusalem:

No man who has a nocturnal emission is to enter any part of My temple until three complete days have passed. He must launder his clothes and bathe on the first day; on the third he must again launder and bathe; then, after the sun has set, he may enter the temple. They are not to enter My temple while unclean, for that would defile it. If a man has intercourse with his wife, he may not enter any part of the temple city (where I shall make My name to dwell) for three days. (11QTemple[a] 45:7–12)

But since the Qumran community regarded themselves as not only a substitute temple but a "Holy of Holies for Aaron," it followed that all members of the community had to live the life of "perfect holiness," never *willfully* engaging in any activity that rendered them unclean, including intercourse. It's not clear whether the Qumran community defined the extent of their human "temple" by geography—up to the border of their settlement, for example—or by membership, such that the "temple" extended to each person who had entered the covenant of their community. But for daily life at Qumran, the distinction would have been insignificant: intercourse and other defiling actions could not take place within the community, period.

The early Church, like the Qumran community, regarded itself as a human Temple. Paul's Letter to the Ephesians impresses on young Christians:

> You are fellow citizens with the saints and members of the household of God, built upon the foundation of the apostles and prophets, Christ Jesus himself being the cornerstone, in whom the whole structure is joined together and grows into a holy temple in the Lord. (Eph 2:19–21)

The Temple was not geographical but extended to every member of the Church. Elsewhere Paul reminds the first Christians:

> Do you not know that your body is a temple of the Holy Spirit within you, which you have from God? (1 Cor 6:19)

Interestingly, the early Church, like Qumran, saw a direct link between the temple-nature of the community and sexual behavior. Because they are the Temple of the Holy Spirit, Paul warns Christians strongly:

> Do you not know that your bodies are members of Christ? Shall I therefore take the members of Christ and make them members of a prostitute? Never! . . . Shun sexual immorality (Gk. *porneia*). Every other sin which a man commits is outside the body; but the sexually immoral man sins against his own body. (1 Cor 6:15, 18; RSV *alt.*)

While the Qumranites required abstention from all intercourse for their temple-members, the Church required abstention only outside of marriage. Intercourse of husband and wife was considered pure in itself: "Let marriage be held in honor among all, and let the marriage bed be undefiled; for God will judge the immoral and adulterous" (Heb 13:4).

That is not to say that early Christians did not place value on celibacy. With the Essenes, and unlike the Pharisees and Sadducees, the young Church had great respect for the celibate state, although for different reasons. For the Essenes, celibacy was part of the larger effort to live a life of perfect ritual cleanliness. For Christians, the issue was not ritual cleanliness but a freedom from the obligations of family life in order to be wholly dedicated to the Lord. This is reflected in Jesus' own teaching: "There are eunuchs who have made themselves eunuchs for the sake of the kingdom of heaven. He who is able to receive this, let him receive it" (Matt 19:12), meaning celibacy for a spiritual goal was a noble state, and those who were able to live it, should. St. Paul, too, in his long discussion of marriage in his letters to Corinth, emphasizes the value of celibacy, which he himself practiced:

> It is well for a man not to touch a woman. . . . I wish that all were as I myself am. But each has his own special gift from God, one of one kind and one of another. To the unmarried and the widows I say that it is well for them to remain single as I do. But if they cannot exercise self-control, they should marry. . . . Yet those who marry will have worldly troubles, and I would spare you that. . . . I want you to be free from anxieties. The unmarried man is anxious about the affairs of the Lord, how to please the Lord; but the married man is anxious about worldly affairs, how to please his wife, and his interests are divided. I say this for your own benefit, not to lay any restraint upon you, but to promote good order and to secure your undivided devotion to the Lord. (1 Cor 7:1–35, excerpted)

The point, then, of Christian celibacy was not ritual cleanliness but "undivided devotion to the Lord." But we shouldn't draw the contrast between Essenes and Christians too starkly, because in Essenism, the concern for ritual cleanliness was not for its own sake but rather for the sake of always being able to worship, which uncleanness prevented. So for the Essenes, too, celibacy was *ultimately* for the sake of "undivided devotion" to the LORD God of Israel.

In the early Church, this "undivided devotion" was expected especially of clergy, and some early Church councils record that celibacy for the leaders of the Church was a tradition going back to the Apostles:

> It is fitting that the holy bishops and priests of God as well as the Levites [= deacons], that is, those who are in the service of the divine sacraments, observe perfect continence, so that they may obtain in all simplicity what they are asking from God; *what the Apostles taught and what antiquity itself observed,* let us also endeavor to keep. . . . It pleases us all that bishop, priest, and deacon, guardians of purity, abstain from conjugal intercourse with their wives, so that those who serve at the altar may keep a perfect chastity. (Council of Carthage, A.D. 397)[19]

Interestingly, the early Church practiced continence for clergy, but this was not necessarily opposed to marriage. Rather, clergy were expected to keep continent after receiving Holy Orders, even if they were married.[20] In some parts of the Church this rule was not well kept, leading to scandal. Siricius, one of the Bishops of Rome during the lifetime of St. Augustine, remarks in one of his letters, "We have indeed discovered that many priests and deacons of Christ brought children into the world, either through union with their wives or through shameful intercourse."[21] Despite that, influential Church Fathers such as St. Augustine, St. Ambrose,

St. Jerome, and St. Hilary were convinced that only the celibate life was compatible with the total dedication that the pastor should have to the Lord and his Bride, the Church. This conviction won the day in the Latin-speaking Church, such that by the time of Pope Leo the Great (400–461), celibacy was the dominant lifestyle of clergy in the West.[22]

Of course, throughout the history of Christianity, there have been many Christians inspired by the lifestyle of Jesus, the Apostles like Paul and John, and many others to embrace the "undivided devotion to the Lord" that a life of singleness affords. These believers were called the "single ones"—in Greek, "single" is *monos,* which was borrowed into Latin as *monachos.* In time, the single Christians gathered into communities called *monasteria,* where they would work, pray, and worship together—unwittingly re-creating the communal life the Essenes at Qumran used to live. In English, the single male Christians became known as "monks" and their dwellings "monasteries." And when, centuries later, the dwelling and the writings of Qumran were rediscovered, Western scholars immediately recognized the deep similarities of lifestyle and referred to the ancient Qumran community as a "Jewish monastery."[23]

Unlike other branches of ancient Judaism, the Essenes practiced celibacy, and at Qumran, Essene men lived together in religious community. Their practice of celibacy sheds light on Jesus' and Paul's teachings on the subject, and the development of celibate religious life in Christianity.

For Further Reading
Broshi, Magen. "Was Qumran, Indeed, a Monastery?: The Consensus and Its Challengers, an Archaeologist's View." Pages 259–273

in Broshi, *Bread, Wine, Walls and Scrolls.* Sheffield, UK: Sheffield Academic Press, 2001.

Cochini, Christian. *Apostolic Origins of Priestly Celibacy.* Translated by Nelly Marans. San Francisco: Ignatius Press, 1990.

Qimron, Elisha. "Celibacy in the Dead Sea Scrolls and the Two Kinds of Sectarians." Pages 287–294 in *The Madrid Qumran Congress: Volume 1.* Studies on the Texts of the Desert of Judah 11/1. Leiden: Brill, 1992.

CHAPTER 10

Marriage in the Scrolls

DURING THE YEARS I SERVED AS A PASTOR OF AN URBAN mission church, I saw a wide variety of Christian opinions on the nature of marriage. I belonged to a Calvinist denomination that, on paper, was opposed to divorce and remarriage, but two blocks down the street was another Calvinist mission church that had no problem with divorce, remarriage, or even sexual activity outside of marriage. A very large, wealthy Pentecostal church from the suburbs sent a bus into our poor inner-city neighborhood every Sunday to gather folks for their services. They strongly stressed reconciling divorced persons with their first spouses, and I remember talking to one of their members who assured me of his confidence that the Lord would work a reconciliation between himself and his wife, even though she had left him and was living with someone else. I had two friends in the neighborhood who were Catholic, and just outside the neighborhood boundaries was a big Catholic parish. My Catholic friends insisted marriage was a sacrament, but I and most other Protestants vehemently denied that anything was a sacrament other than Baptism and the Lord's Supper. In all, among the half dozen or so tiny churches in the old neighborhood where I served as a pastor, there was a wide variety of views on marriage, its purpose, how permanent it was, whether sex should only take place within it, whether it was a sacrament, and other matters related to this institution.

In Jesus' day, too, there was a wide variety of views on different aspects of marriage and sexuality among the Jewish sects. Everyone agreed that sex should only take place within marriage, but beyond that, most details were disputed. For example, on the issue of the permissibility of divorce, there wasn't even agreement within the Pharisaic sect. There were two major schools of thought among the Pharisees, named after their founders, Rabbi Shammai and Rabbi Hillel. Shammai tended toward a strict, literal application of the law of Moses, whereas Hillel sought to find legal principles that would make the law easier to observe in practice. They sparred over the interpretation of Moses' permission for divorce in Deuteronomy:

> When a man takes a wife and marries her, if then she finds no favor in his eyes because he has found some indecency in her, and he writes her a bill of divorce and puts it in her hand and sends her out of his house, and she departs out of his house, and if she goes and becomes another man's wife, and the latter husband dislikes her and writes her a bill of divorce and puts it in her hand and sends her out of his house, or if the latter husband dies, who took her to be his wife, then her former husband, who sent her away, may not take her again to be his wife, after she has been defiled; for that is an abomination before the LORD, and you shall not bring guilt upon the land which the LORD your God gives you for an inheritance. (24:1–4)

If one observes carefully, one sees that this is not a command to divorce, or even a permission to write a divorce note for one's wife. Formally, the only instruction Moses gives here is that a divorced wife may not go back to her first husband after she has married another man. Be that as it may, the law does tacitly acknowledge divorce and the legal procedure by which it occurs.

The schools of Pharisaic thought disagreed on what the "indecency" in the first verse meant. Shammai argued it meant some grave impurity, like an adulterous act, and short of that, no man ought to divorce his wife. Hillel, on the other hand, argued it could mean just about anything, even that the husband didn't like the way his wife cooked breakfast. One famous rabbi of the Hillel school, Akiba, said divorce was permissible for any reason, even if a husband just wanted a younger, prettier wife.[1]

The debates between these schools were raging in the days of Jesus. So in Mark 10, a group of Pharisee scholars come to Jesus to find out his position on the controversy:

> And Pharisees came up and in order to test him asked, "Is it lawful for a man to divorce his wife?" He answered them, "What did Moses command you?" They said, "Moses allowed a man to write a certificate of divorce, and to put her away." But Jesus said to them, "For your hardness of heart he wrote you this commandment. But from the beginning of creation, 'God made them male and female.' 'For this reason a man shall leave his father and mother and be joined to his wife, and the two shall become one flesh.' So they are no longer two but one flesh. What therefore God has joined together, let not man put asunder." And in the house the disciples asked him again about this matter. And he said to them, "Whoever divorces his wife and marries another, commits adultery against her; and if she divorces her husband and marries another, she commits adultery." (10:2–12)

Jesus' position on marriage expressed here is even more conservative than that of the School of Shammai. Jesus teaches that marriage is *indissoluble*—it can't be broken once contracted. Moses had made a concession to the hard-heartedness of Israelite men who were unwilling to remain faithful to their wives. But Jesus goes all the way back to the account of creation, before human sin entered the world, and bases his theology of marriage on God's design and intent for man and woman "from the beginning." The union of man and woman in marriage is designed and blessed by God, and no human being has the authority to break that union.

Interestingly, Jesus' teaching on marriage resembles none of the schools of Pharisaic thought as much as it does Essene teaching. For example, the Damascus Document criticizes other branches of Judaism for falling into *fornication,* that is, unlawful sexual activity:

> The "Builders of the Wall" . . . are caught in . . . fornication, by taking two wives in their lifetimes, although the principle of creation is "male and female He created them" (Gen 1:27) and those who went into the ark "went into the ark two by two" (Gen 7:9). Concerning the Leader it is written "he shall not multiply wives to himself" (Deut 17:17). (CD 4:19–5:2)

The "Builders of the Wall" are probably the Pharisees.[2] The Pharisees prided themselves in "building a wall around the law," that is, adding restrictions to one's lifestyle to avoid even getting close to actually breaking the laws of Moses. The Essenes criticize these "wall-building" Pharisees for "taking two wives in their lifetimes," which could refer both to bigamy and to divorce and remarriage, since the divorced-and-remarried man would have had two (or more) wives in his lifetime. The law of Moses actually permitted both bigamy (Exod 21:10) and divorce (Deut 24:1–4), so what's fascinating is that the Essenes make the same interpretive move that Jesus makes: they reject the plain sense of the law of Moses in order to go back to earlier biblical texts that represent "the principle of creation" (Heb. *yasôd ha-brî'ah*). In this case they point to the *same text Jesus cites*: "male and female he created them" (Gen 1:27). The point is, God created a balanced pair of male and female: one man (Adam) and one woman (Eve). This indicates God's intention that a man be paired with only one woman. Had God wanted a man to have more than one wife, he would have created one man and several women.

The Essenes backed up this interpretation by citing the account of the Flood, in which the animals all went on Noah's ark "two by two" (Gen 7:9). This indicates that God's intention is an even balance of male and female, an intention that can be seen even in the animal world. Finally, Moses himself—although permitting divorce and bigamy among the common people—forbade the leader of the people from having more than one wife, when he insists that the king "shall not multiply wives to himself" (Deut 17:17). The Essenes took this command very strictly—anything more than one wife was "multiplying wives." What's good for the leader is good for the people: so if the leader ought not to multiply wives, neither should the people.

The view of marriage described in the Damascus Document would, therefore, if consistently applied, lead to the same conclusions that Jesus reaches in Mark 10: divorcing one's wife and marrying another in her lifetime is unlawful and therefore "adultery."[3] So the Pharisees, coming to Jesus to get his views on marriage, would have been surprised that he sides not with Hillel or Shammai but with the very strict views of their Essene opponents. Again, it's quite striking that both the Gospels and the Dead Sea Scrolls dispute with the Pharisees over marriage using the same text (Gen 1:27) and the same interpretive principle (the order of creation)!

While the accounts of the Essenes in Philo, Josephus, and Pliny would lead one to conclude that nearly all the Essenes were celibate males, Josephus does mention that one branch of the order did practice marriage:

> Moreover, there is another order of Essenes, who agree with the rest as to their way of living, and customs, and laws, but differ from them in the point of marriage, as thinking that by not marrying they cut off the principal part of the human life, which is the prospect of succession; nay rather, that if all men should be of the same opinion, the whole race of mankind would fail. . . . But they do not use to accompany with their wives when they are with child, as a demonstration that *they do not marry out of regard to pleasure, but for the sake of posterity.* Now the women go into the baths with some of their garments on, as the men do with somewhat girded about them. And these are the customs of this order of Essenes. (*War* 2:160–161; emphasis mine)

Josephus emphasizes that even the married Essenes practiced modesty (wearing some clothing in the baths) and did not engage in intercourse simply to satisfy lust. Some scholars have cast doubt on Josephus's portrayal of the Essenes, arguing that there are no references in the Scrolls to avoiding intercourse during pregnancy, or some of the other practices Josephus mentions in this passage.[4] On the other hand, we can't expect that every single custom of the Essenes would be documented in the Scrolls they left us, and there was absolutely no motivation for Josephus to have invented the details he records. Furthermore, the principle that "they do not marry out of regard to pleasure, but for the sake of posterity" is, in fact, documented at Qumran, but the fact is frequently overlooked because of a lack of familiarity with the document in question.

We are speaking of the Book of Tobit, which is accepted as a biblical book by Eastern Orthodox Christians and also Catholics, but not by rabbinic Judaism or the Protestant traditions. Five copies of Tobit were found among the scrolls of Qumran, which is a significant number.[5] That's only one fewer than the number of copies of Jeremiah or Ezekiel (six each), and *more* than were found for about a dozen books modern Jews and Christians would consider biblical, including: Job (4), Ruth (4), Song of Songs (4), Lamentations (4), 1–2 Samuel (4), Judges (3), 1–2 Kings (3), Joshua (2), Proverbs (2), Ecclesiastes (2), 1–2 Chronicles (1), Ezra (1), Nehemiah (0), and Esther (0).[6]

Compared to modern Jews and Christians, the Essenes at Qumran almost certainly had a different list of "biblical" books, that is, books they considered inspired or divine Scripture. For example, we have found among the Scrolls about fifteen copies of the *Book of Jubilees* (a rewriting of Genesis and Exodus) and remains of twelve manuscripts of the book we now call *1 Enoch* (consisting of revelations given to the patriarch Enoch).[7] Since both these books claim to be inspired, their popularity at Qumran probably means the Qumranites considered them Sacred Scripture. (Interestingly, both books are considered biblical by the Ethiopic Orthodox Church to this day.) On the other hand, no copies of Esther were found at Qumran, and the Festival of Purim that Esther describes was neither mentioned nor observed there. So it is highly unlikely that the Qumranites considered Esther to be "biblical."

Getting back to Tobit, the relatively large number of copies found at Qumran suggests they did consider this an inspired book. The book tells the life story of the man for which it is named, Tobit, an Israelite descended from Naphtali who lived in the seventh century B.C. (600s) as an exile in the Assyrian capital, Nineveh. Tobit experienced misfortune in his life, despite being a righteous man, and wound up blinded and impoverished. Trying to provide for his family, he sent his son, Tobias, to recover some money that he had left a long time ago with a relative in Media (i.e., Persia, modern Iran). Tobias, guarded by the angel Raphael, has a long adventure in which he recovers the money but also marries his beautiful and wealthy cousin Sarah, who has had more than her own share of misfortune. Sarah was plagued by a demon who slew multiple fiancés of hers on their wedding nights, before any of them could consummate. Thus, in the course of the narrative of Tobit, when Tobias weds Sarah and they retire to the nuptial chamber, he prays a famous prayer for God's protection and blessing of their marriage:

> When the door was shut and the two were alone, Tobias got up from the bed and said, "Sister, get up, and let us pray that the Lord may have mercy upon us." And Tobias began to pray, "Blessed art thou, O God of our fathers, and blessed by thy holy and glorious name for ever. Let the heavens and all thy creatures bless thee. You made Adam and gave him Eve his wife as a helper and support. From them the race of mankind has sprung. You said, 'It is not good that the man should be alone; let us make a helper for him like himself.' And now, O Lord, *I am not taking this sister of mine because of lust, but with sincerity.* Grant that I may find mercy and may grow old together with her." And she said with him, "Amen." Then they both went to sleep for the night. (Tobit 8:4–9)

This passage projects a delicate and refined view of the nature of marriage and the relationship of husband and wife. Tobias calls Sarah "sister," emphasizing companionship, friendship, and equality rather than sexual passion and domination. Tobias also appeals to the same passages of the creation narratives in Genesis 1–2 that Jesus and the Damascus Document appeal to for their theologies of marriage. Finally, Tobias denies that the purpose of his marriage is lust; rather he is taking his kinswoman "with sincerity." By remarking that they both went to sleep, the text suggests they did not even consummate that night.

The classical authors who write about the Essenes agree that they rejected sexual lust. Pliny describes them as "without women, rejecting every sexual passion."[8] Josephus says they "reject pleasures as an evil, but esteem continence, and the conquest over our passions, to be virtue" (*War* 2:120), and even those who procreate "do not marry out of regard for pleasure"(*War* 2:161). Philo describes them as men who "are no longer carried away by the impetuosity of their bodily passions, and are not under the influence of the appetites"(*Hypothetica* 11:3), and "practice continence in an eminent degree" (*Hypothetica* 11:14). The Essenes' emphasis on control of the physical passions is one of the reasons they valued the Book of Tobit, with its nonsensual, companionate view of the relationship of husband and wife.

The Book of Tobit continued to be cherished by the early Christians: it was frequently quoted by Church Fathers and included in the lists of biblical books that come down to us from St. Augustine and early Church councils at Rome (382), Hippo (393), and Carthage (397, 419).[9] To this day, it is a favorite book for the Scripture readings at Catholic weddings.

The rejection of sexual lust evident among the Essenes and in works like Tobit can also be seen in the Gospels and other New Testament writings. Jesus teaches in the famous "Sermon on the Mount":

> You have heard that it was said, "You shall not commit adultery." But I say to you that everyone who looks at a woman lustfully has already committed adultery with her in his heart. If your right eye causes you to sin, pluck it out and throw it away; it is better that you lose one of your members than that your whole body be thrown into hell. (Matt 5:27–29)

Here Jesus teaches that the commandment against adultery, if properly understood, prohibits those things that are the seedbed of sexual immorality, like the lustful ogling of women. This kind of lust needs to be combated, even if doing so requires painful sacrifices. Jesus, of course, does not mean one should literally gouge out one's eyes: this is a use of *hyperbole,* a literary device of overstatement for the sake of emphasis. He means, "One must make whatever sacrifice is necessary to ensure that one does not end up in hell."

St. Paul follows in this same Jewish tradition of sexual purity, even within marriage, when he writes to the Christians in Thessaloniki:

> For this is the will of God, your sanctification: that you abstain from unchastity; that each one of you know how to take a wife for himself in holiness and honor, *not in the passion of lust like heathen who do not know God;* that no man transgress, and wrong his brother in this matter, because the Lord is an avenger in all these things, as we solemnly forewarned you. For God has not called us for uncleanness, but in holiness. (1 Thes 4:3–7; emphasis mine)

When St. Paul contrasts a Christian approach to marriage with the "passion of lust like heathen who do not know God," he is expressing toward Greco-Roman sexual culture a disgust that was shared by the Essenes, other groups of Jews, and the early Christians.

Sex in the Greco-Roman world was cheap and readily available for the wealthy men who ran society, and women were not highly valued. The view upper-class men had of women is aptly summarized in this famous quote found in the works of the Athenian orator Demosthenes (384–322 B.C.): "Mistresses we keep for the sake of pleasure, concubines for the daily care of our persons, but wives to bear us legitimate children and to be faithful guardians of our households."[10]

Demosthenes fails to mention that they also had boys, as the preferred form of sexual relationship was between adult men and adolescent males.[11] This kind of homosexual pedophilia—technically *ephebophilia*, love between men and adolescent boys—was ubiquitous among the Greek aristocracy. Plato famously had reservations about this practice—"Platonic love" referred originally to nonsexual friendship between *men and boys*, not men and women.[12] Plato argued that if men truly loved the boys, they would develop a friendship with them that was intellectual—a true meeting of the minds, the mutual admiration of noble souls.[13]

But most Greek men ignored Plato's advice and continued to pursue erotic relationships with boys. Relationships with women had less potential for the fullest realization of love, because women were thought unequal to men in virtue, reason, and other attributes.[14] Prostitution with both boys and women was incorporated into religious practice, boys associated with the temples of Apollo, and women with temples of the goddess Aphrodite (Venus in Roman mythology). Corinth—the Greek city to which St. Paul addressed at least two of his letters—was famous for its massive temple to Aphrodite. Around the time of the birth of Jesus, the classical geographer Strabo wrote of Corinth:

> The temple of Aphrodite was so rich that it employed more than a thousand courtesans, whom both men and women had given to the goddess. Many people visited the town on account of them, and thus these courtesans contributed to the riches of the town: for the ship captains frivolously spent their money there, hence the saying: "The voyage to Corinth is not for every man."[15]

Judging from the well-preserved remains of Pompeii, the conditions under which these ancient "courtesans" worked were degrading: dark, narrow alleys lined with rooms or stalls whose only furniture was a single cot, with "business" going on twenty-four hours a day.[16]

Jews and early Christians disdained this whole trade and would not countenance any kind of intercourse outside of marriage. It's not at all a coincidence that St. Paul speaks the most about sexual morality and the temple-nature of the Church in his first letter to the Corinthians, where he contrasts the Church-as-Temple or the Christian-as-Temple with the kind of temple immorality that characterized Corinthian culture:

> Do you not know that your bodies are members of Christ? Shall I therefore take the members of Christ and make them members of a prostitute? Never! Do you not know that he who joins himself to a prostitute becomes one body with her? For, as it is written, "The two shall become one flesh." But he who is united to the Lord becomes one spirit with him. Shun sexual immorality. Every other sin which a man commits is outside the body; but the sexually immoral man sins against his own body. Do you not know that your body is a temple of the Holy Spirit within you, which you have from God? You are not your own; you were bought with a price. So glorify God in your body. (1 Cor 6:15–20 RSV *alt.*)

St. Paul contrasts two temple systems. There was the Temple of Aphrodite, where female slaves had been dedicated to the goddess and could be "bought with a price." Over against it was the Temple of God, the Church, whose members were "slaves of God" who had already been "bought with [the] price" of Jesus' blood. These two systems were diametrically opposed and could not mix.

We also see here parallels to Essene thought. The fact that the Qumranites considered their community to be an alternative temple to the Jerusalem Temple, with the Holy Spirit flowing through the community, led them to live continually by the standards of Temple cleanliness, abstaining from all relations. St. Paul considers the Church to be a replacement for the Jerusalem Temple, both corporately and individually, since the Holy Spirit dwells within each member. Therefore each member of the community must live a sexually pure life. A key difference is that, for the Qumranites, all intercourse rendered one ritually unclean, whereas St. Paul is concerned not about ritual cleanliness but about moral purity. For St. Paul and Christianity generally, relations between the married did not defile either ritually or morally, but all other intercourse was morally defiling.

The few documents concerned with marriage that we've recovered from Qumran reflect a fairly positive view of matrimonial life. We have one document that appears to be a fragmentary description of a wedding ceremony, in which the whole community— young and old, men and women—would gather for a joyful celebration, to witness the commitment of the bride and groom to each other, and to invoke blessings on the new couple.[17] The celebratory tone of this document should not surprise us, because many texts of the Old Testament reflect a high view of marriage. The Book of Proverbs, for example, urges men to avoid flirtatious women, to stay faithful to the "wife of [one's] youth" (i.e., one's first and ideally *only* wife), and to find joy in the relationship with her:

> *Drink water from your own cistern,*
> *flowing water from your own well.*
> *Should your springs be scattered abroad,*
> *streams of water in the streets?*
> *Let them be for yourself alone,*

and not for strangers with you.
Let your fountain be blessed,
and rejoice in the wife of your youth:
a lovely hind, a graceful doe.
Let her affection fill you at all times with delight,
be infatuated always with her love.
Why should you be infatuated, my son,
with a loose woman,
and embrace the bosom of an adventuress? (Prov 5:15–12)

The same book, in its climactic chapter, portrays a faithful wife and mother as the quintessential embodiment of the virtue of wisdom (31:10–31) and speaks of how her husband praises her: "Many women do excellent things, but you surpass them all!" (31:29). Indeed, faithfulness to one's spouse is the paradigmatic act of wisdom in Proverbs 1–9, as well as in other places in the wisdom literature.[18]

An instruction on marriage discovered at Qumran (4Q416) develops these biblical ideals of joy, affection, and fidelity in marriage. The instruction is addressed first to grooms and then to brides, and gives them advice about how to live their future state. It emphasizes the divine nature of marriage even more than do the ancient biblical texts. For example, Genesis 2:24 says, "A *man* separates from his father and his mother and clings to his wife, and they become one flesh"; but the Qumran scroll attributes the acts of *separating* from one's parents and *clinging* to one's spouse directly to *God*:

From her mother He (i.e., God) has separated her (i.e., your wife), and to you she shall cling and she will be to you as one flesh. Your daughter he will separate (in order to cling) to another, and your sons (he will separate) for the daughters of your friend.[19]

Jesus shares this view. Again, although Genesis 2:24 describes a "man" as "separating" and "clinging" to his wife, Jesus attributes the resulting bond to divine agency: "What God has joined together, let not man separate" (Mark 10:9). Like the Essenes, Jesus understands God in his providence as the true agent behind the process of betrothal and marriage.[20]

The document 4Q416 continues its advice to a young husband:

> You and the wife of your bosom will become a union (Heb. *yahad*) because she is the flesh of your nakedness. (4Q416 2 iv 5)

The language reflects great intimacy: the wife is "of your bosom"—an image of embracing someone to one's breast—and she is "the flesh of your nakedness," that is, as intimate as one's own unclothed body. It is also striking that the Essenes use the same word for the marital union that is employed for a sacred covenant community like Qumran: *yahad.* This word can be translated literally as "union" or "unity" in English, since it derives from the Hebrew word for "one," *'ehad.* The marital bond between the husband and wife is a "holy covenant" (Heb. *berîth qôdesh*). Addressing the wife directly, the Scroll says: "In his (i.e., your husband's) bosom is your blessing. . . . Beware lest you neglect the holy covenant." (4Q415 2:3–4).[21]

One can see that the fact that the Qumran group constituted a *yahad* bound together by a holy covenant, and that each husband and wife constituted a *yahad* bound together by a holy covenant, suggests there is a kind of mystical relationship between the sacred covenant community as a whole and each married couple. The two "covenant communities" reflect or mirror one another. This idea develops naturally from the ancient Israelite prophets, who frequently used the metaphor of husband and wife to describe God's covenant relationship with Israel (e.g., Hosea 2).

It's precisely this concept, that the covenantal union of husband and wife reflects the covenantal union of God and his people, that we find developed magnificently in St. Paul's most famous teaching on the union of spouses, Ephesians 5:

> Wives, be subject to your husbands, as to the Lord. For the husband is the head of the wife as Christ is the head of the church, his body, and is himself its Savior. As the church is subject to Christ, so let wives also be subject in everything to their husbands.
>
> Husbands, love your wives, as Christ loved the church and gave himself up for her, that he might sanctify her, having cleansed her by the washing of water with the word, that he might present the church to himself in splendor, without spot or wrinkle or any such thing, that she might be holy and without blemish. Even so husbands should love their wives as their own bodies. He who loves his wife loves himself. For no man ever hates his own flesh, but nourishes and cherishes it, as Christ does the church, because we are members of his body. "For this reason a man shall leave his father and mother and be joined to his wife, and the two shall become one flesh." This mystery is a profound one, and I am saying that it refers to Christ and the church; however, let each one of you love his wife as himself, and let the wife see that she respects her husband. (Eph 5:22–33)

Modern readers often get stuck on Paul's injunction for wives to "be subject" to their husbands, which appears to violate our egalitarian ideals of the relationship between the sexes. But this injunction would scarcely have raised an eyebrow in antiquity, when most legal responsibilities were invested in the man, and husbands were often much older than their wives.[22] What *would* have caught the eye of the ancient reader, however, is that wives are addressed directly, as moral agents in their own right (vv. 22–24). This can also be found in the Qumran instruction on marriage.[23] Like the older Israelite Scriptures, neither the Scrolls nor Paul *ever* commands husbands to *make* their wives submit. Both exhort wives to do so of their *own free will.*

But the ancient reader would find even more striking the fact that the majority of the passage expounds on the *love* that husbands should have for their wives, which should be modeled on Christ's love for the Church—in other words, a love even to the point of death, even to the point of self-sacrifice for the beloved: "Christ loved the church and gave himself up for her." This is striking, since marriage wasn't necessarily associated with love in Greco-Roman culture.[24] Yet Paul's words go beyond what we see at Qumran or even in the Old Testament, for although many texts (e.g., Prov 5:18–19) encourage or reflect love of a husband for his wife, they stop short of explicit self-sacrifice.

Other aspects of Paul's teaching sound very familiar, however. The stress on the one-flesh intimacy of husband and wife found in Genesis 2:24 is reflected in St. Paul's description of the wife as the husband's "own body" and "own flesh," and reminds us of 4Q416, "She is the flesh of your nakedness." And the suggested relationship between the *yahad* of the holy society and the *yahad* of the spousal couple becomes completely explicit: "Husbands, love your wives, as Christ loved the church . . . 'the two shall become one flesh.' This mystery is a profound one, and I am saying that it refers to Christ and the church" (Eph 5:25, 31–32). Throughout the passage, Paul moves easily between speaking about the covenant between spouses and the covenant between Christ and the Church: "No man ever hates his own flesh, but nourishes it and cherishes it, as Christ does the church, because we are members of his body" (vv. 29–30). Matrimony takes on a new significance as a sacred symbol, or icon, of the new covenant. For this reason Paul refers to it as a "mystery," Greek *mysterion,* which in Latin becomes *sacramentum,* from which we get the word "sacrament." Thus Ephesians 5:32 could be translated, "This sacrament is a profound one, and I am saying that it refers to Christ and the Church." Not all Christians recognize matrimony as a sacrament, but somewhat ironically it is the only one of the traditional Christian sacraments to be called a "sacrament" in Scripture.

Some Greco-Roman moral philosophers had positive things to say about marriage and the relationship of husband and wife,[25] and certainly the Israelite sacred tradition included very beautiful portrayals of this bond, but Paul's vision of husbands loving their wives with a sacred, self-sacrificial love modeled on the divine love of the Messiah for his people goes beyond those of his predecessors. Developing Paul's thought, the early Church would come to place great value on a life of celibacy, but nonetheless honor matrimony as a holy institution through which God communicates his grace to husband and wife. While honoring *both* matrimony and celibacy may seem paradoxical, there was an inner logic to it: since matrimony was *so good* in itself, to give it up for the sake of the kingdom of heaven was a very noble sacrifice.

Pauline teaching, and Christian belief about marriage generally, had an interesting effect on the development of Western civilization. Unlike Greco-Roman culture, the Church required sexual fidelity and exclusivity not just from wives but also from husbands, and rejected institutions that were nonreciprocal: polygamy, concubinage, prostitution.

Eventually, marriage between a man and a woman replaced the erotic relationship between an older and a younger man as the cultural ideal of the most intimate and satisfying bond between two human persons. This changed the way women were viewed culturally and philosophically: now they were seen as prospective partners in whom a man could find a relationship of completion and wholeness that participated in divine love, God's own nature. The whole genre of "romance" narratives in Western culture—whether expressed in music, novels, or (more recently) movies—grew out of this Christian "romanticization" of marriage.

Like early Christians, the Essenes had strong views on marriage, and discouraged divorce, polygamy, and promiscuity. Some of their views on marriage derived from the Book of Tobit, which encourages companionship and fidelity between spouses and downplays eroticism. Some Scrolls call marriage a "holy covenant," and resonate with Paul's teaching on marriage in Ephesians 5. This Judeo-Christian culture of sexuality and marriage was in stark contrast to that of Greco-Roman society.

For Further Reading

Fitzmyer, Joseph. "Marriage and Divorce." Pages 511–515 in *Encyclopedia of the Dead Sea Scrolls,* Volume 1. Edited by Lawrence H. Schiffman and James C. VanderKam. Oxford: Oxford University Press, 2000.

Hahn, Scott. *The First Society: The Sacrament of Matrimony and the Restoration of the Social Order.* Steubenville, OH: Emmaus Road Publishing, 2018.

Shemesh, Aharon. "Marriage and Marital Life in the Dead Sea Scrolls." Pages 589–600 in *The Dead Sea Scrolls and Contemporary Culture.* Edited by Adolfo Roitman, Lawrence Schiffman, and Shani Tzoref. Studies on the Texts of the Desert of Judah 93. Leiden: Brill, 2011.

PART FIVE

HOLY ORDERS
AND THE SCROLLS

CHAPTER 11

Priesthood and the Scrolls

CHURCH GOVERNMENT IS YET ANOTHER ASPECT OF CHURCH life about which modern Christians have a wide variety of opinions. The Christian denomination I served as pastor for a number of years was typical of many Protestant groups in recognizing two orders of church officers: *elders* and *deacons*. But I remember my Church government professor in seminary telling the class one day, "The basic principle of our Church government is: no bishops need apply!" That was in contrast to the really old Christian traditions, like the various Eastern Orthodox and the Catholic Church, in which the bishop was the central figure in the authority structure of the church. On the other end of the spectrum, I had a friend in college who joined a very tight-knit and semisecretive Christian group located largely in a suburb of Indianapolis. To me, it seemed a bit like a cult, and I ended up debating with the "pastor" of my friend's group for some time. I say "pastor" because this man, who produced all the educational materials for the group and did all their teaching, denied that the idea of having a pastor was biblical. He argued that there were no biblical roles of leadership in the Church, but all Christians were equal. This was somewhat ironic, because he exercised very strong authority over the rest of the members of his group, and functioned for all intents and purposes as what other Christians would call a "pastor" or even a "bishop."

So there is a wide variety of views out there on how and by whom the Church should be run, and the average American Christian has probably done some church hopping at some point in their life and been exposed to different systems of church governance. But what was the situation originally? How was the early Church governed? Where did the traditional roles like "deacon," "elder," "priest," and "bishop" come from? Here again, it's unsurprising that we find some strong parallels between how the Qumran community organized itself and the descriptions of Church leadership in the New Testament and early Fathers. In what follows, we will first look at the leadership system of the Qumran community and then draw the parallels to early Christianity.

The Qumran community saw itself as the restoration of the ancient sacred nation of Israel, and the pattern of religious leadership for ancient Israel had been founded by Moses, who established essentially three levels of clergy: the Levites, the priests, and the High Priest. The Levites constituted the most basic level of clergy. All the males of the tribe of Levi were eligible to help perform the duties of the sanctuary, which was first the Tabernacle and then later the Temple. According to the Book of Numbers, the Levites had responsibility for caring for and transporting the furnishings and structures of the Tabernacle, and assisting the priests in the offering of sacrifices (Num 3:5–11; 4:1–49; 8:5–26). Later, when David located the sanctuary permanently in Jerusalem, the Levites were no longer needed to transport the sacred tent, so David gave many of them new duties as singers and choir leaders for worship (1 Chr 16:4–6).

Within the tribe of Levi, the family of Aaron had greater responsibility and authority, and they functioned as priests (Exod

28–31). They actually offered the animal sacrifices, made decisions about ritual matters, and could enter the inner rooms of the Tabernacle and later the Temple.

Finally, Aaron himself, and later his most senior heir, functioned as High Priest. He performed sacrifices like the other priests, but in addition there were liturgies that only he could perform: for example, on the holiest day of the year, Yom Kippur, or the Day of Atonement, only the High Priest could enter the holiest room of the Temple, the Holy of Holies, and sprinkle the blood of the lamb on the Ark of the Covenant to make ritual atonement for the whole nation of Israel (Lev 16). Many other duties were reserved for him alone, and he had ultimate responsibility for and authority over the entire system of worship (the liturgy) that was celebrated in the Temple. At various times in Israel's history, when there was no king, the High Priest also served as the political leader of the community.

Now the Essenes generally, and especially the Qumranites, were very concerned about priesthood, and there is no reason to doubt that their leadership consisted largely of priests whose bloodlines went back to the House of Aaron and the later priestly lines of descent that are recorded in Scripture. During the reign of Solomon, the greatest of Israel's kings, the High Priesthood was held by a certain descendant of Aaron by the name of Zadok (1 Kings 2:35). Later, the prophet Ezekiel would insist that only the descendants of Zadok should exercise the priestly ministry, because they alone had remained faithful during periods of religious corruption in Israel (Ezek 40:46). For this reason, by the time of the Qumran community and Jesus' ministry, prospective priests were eager to claim descent from Zadok. In fact, this famous priest gave his name to the Sadducee party, since "Sadducee" is a Greek transliteration of the Hebrew *zadoqîm,* meaning "Zadokites," descendants of Zadok. It is, in fact, unlikely that the

Sadducees had a good Zadokite bloodline, but they had to claim it in order to present themselves as legitimate priests.[1]

The Qumran group also claimed their leaders were Zadokites, and the Scrolls make several mentions of them. The *Community Rule* specifies that business meetings of the community will be guided by the Zadokites:

> Their discussions shall be under the oversight of the Sons of Zadok—priests and preservers of the Covenant—and according to the majority rule of the men of the Yahad, who hold fast to the Covenant. (1QS 5:2–3)

One popular theory about the origin of the Qumran community holds that Jonathan Apphus, one of the Maccabees, drove out the legitimate Zadokite high priestly family when he (Jonathan) assumed the title of High Priest around 152 B.C., and the displaced Zadokites went into exile at Qumran and elsewhere.[2] Some have identified the "Teacher of Righteousness"—the founder of the Qumran community—with the Zadokite High Priest that Jonathan removed, although scholars debate this.[3]

What we do know is that the Qumran community had two basic orders of leadership, whom they called "priests" and "Levites," and then the regular "laity." For example, here's a description of the annual procession and ceremony when new members were inducted:

> They shall do as follows annually, all the days of Belial's dominion: the priests shall pass in review first, ranked according to their spiritual excellence, one after another. Then the Levites shall follow, and third all the people by rank, one after another, in their thousands and hundreds and fifties and tens. Thus shall each Israelite know his proper standing in the Yahad of God. (1QS 2:19–22)

The Qumranites really expected the triple religious leadership of High Priest, priests, and Levites described in the Books of Moses to be restored when the Messiahs of Aaron and Israel appeared. In the meantime, they tried to arrange their local communities as "camps"—intentionally using the biblical word "camp" (Heb. *maheneh*), which once described the community of Israel as it was sojourning through the Wilderness:

> The rule of dwelling in all the camps. All shall be mustered by their names: the priests first, the Levites second, the children of Israel third, the "strangers"[4] fourth. (CD 14:3–4)

Of course, in the idealized system Moses set up for the wilderness camp of Israel, there was one overall authority, where the "buck stopped"—the High Priest. There could not be more than one High Priest in all of Israel, but for every individual Essene "camp" throughout the land of Israel, the role of central authority was held by a man the Essenes called "the Overseer" (Heb. *mebaqqer*).[5] This Overseer was tasked with examining all prospective candidates for the community, instructing the members in the proper interpretation of the law, governing the disposal of the common purse, caring for the weak and vulnerable of the community, giving marriage advice, and many other tasks.

> This is the rule for the Overseer of a camp. He must teach the general membership about the works of God, instruct them in His mighty miracles, relate to them the future events coming to the world with their interpretations; he should care for them as a father does his children, taking care of all their problems as a shepherd does for his flock. He should loosen all their knots, that there be no one oppressed or crushed in his congregation. He shall observe everyone who is added to his group as to his actions, his intelligence, his ability, his strength, and his

wealth and write him down by his place according to his share in the allotment of Light. No members of the camp are allowed to bring anyone into the group except by permission of the Overseer of the camp; and none of the members of God's covenant should do business with corrupt people, except hand to hand. No one should do any buying or selling unless he has informed the Overseer who is in the camp and taken counsel (with him), lest they err unwittingly. Likewise with any man who marries a woman: let it be with the counsel (of the Overseer); and likewise let him instruct a man who wishes to divorce. He shall educate their sons and daughters and young children in a spirit of meekness and love of mercy. He must not bear against them a grudge in anger and wrath for their transgressions. (CD 13:7–19)

We should note that the Overseer is described as both a "father" and a "shepherd" in this passage. Also, it so happens "overseer" is almost the exact equivalent of the Greek word *episkopos,* from which we get the English word "bishop."[6] Many scholars have noted a strong similarity between the role of the Overseer in the Essene "camps" and the role of the bishop in the early Christian churches. For example, St. Paul writes to his protégé Titus as follows:

This is why I left you in Crete, that you might amend what was defective, and appoint presbyters (Gk. *presbuteroi*) in every town as I directed you, if any man is blameless, the husband of one wife, and his children are believers and not open to the charge of being profligate or insubordinate. For a bishop, as God's steward, must be blameless; he must not be arrogant or quick-tempered or a drunkard or violent or greedy for gain, but hospitable, a lover of goodness, master of himself, upright, holy, and self-controlled; he must hold firm to the sure word as taught, so that he may be able to give instruction in sound doctrine and also to confute those who contradict it. (Titus 1:5–9)

St. Paul gives us more of a description of the qualities of a suitable bishop than a detailed description of his duties, which is what the Damascus Document provides. However, reading between the lines of Paul's description, we can tell that the bishop had financial responsibility for the congregation, as he is called a "steward" (Gk. *oikonomos*), a man who handled the business affairs for a wealthy landowner (cf. Luke 16:1–8). He also must have been responsible for hosting visitors, strangers, and/or the poor, because Paul insists he must be "hospitable," both here and in 1 Timothy 3:2. Finally, like the Overseer, the bishop is the primary teacher of the community, so he must be "able to give instruction in sound doctrine."

In Paul's letter to Titus, we can see that the terms "presbyter" (lit. "elder") and "bishop" (lit. "overseer") were roughly synonymous in the early period. Elsewhere, Peter describes the presbyters as shepherds: "So I exhort the presbyters among you, as a fellow presbyter . . . *tend the flock* of God that is your charge . . . being *examples to the flock*. And when the chief Shepherd is manifested you will obtain the unfading crown of glory" (1 Pet 5:1–4). John also seems to be referring to the presbyters of the early Church when he says, "I am writing to you, *fathers,* because you know him who is from the beginning" (1 John 2:13).[7] These are the beginnings of the Christian practice of referring to a congregational leader as "pastor" (Latin for "shepherd") or "father."

However, a generation after St. Paul, the terms "presbyter" and "bishop" began to be distinguished. The term "bishop" was reserved for the chief presbyter in a city, who was in charge of the whole community of Christians there, just as the Overseer was in charge of all the Essenes in a "camp." By the time of Ignatius of

Antioch, the Christian bishop of the Syrian city of Antioch, the Christian communities were organized in a way very similar to the older Essene camps. As the Essenes had an Overseer assisted by priests and Levites, so these early churches had a bishop who presided over the community, assisted by the presbyters and the deacons. Just as the Damascus Document insisted that the Overseer approve of any business affecting the community, so Ignatius, writing in A.D. 106 (about ten years after the death of St. John the Apostle), advises the church in the Asian city of Smyrna (now Izmir, Turkey) to obey their bishop in everything:

> You must all follow the bishop, as Jesus Christ followed the Father, and follow the presbytery as you would the apostles; respect the deacons as the commandment of God. Let no one do anything that has to do with the church without the bishop. Only that Eucharist which is under the authority of the bishop (or whomever he himself designates) is to be considered valid. Wherever the bishop appears, there let the congregation be; just as wherever Jesus Christ is, there is the catholic church.[8] It is not permissible either to baptize or to hold a love feast without the bishop. But whatever he approves is also pleasing to God, in order that everything you do may be trustworthy and valid. (*Smyrneans* 8:1–2)

By Ignatius's day, it was unthinkable that any Christian community would not have the three ranks of leadership: bishop, presbyters, and deacons:

> Similarly, let everyone respect the deacons as Jesus Christ, just as they should respect the bishop, who is a model of the Father, and the presbyters as God's council and as the band of the Apostles. Without these no group can be called a "church."[9] (*Trallians* 3:1)

The similarity with the pattern Overseer, priests, and Levites is strong enough that some scholars have proposed that there was heavy Essene influence in Syria and Asia Minor, where Ignatius ministered, and this shaped the life of the early Church.[10] That may be the case, but it's more likely both the Essenes and the early Christians were building on the model of High Priest, priests, and Levites from the Old Testament. This is quite explicit in the letter of Clement, the Bishop of Rome, to the church in Corinth, from around A.D. 80. Discussing a dispute about Christian clergy and how they should be chosen for office, Clement describes the Christian leaders as if they were the High Priest, priests, and Levites of the Old Testament:

> Since, therefore, these things are now clear to us . . . we ought to do, in order, everything that the Master has commanded us to perform at the appointed times. Both where and by whom he wants them to be performed, he himself has determined by his supreme will. . . . For to the *high-priest* the proper services have been given, and to the *priests* the proper office has been assigned, and upon the *Levites* the proper ministries have been imposed. The layman is bound by the layman's rules. Let each of you, brothers, in his proper order give thanks to God, maintaining a good conscience, not overstepping the designated rule of his ministry, but acting with reverence.[11]

We note the emphasis on each Christian keeping to the duties appropriate to his own rank, in a way very similar to the insistence of the Damascus Document and *Community Rule* that ceremonies be observed with each member of the community keeping to his appropriate place by status and seniority: "Thus shall each Israelite know his proper standing in the *Yahad* of God, an eternal society. None shall be demoted from his appointed place, none promoted beyond his foreordained rank" (1QS 2:22–23). The occasion for the writing of 1 Clement was, in fact, the unjust demoting of some of the presbyters of the church in the city of Corinth.

We can see, then, how the analogy between the threefold clerical leadership of the Old Testament and the threefold leadership of the early Church could lead the early Christians to perceive their leaders as a new priesthood that had succeeded to the priesthood of the Old Testament. But the question remains: was this a misunderstanding? Were the offices of leadership in the early Church merely functional roles, and in time did Christians superstitiously impute a certain sacredness to the persons who filled them? Or is there indication that Jesus himself intended to establish a new priesthood for his community? That's the question we will take up in the next chapter, by closely examining several New Testament texts.

The governing structures of the early Church and the Qumran community were similar, each consisting of three orders of leadership. In Qumran these were the Overseer, the priests, and the Levites; for Christians it was the bishop, the presbyters, and the deacons. The inspiration for both comes from the Old Testament and the pattern of High Priest, priests, and Levites. Essene converts to Christianity would have been used to this structure, and it would not have taken much time at all for the first Christians to organize themselves this way, as the pattern was already established.

For Further Reading

Daniélou, Jean. "The Syrian Church and the Zadokites." Pages 118–121 in Daniélou, *The Dead Sea Scrolls and Primitive Christianity.* Translated by Salvator Attanasio. Baltimore: Helicon Press, 1958.

Reicke, Bo. "The Constitution of the Primitive Church in Light of Jewish Documents." Pages 143–156 in *The Scrolls and the New Testament*. Edited by Krister Stendahl. New York: Harper, 1957.

Thiering, B. E. "*Mebaqqer* and *Episkopos* in the Light of the Temple Scroll." *Journal of Biblical Literature* 100 (1981): 59–74.

CHAPTER 12

Priesthood in the Gospels

ALTHOUGH THE ESSENES OF QUMRAN HAD HEREDITARY
priests, "sons of Zadok," among their leadership, various texts
from the Scrolls attribute a kind of priesthood to everyone in the
covenant community. So the Damascus Document, commenting
on the "priests" mentioned in Ezekiel 44:15, asserts:

> The "priests": these are the repentant ones of Israel. (CD 4:2)

In other words, the "priests" are the members of the Essene
movement.

Likewise, when we start looking for references to priesthood in
the New Testament, we immediately notice several texts that regard all the members of the new covenant community as sharing
a priestly status:

> Come to him, to that living stone, rejected by men but in
> God's sight chosen and precious; and like living stones be
> yourselves built into a spiritual house, to be a *holy priesthood,*
> to offer spiritual sacrifices acceptable to God through Jesus
> Christ. (1 Pet 2:4–5)

> To him who loves us and has freed us from our sins by his
> blood and made us a kingdom, *priests to his God and Father,*

to him be glory and dominion for ever and ever. Amen. (Rev 1:5–6)

This idea of the whole community being a priesthood goes back to the promises of God to his people at Mt. Sinai:

Now therefore, if you will obey my voice and keep my covenant, you shall be my own possession among all peoples; for all the earth is mine, and you shall be to me a *kingship of priests* and a holy nation. (Exod 19:5–6, my translation)

The Hebrew phrase "kingship of priests" can be taken in the sense of either "kingly priesthood" or "kingdom of priests," and we see that different New Testament texts take it in both directions.[1] Regardless, the early Christians believed that the promise to Israel at Sinai was now fulfilled in the community that gathered around Jesus the Messiah.

This idea of every member of the community sharing in a priestly status was also very evident at Qumran. The Qumran community was a substitute for the Temple, and every member lived by priestly purity, which included a lifestyle of celibacy and dressing in white linen. Let's look at the description of the *Yahad* in the *Community Rule*:

When such men as these come to be in Israel, then shall the party of the *Yahad* truly be established, an "eternal planting," a temple for Israel, and—mystery!—a Holy of Holies for Aaron; true witnesses to justice, chosen by God's will *to atone for the land.* . . . They will be "the tested wall, the precious cornerstone" (Isa 28:16) whose foundations shall neither be shaken nor swayed, a fortress, a Holy of Holies for Aaron, all of them knowing the Covenant of Justice and thereby *offering a sweet savor.* They shall be *a blameless and true house* in Israel. . . .

They shall be accepted *to atone for the land.* (1QS 8:4–10; emphasis mine)

The *Community Rule* applies all sorts of Temple language to the *yahad*—"eternal planting," "temple for Israel," "Holy of Holies for Aaron," "tested wall," "precious cornerstone," "fortress," "true house"—and attributes to the *yahad* the priestly role of "offering a sweet savor" and "aton[ing] for the land." The parallels with New Testament descriptions of the Church in 1 Peter 2:4–9 and Ephesians 2:14–22 are obvious, and we will discuss those parallels further in chapter 14.

So from the beginning, there was in the Christian movement— as among the Essenes—a concept of the "priesthood of all believers" that is clearly expressed in both the New Testament and the Church Fathers. For example, St. Paul presumes that Christians have a priestly role when he says:

I appeal to you therefore, brethren, by the mercies of God, to present your bodies as a living sacrifice, holy and acceptable to God, which is your spiritual worship. (Rom 12:1)

Commenting on this verse, the Church Father St. Peter Chrysologus (A.D. 380–450) remarks:

By this exhortation of his, Paul has raised all men to priestly status. How marvelous is the priesthood of the Christian, for he is both the victim that is offered on his own behalf, and the priest who makes the offering![2]

But just as the ancient Israelites, though a priestly people, still had men set aside for ritual duties whom they called "priests," and just as the Qumranites, though all dressed in priestly linen, still had "priests" and "Levites" among them, so in the early Church there were those set aside and given spiritual authority for certain sacred tasks. The traditional Christian term for this specialized priesthood is the *ministerial priesthood,* distinguished from the *common priesthood* of each member of the community.

Already in Jesus' ministry, we see him claiming a special status—indeed, a ministerial priestly status—for himself and the Twelve Apostles:

> At that time Jesus went through the grainfields on the Sabbath; his disciples were hungry, and they began to pluck heads of grain and to eat. But when the Pharisees saw it, they said to him, "Look, your disciples are doing what is not lawful to do on the Sabbath." He said to them, "Have you not read what David did, when he was hungry, and those who were with him: how he entered the house of God and ate the bread of the Presence, which it was not lawful for him to eat nor for those who were with him, but only for the priests? Or have you not read in the law how on the Sabbath the priests in the temple profane the Sabbath, and are guiltless? I tell you, something greater than the temple is here. (Matt 12:1–6)

The two examples Jesus cites to defend his and his Apostles' right to thresh grain on the Sabbath are both priestly in nature: David and his men performing a priestly act of eating the bread of the Presence (1 Sam 21:1–6) and the priests in the Temple working on the Sabbath day as part of their priestly service. Rabbi Jacob Neusner, a renowned scholar of the Bible and ancient Judaism, comments on this passage:

> He [Jesus] and the disciples may do on the Sabbath what they do because *they stand in the place of the priests in the Temple;* the holy place has shifted, now being made up of the master and his disciples.[3]

Neusner correctly sees that Jesus claims a priestly status for himself and his disciples, and that the community he is forming is a new Temple. This made sense within the historical context of Jesus' ministry, because other groups—like the Qumran Essenes—were also forming priestly societies meant to replace the Temple.

We see additional priestly imagery a little later in Matthew. Peter's famous confession of Jesus as the Christ at Caesarea Philippi is filled with images of priesthood and Temple. The wordplay in the passage is very important but is lost in English, so I've included key Greek words in parentheses:

> Now when Jesus came into the district of Caesarea Philippi, he asked his disciples, "Who do men say that the Son of man is?" And they said, "Some say John the Baptist, others say Elijah, and others Jeremiah or one of the prophets." He said to them, "But who do you say that I am?" Simon Peter replied, "You are the Christ, the Son of the living God." And Jesus answered him, "Blessed are you, Simon Bar-Jona! For flesh and blood has not revealed this to you, but my Father who is in heaven. And I tell you, you are Rock (*petros*), and on this rock (*petra*) I will house-build my assembly (*ekklesia*), and the gates of Hades shall not prevail against it. I will give you the keys of the kingdom of heaven, and whatever you bind on earth shall be bound in heaven, and whatever you loose on earth shall be loosed in heaven." (Matt 16:13–19 RSV, *alt.*)

Jesus changes Simon's name to "Rock" (Greek *petros,* Aramaic *kephas*) and speaks of "house-building" (*oikodomêsô*) his "assembly" (*ekklesia*) on this Rock-of-Simon. The image of the rock picks up various Old Testament prophecies of a rock or stone on which the end-times Temple would be built.[4] The term "house-building" picks up the image of the Temple as "House of God" or "Holy House."[5] The term "assembly"—in Greek, *ekklesia*—is a translation of the Hebrew term *qahal,* a word used several times in the Psalms to refer to the worshipping assembly of Israel gathered in the Temple but also used frequently in the Scrolls either as a synonym for the entire new covenant community[6] or for the end-times assembly of Israel for worship.[7] Later, of course, *ekklesia* will be translated "church."[8] The reference to the "gates of Hades" is another Temple image, because the Jewish worldview at the time held that the Temple was built upon a great rock,[9] which blocked up the shaft leading down to Hades, the realm of the dead or "hell." Jesus is building a human temple, and the "foundation stone" of that temple is the "Rock" (Peter) who will block up the shaft to Hades.[10] So everything in Matthew 16:18 is Temple imagery.

The following verse is filled with priestly imagery. Jesus says to Peter, "I will give you the keys of the kingdom of heaven" (Matt 16:19). We know from Isaiah 22:22 that the "keys of the kingdom" were carried by the royal steward, the first officer of the kingdom after the king himself. Jesus the king is making Peter his royal steward.[11] Interestingly, the royal steward wore priestly garments, and it seems that the office was usually filled by a priest from the tribe of Levi.[12]

The royal steward was so important because he carried the keys to the palace and thus controlled access to the king. Isaiah says of the royal steward, "what he shall open, none shall shut, and what he shall shut, none shall open" (Isa 22:22). But Jesus is building a Temple-kingdom of persons, not of stones. So to Peter he says something similar, yet a little different: "whatever you bind on earth shall be bound in heaven, and whatever you loose on earth shall be loosed in heaven" (Matt 16:19). These terms "bind" and "loose" had a very specific meaning in the Judaism of Jesus' day.[13] They referred to the act of making an authoritative decision about the interpretation of God's law. In Judaism, the interpretation of the law is called *halakhah,* and the authority to interpret is *hal-*

akhic authority. To "bind" was to forbid something, to "loose" was
to permit it. For example, the law of God says to rest on the Sabbath, and not to work. But is starting a fire "working"? Most rabbis said yes, so starting a fire was "bound." By contrast, getting an
animal out of a pit was not considered "work," so it was "loosed"
(see Matt 12:11).

In the time of Jesus, the party of the Pharisees did most of the
"binding" and "loosing" for the common Jews in Judea. Josephus
says of them that, when they enjoyed royal favor, "they banished
and reduced whom they pleased; they bound and loosed at their
pleasure" (*War* 1:111). Rabbi Kaufmann Kohler says, "This does
not mean that . . . they merely decided what . . . was forbidden or
allowed, but that they possessed and exercised the power of tying
or untying a thing by the spell of their divine authority."[14]

The Scriptures, however, had not given this authority to the
Pharisees or the rabbis generally, but to the Levitical priests. Moses
commanded that if there was a dispute about the interpretation
of the law, one was to travel to the sanctuary and get the decision of the Levitical priests, and their decision was absolutely
binding on pain of death (Deut 17:8–13)—in other words, the
priests' interpretation of the law was as binding as the law itself. In
keeping with this principle, God commands Haggai the prophet
to go consult the priests about the interpretation of the laws of
cleanliness (Hag 2:10–13). The Hasmonean (i.e., Maccabean) dy-
nasty, however, unlawfully took over the high priesthood around
150 B.C., which shook the confidence of the people in priestly
authority. The Pharisees moved in to fill this religious authority
vacuum, and especially when they had political backing from the
king, they effectively usurped the priestly role of "binding" and
"loosing."

The Essenes, whose leadership probably consisted of Zadokite
priests of good bloodline, resented this Pharisaic usurpation and
wrote vigorously against the Pharisaic interpretation of the law.[15]

They insisted that it was *Levi*—the priestly tribe—whom God had appointed "to bind [and loose]" and the people of Israel must "live by the judgment of the Sons of Zadok, the priests, and the men of their covenant," that is, by their interpretation of the law.[16]

Jesus, on the other hand, bestows this priestly power to "bind and loose" neither on the Pharisees nor on the Levitical priests, but on Peter, his royal steward (Matt 16:19), and the Apostles with him (Matt 18:18). This placed Peter and the Apostles de facto in a "priestly" role with respect to the rest of the "assembly" or church that Jesus was forming.

The interpretation of the law was only one priestly duty. A more important one was offering sacrifice. At the Last Supper, we observe Jesus in a priestly role, teaching the Apostles how to offer the new Passover, the new "memorial" or "remembrance" sacrifice consisting of his body and blood under the signs of bread and wine. The oldest record of Jesus' words is from St. Paul: "This cup is the new covenant in my blood. *Do this,* as often as you drink it, as my memorial sacrifice" (1 Cor 11:25).[17]

Jesus also says to the Apostles, "I covenant to you, as my Father covenanted to me, a kingdom, that you may eat and drink at my table in my kingdom, and sit on thrones judging the twelve tribes of Israel" (Luke 22:29–30). We noted in chapter 8 that this refers to the kingdom of David, which was founded on a covenant. Interestingly, the Essenes perceived the relationship between the Davidic kingdom and God's covenant, for they write:

> And the one who sits on the throne of David shall never be cut off, because the "ruler's staff" is *the covenant of the kingdom* . . . until the Righteous Messiah, the Branch of David, has come. For to him and to his seed *the covenant of the kingdom* of His people has been given for the eternal generations, because he has kept [. . .] the Law with the men of the Yahad. (4Q252 5:2–5)

"Eating and drinking at the king's table" was a privilege reserved for the king's sons, as we see from 2 Samuel 9:11: "Mephibosheth ate at David's table, like one of the king's sons." The sons of David were princes who judged legal cases that were brought to Jerusalem. Jesus' words about the Apostles sitting on thrones judging the tribes clearly allude to Psalm 122:3–5, which speaks of the thrones where the Davidic princes sat to judge cases:

> Jerusalem, built as a city which is bound firmly together,
> to which the tribes go up, the tribes of the Lord. . . .
> There thrones for judgment were set,
> *the thrones of the house of David.* (RSV; emphasis mine)

Now David himself was a "priest forever after the order of Melchizedek" (Ps 110:4), since he succeeded to the throne of Jerusalem, the throne once held by the priest-king Melchizedek (Gen 14:18).[18] That priesthood was shared by his sons: "David's sons were priests" (2 Sam 8:18).[19] The Apostles, likewise, as covenant sons of Jesus, share in his priesthood. One of the roles of priesthood was to mediate the forgiveness of sins, as we can see from the statement that is repeated throughout Leviticus: "the priest shall make atonement for him . . . and he shall be forgiven."[20] After his resurrection, Jesus confers on the Apostles this priestly role of mediating forgiveness: "Receive the Holy Spirit. If you forgive the sins of any, they are forgiven. If you retain the sins of any, they are retained" (John 20:22–23).

So we've seen in this chapter that the New Testament texts describe Jesus establishing the Apostles as a new priesthood for his new covenant community, as they take on the roles of interpreting the law, offering sacrifice, and mediating the forgiveness of sins, all of which were performed by the Levitical priests of the Old Covenant. The early Church was like Qumran in being a priestly people that still had ministerial priests. Moreover, as we are about to see, the New Testament and other Christian writings show how the early Church thought this ministerial priesthood did not die with the Apostles but was transferred to subsequent generations of leadership.

The Qumran community was a "priesthood within a priesthood," a priestly society that still had within it men set aside for sacred duties. We see the same pattern in early Christianity. Reading the Gospel through Essene eyes helps us to recognize the priestly overtones of Jesus' own actions and the responsibilities he gives to the Apostles: the authority to interpret the law ("binding and loosing"), to offer the memorial sacrifice, and to mediate the forgiveness of sin—roles performed by the priesthood under the Mosaic covenant.

For Further Reading

Cross, Frank Moore, Jr. "The Order and Liturgical Institutions of the 'Apocalyptic Communities.'" Pages 230–238 in Cross, *The Ancient Library of Qumran.* Garden City, NY: Anchor Books, 1961.

Kohler, Kaufmann. "Binding and Loosing." Page 215a in *The Jewish Encyclopedia,* Volume 3. Edited by Isidore Singer. New York: Funk and Wagnalls, 1906. Online: http://www.jewishencyclopedia.com /articles/3307-binding-and-loosing.

Ratzinger, Joseph/Benedict XVI. "The Disciples." Pages 169–182 in Ratzinger, *Jesus of Nazareth: From the Baptism in the Jordan to the Transfiguration.* Translated by Adrian J. Walker. New York: Doubleday, 2007.

CHAPTER 13

Priesthood in the Early Church

HOW DID THE EARLY CHURCH COME TO UNDERSTAND ITS leaders not simply as civil functionaries of the community but truly as *priests*: sacred persons consecrated to God, with cultic duties?

In Acts 1, we see that the Apostles were conscious of filling an office or role that could be filled by another after their death. After the death of Judas, Peter insists another should be appointed to his office, citing Psalm 109:8: "His bishoprick let another take" (Acts 1:20 KJV). I'm using the old King James Version here, because it accurately reveals that the word used for the apostolic office (Gk. *episkopên*) is the same root for the word used for early Christian leaders, the bishops (Gk. *episkopoi*), as we have seen. So the Apostles cast lots—as many scholars have noted, a priestly way of determining God's will[1]—and Matthias is chosen to "take part in the diaconate (Gk. *diakonias*) and the apostleship," using a word for ministry directly related to the title for the second-tier leadership of the early Church, the deacon (Gk. *diakonos*). It's important to observe the Greek words used to describe the role the Apostles have, because doing so helps us understand how the early Christians understood the roles of their leaders, the bishops and deacons, as rooted in the ministry of the Apostles.

Later in Acts, a dispute arises because some widows are being neglected in "the daily diaconate of food" (Acts 6:1, my translation). The Twelve gather the Church and say, "It is not right that we should give up preaching to serve (Gk. *diakonein*) tables" (1:2). So the Church chooses seven men for this duty, and the Apostles appoint them to it: "These they set before the apostles, and they prayed and *laid their hands* on them" (6:6). "Laying hands" on persons was an Old Testament sign of consecrating them to a sacred role. In fact, the closest Old Testament parallel to Acts 6:6 is Numbers 8:10–11: "When you present the Levites before the LORD, the people of Israel shall *lay their hands upon the Levites,* and *Aaron shall offer the Levites* before the LORD . . . that it may be theirs *to do the service* of the LORD." So the early Christians saw these seven men as the first deacons, and as taking over the role of the Old Testament Levites.

But there was another order of Church leaders appointed by the Apostles, and these went by the name "presbyters," or "elders":

> And when they [Paul and Barnabas] had appointed presbyters for them in every church, with prayer and fasting they committed them to the Lord in whom they believed. (Acts 14:23)

The word "appointed" here means literally "extended their hands upon" them.[2] It refers to the same kind of "laying on of hands" that we saw for the deacons in Acts 6—again, a gesture indicating that something or someone was being consecrated to God for a sacred purpose. The fact that these men were appointed by the Apostles by the laying on of hands indicates that they were not *merely* the older or oldest members of the congregation but rather held an office called "presbyter." Paul refers to the time when his protégé Timothy, even though he was young (1 Tim 4:12), received the laying on of hands from the presbytery, that is, the body of presbyters:

Do not neglect the gift you have, which was given you by prophetic utterance when the presbytery[3] laid their hands upon
you. (1 Tim 4:14)

From other parts of Acts, we learn that these presbyters shared
in the governance of the Church already during the lifetime of the
Apostles. The Apostles gave them, as it were, "on the job training"
in guiding Church affairs. The first large Church council in Jerusalem, recorded in Acts 15, was composed of the "Apostles and
the presbyters" (Acts 15:6), and the decision they reached—that
the Gentiles did not need to be circumcised—was promulgated
in the name of "the brethren, both the Apostles and the presbyters" (Acts 15:23). Peter, the chief of the Apostles, refers to himself
as a presbyter: "So I exhort the presbyters among you, as a fellow
presbyter and a witness of the sufferings of Christ: Tend the flock
of God that is your charge" (1 Pet 5:1–2).

Since the Apostles referred to themselves as fulfilling the role of
presbyters, and since the Apostles appointed the first presbyters,
and since the presbyters collaborated with the Apostles in governing the early Church, it was natural that, after the death of the
Apostles themselves, the early Christians saw the presbyters as the
successors of the Apostles, who continued to exercise their authority. So Irenaeus, the Church Father, writing around A.D. 150, tells
Christians of the time: "It is incumbent to obey the presbyters
who are in the Church—those who, as I have shown, possess the
succession from the apostles."[4] But since, as we have seen, the
Apostles themselves were given a priestly role by Jesus—including
the authoritative interpretation of the law, the offering of sacrifice,
the blessing of sacred meals, and the mediation of the forgiveness
of sins—it was natural that the early Christians came to see the
successors of the Apostles, the presbyters, as carrying on this ministerial priestly role. Hints of this are already in the New Testament itself, as when James gives instructions concerning the sick:

Is any among you sick? Let him call for the presbyters of the
church, and let them pray over him, anointing him with oil in
the name of the Lord; and the prayer of faith will save the sick
man, and the Lord will raise him up; and if he has committed
sins, he will be forgiven. (James 5:14–15)

This ritual of prayer and anointing with oil to heal and forgive
a sick person is parallel to certain Old Testament rituals like the
cleansing of a man healed of a skin disease, in which the priest
would *anoint with oil* and *make atonement* for the healed person
so that they could become clean once more (see Lev 14:1–20).
The presbyters of the Church take over the priestly task of anointing and forgiving sins for the sick person, only more so, since the
Old Testament priest intervened *after* the man was healed, whereas
the ministry of the New Testament presbyters *causes* the healing.
This action of the presbyters eventually became formalized as the
sacrament some Christians call "Anointing of the Sick" or "Last
Rites."

At first the terms "presbyter" and "bishop" were used synony-
mously, but as we have seen, already by the time of Ignatius of
Antioch (early A.D. 100s), the term "bishop" usually meant the
chief presbyter in a local church, who had final supervision over
the whole region. Since they were the chief presbyters, the bishops
had a very close connection to the ministry of the Apostles in the
eyes of the early Christians. So about fifty years after the death of
the Apostle John, Irenaeus could still boast that "we are in a position to reckon up those who were by the apostles instituted bishops in the Churches, and [to demonstrate] the succession of these
men to our own times."[5]

This succession from the Apostles to the bishops of the early
Church has a kind of precursor at Qumran. If the theory is correct
that the Teacher of Righteousness was the legitimate High Priest
of the Jerusalem Temple forced out by the Maccabean king Jona-

than Apphus in the 150s B.C., and left to found (or refound) the Qumran community, then the organizer of Qumran was himself a High Priest and the unquestioned interpreter of the law for the community members.[6] After the death of the Teacher of Righteousness, however, all his roles and responsibilities fell to the Overseer who was appointed after him. Thus, the Overseers of Qumran were, in a sense, the successors of the Teacher of Righteousness, himself the legitimate High Priest. One could say, then, that the Overseers inherited a High Priestly role.

It has taken us some time to "connect all the dots" between the Old Testament priesthood, Jesus and the Apostles, and the Apostles' successors and co-workers, the presbyters and bishops. Jesus claimed prerogatives of the Old Testament priesthood for himself and his Apostles, and the Apostles shared these rights and responsibilities with the presbyters, whom they chose to collaborate with themselves and succeed themselves. So just as Essene communities were governed by the Overseer, a priestly class, and a Levitical class, the early Church came to see the bishop, the presbyters, and the deacons as fulfilling the ancient pattern of High Priest, priests, and Levites established by Moses. The leaders of the Christian community, having been consecrated for the priestly ministry once exercised by the Apostles themselves, were not considered simply functionaries or officers who, for merely practical reasons, performed duties on behalf of the whole community. Rather, they were sacred persons consecrated by the laying on of hands for a sacred duty: what we usually call "priests" in the English language.

After the death of the priestly Teacher of Righteousness, the successive Overseers at Qumran continued to exercise his leadership over the community. We see a similar kind of succession in early Christianity, as the leadership role of the

Apostles is continued by the Christian presbyters and, in time, especially by the bishops. The early Christians saw the priestly duties Jesus gave the Apostles as continued by those who succeeded them.

For Further Reading

Daniélou, Jean. "Essenian Practices in the Community of Jerusalem." Pages 37–47 in Daniélou, *The Dead Sea Scrolls and Primitive Christianity*. Translated by Salvator Attanasio. Baltimore: Helicon Press, 1958.

Dupuis, Louis George. *The Apostolic Succession in the Holy Scriptures*. Burbank, CA: National Literary Guild, 1984.

Quinn, Jerome D., and William C. Wacker. *The First and Second Letters to Timothy,* pp. 267–271. Grand Rapids, MI: Eerdmans, 2000.

PART SIX

THE CHURCH
AND THE SCROLLS

CHAPTER 14

Did St. Paul Write Anything About the Church?

DID ST. PAUL—OR ANY OF THE APOSTLES, FOR THAT matter—actually write anything about the Church?

One of the things I've noticed over the years is the difference in beliefs between the typical American congregation and the typical American university religion department. If one visits a reasonably healthy, active local Christian church—whether Protestant, Catholic, or otherwise—one will find that most laypeople assume that the authors whose names are on biblical books actually did write those books. Thus, the Apostle John wrote the Gospel of John, Paul wrote the letters that bear his name, and so on. However, in most university religion departments, the standard assumption is exactly the opposite: no one named as the author of a biblical book is thought to have actually written it, and the entire Bible—with the exception of some of the letters of Paul (more on that to come)—is believed to be *pseudepigraphal* (soo-dah-PIG-grah-full) meaning "written under a false name."

I experienced a memorable example of this phenomenon in my own life. In the first semester of my doctoral program, I was required to take a course in New Testament studies. Now, my focus was the Old Testament. So I found myself as the only "Old Testament guy" in a class of New Testament doctoral students, and one day the class discussion turned to Paul's Letter to the Ephesians.

About fifteen minutes into the conversation, I realized that everyone in the room considered it proven that Paul had *not* written this letter. I was a bit surprised. I knew that Paul's authorship of Ephesians was disputed but was also aware of several scholars who defended him as the actual writer.[1] So why was everyone so confident he *hadn't* written it? Had something been discovered recently that I was unaware of? Being foolish, I raised my hand tentatively, and the professor called on me. "You'll have to excuse me," I began, "because I'm an Old Testament student and haven't worked in Pauline studies for a while. But could someone remind me of the reasons that we *know* Paul could not have written Ephesians?"

It was immediately obvious that I had committed a social faux pas. The room was silent. Someone cleared his throat. The New Testament students shuffled their feet and avoided eye contact. The professor was caught off guard. "Well," he said slowly, "the last person to defend Paul's authorship was Markus Barth,"[2] and then he mentioned a few other scholars who discussed the issue of authorship, before returning the class to the conversation that had been going on before I asked the stupid question. It was obvious, though, that the professor didn't actually *know* the reasons most Bible scholars did not believe Paul wrote this letter. I don't fault him for this. He wasn't a Paul specialist, and the field of biblical studies is incredibly large and complicated. It's impossible to master all the arguments for the different positions commonly held in it. Frequently, for matters outside his or her own specialty, all a scholar will know is that there is a general consensus on an issue.

I later did find out the reasons Ephesians is not thought to be from Paul. In the nineteenth century, there was a very influential German Bible scholar by the name of Ferdinand Christian Baur, who shared many views with the well-known German philosopher G.W.F. Hegel.[3] Hegel had a theory about the development of human culture. He argued that movements periodically would arise espousing a certain new idea or concept, which he called a "thesis." These movements would invariably provoke a reaction or opposition from another group (or groups) who would espouse a contrary idea, which Hegel called an "antithesis." Then, the two groups would struggle for a while, and out of that conflict would arise a third group that somehow reconciled the disagreements between the "thesis" and the "antithesis" to produce a "synthesis." This pattern, *thesis-antithesis-synthesis,* was how Hegel saw human history developing.

Of course, Hegel was wrong, and no one seriously follows his thought anymore. Human history doesn't follow nice, neat patterns developed by philosophers. However, Hegel was very fashionable among intellectuals for a while, and he certainly represented a whole current of thought that included F. C. Baur, who applied a Hegel-like pattern to the origins of Christianity. Baur argued that first there was a Jewish-Christian movement, headed by Peter, which saw Jesus as the Jewish Messiah but continued to practice the law of Moses (= thesis). This provoked a reaction, a Gentile-Christian movement headed by Paul, which saw Jesus as a universal savior and dispensed with the practice of the law (= antithesis). The struggle between these two eventually produced a *synthesis,* which Baur called "early Catholicism" (German *Frühkatholismus*), the Church that we know from the Fathers.

Unfortunately for Baur, the New Testament did not support his model. Already in Paul's letters, for example, one finds the so-called synthesis of "early Catholicism." So Baur did what many German Bible scholars have done in the modern period: he rearranged the data to support his theory. The letters of Paul that have a high view of the Church can't really be from Paul, since they represent the "synthesis," and Paul belongs to the "antithesis." So Baur argued that only Romans, 1 and 2 Corinthians, and Galatians were actually from St. Paul. These were the "principle letters" (German *Hauptbriefe*). All the others were false writings composed by later "early Catholic" authors under Paul's name. Baur threw Ephesians especially into this category, because it, perhaps more than any of Paul's letters, emphasizes the role of the Church in salvation. Paul—according to Baur—could never have had such a high view of the Church.

Baur and his followers did get some pushback from biblical scholars who questioned whether there was enough independent evidence that Ephesians and other letters were not from Paul. So Baur and his allies called attention to unique features of Ephesians: it has long, redundant sentences, and some uncommon words not used in the rest of Paul's letters. This was sufficient proof, according to Baur, that it could not come from Paul.

But all of Paul's letters have unique features, and employ at least some words not found in his other correspondence. According to statistics, the vocabulary of Ephesians does not differ significantly from that of the rest of Paul's letters: its percentage of unique words compares very closely with that of Galatians, for example, which is similar in length, and which everyone acknowledges as Paul's own work.[4] Galatians, in fact, has many peculiarities compared with the rest of Paul's correspondence, yet—for sociological and theological reasons—has never been challenged as authentically Pauline.[5]

Moreover, the style of any given ancient author changes over time and can also differ according to the purpose for which he is writing and the audience he is addressing. Ancient rhetoricians distinguished between the plain or "subdued" style, the moderate or "temperate" style, and the grand or "majestic" style. Any trained speaker or writer in antiquity was supposed to be able to write and speak in any of the three, depending on what was appropriate for the occasion.[6] Ephesus was in Asia Minor, and the style of Greek preferred there—called "Asianism"—was a majestic style, highly ornamented and "baroque." So Paul adapted his style to the tastes of his intended audience.[7] Finally, famous ancient persons often got help with their compositions, just as politicians today have secretaries and speechwriters. These assistants—called *amanuenses*—could influence the style of the document produced, so maybe Paul collaborated with someone like Tychicus (Eph 6:21–22) in composing the letter.

The point is, we have the resources to explain Ephesians' differences in style without having to deny Paul's authorship. Why, then, do many still insist it can't be from Paul? According to the late Swiss New Testament scholar Bo Reicke, the reason is this paradigm inherited from the period of Hegel and Baur, which makes it impossible to think that Jesus and Paul envisioned a Church. Speaking of Ephesians along with Colossians, 1 Timothy, and Titus, Reicke comments:

> What has especially led critical scholarship to doubt the Pauline authorship of these epistles is their emphasis on the "church" as the subject of Paul's concern.[8]

Baur was at the peak of his career about a century before the discovery of the Dead Sea Scrolls, and thus he had no access to Jewish writings from Israel that were contemporary with the lives of Jesus and Paul. Now that we have the Scrolls and can compare them to the New Testament writings, do they support the view that the Church, as Ephesians describes it, could only have been imagined after Paul's lifetime?

We can't answer that question without making a close comparison of passages of Ephesians with the Dead Sea Scrolls. I find it fascinating that so many of the "distinctive concepts" that Paul advances in Ephesians have parallels in the Scrolls.

For example, Paul stresses the idea of God's providence and predestination more in Ephesians than in other letters, especially in the first chapter:

Blessed be the God and Father of our Lord Jesus Christ, who has blessed us in Christ with every spiritual blessing in the heavenly places, even as he chose us in him before the foundation of the world, that we should be holy and blameless before him. He destined us in love to be his sons through Jesus Christ, according to the purpose of his will. (Eph 1:3–5)

Fascinatingly, the passages of the Scrolls that most stress the concept of predestination *also* occur in contexts associated with *God's blessing* and *holiness of life*. So the *Community Rule* insists:

The priests are to *bless* all those foreordained to God (lit. "of the lot of God"), who *walk faultless in all of His ways*, saying "May He *bless* you with every good thing and preserve you from every evil. *May He enlighten your mind with wisdom* for living, be gracious to you with the knowledge of eternal things." (1QS 2:1–3; emphasis mine)

The connection of predestination with the blessing of *wisdom* and *enlightenment* of mind is also found in Ephesians, for Paul goes on to pray that God "may give you *a spirit of wisdom and of revelation* in the knowledge of him, having *the eyes of your hearts enlightened*" (Eph 1:15–18). In other words, the blessings that Paul prays down on the Ephesian Christians are very similar in content and theology to the blessings the priests of Qumran invoked on the "elect of God" who composed the membership of the community. The Qumranites shared with Paul a robust sense that God guided all things according to his foresight and plan:

All that is now and ever shall be originates with the God of knowledge. Before things come to be, He has ordered all their designs, so that when they do come to exist—at their appointed times as ordained by His glorious plan—they fulfill their destiny, a destiny impossible to change. He controls the laws governing all things, and He provides for all their pursuits. He created humankind to rule over the world, appointing for them two spirits in which to walk until the time ordained for His visitation. These are the spirits of truth and falsehood. (1QS 3:15–19)

What the Essenes refer to as the "glorious plan" of God, St. Paul now claims has been revealed in Jesus Christ:

For he has made known to us in all wisdom and insight the mystery of his will, according to his purpose which he set forth in Christ as a plan for the fullness of time, to unite all things in him, things in heaven and things on earth. In him, according to the purpose of him who accomplishes all things according to the counsel of his will, we who first hoped in Christ have been destined and appointed to live for the praise of his glory. (Eph 1:9–12)

Thus, for Paul it is not the men of the Qumran community nor any of the other Essenes but those who have hoped in Christ who are the true "men of the lot of God," having been "destined and appointed to live for the praise of his glory."

Another parallel between the Qumranites' view of their community and Paul's view of the Church is the union of its members with angels "in heavenly places." Paul says to his fellow Christians that God has "made us alive together with Christ . . . and raised us up with him, and *made us sit with him in the heavenly places* in Christ Jesus" (Eph 2:5–6). Likewise, Paul thanks God that to him "this grace was given . . . to make all men see what is the plan of the mystery hidden for ages in God who created all things; that through the church the manifold wisdom of God might now be made known *to the principalities and powers in the heavenly places*"

(Eph 3:8–10). The "principalities and powers" are terms for angelic beings.

This notion of the members of the covenant community being lifted up to worship with the angels is prevalent at Qumran. The British scholar Crispin Fletcher-Louis has established his scholarly reputation by studying this theme.[9] A good example of this is the *Rule of Benedictions,* in a section in which the "Instructor"[10] of the community is to bless the priests:

> May you abide forever as an Angel of the Presence in the holy habitation, to the glory of the God of hosts. May you serve in the temple of the kingdom of God, ordering destiny with the Angels of the Presence, a party of the *Yahad* [with the Holy Ones] forever, for all the ages of eternity! (1Q28^b 4:21)

Likewise, the document known as the Songs of the Sabbath Sacrifice (4Q400–407) contains liturgical instructions in which the "Instructor" of the community directs both the angels and the community members in a heavenly liturgy in which both participate:

> A text belonging to the Instructor. The song accompanying the sacrifice on the first Sabbath, sung on the fourth of the first month: "Praise the God of . . . , you angels (Heb. *'elohim*) of utter holiness; rejoice in his divine kingdom. For He has established utter holiness among the eternally holy ones, that they might become for Him priests of the inner sanctum in His royal temple, ministers of the Presence in His glorious innermost chamber. In the congregation of all the wise angels (*'elohim*), and in the councils of all the divine spirits, He has engraved His precepts to govern all spiritual works, and His glorious laws for all the wise angels, that sage congregation

honored by God, those who draw near to knowledge. (4Q400
1:1–6)

"Eternally holy ones" seems to be a reference to "the men of
perfect holiness," i.e., the celibate members of the Qumran community, who now function as "priests" in the heavenly Temple,
along with the "congregation of the angels," using the Hebrew
word 'elohim to mean "angels," as it frequently does in the Bible.[11]
Fletcher-Louis argues that the Qumranites believed they were
transformed spiritually, through their worship, into angelic priests
in God's heavenly Temple. Something at least close to that must
have been the case.

One of the strongest correlations between the Church in Ephesians and the *yahad* in Qumran is the Temple-nature of both communities. Paul makes clear that the Church is a new Temple where
God is now worshipped. The Temple in Jerusalem had a dividing
wall inside it that kept Gentiles out of the inner parts, where only
Jews could go. Paul says that in the new Temple of the Church,
there is no longer a dividing wall:

> Therefore remember that at one time you Gentiles . . . were
> separated from Christ. . . . But now in Christ Jesus you . . .
> have been brought near in the blood of Christ. For he is our
> peace, who has made us both one, and *has broken down the
> dividing wall of hostility,* that he might create in himself one
> new man in place of the two. (Eph 2:11–14)

Paul's language of "one new man in place of the two" is a reference to Adam and the creation story. Adam was the original "new
man," and through his marriage with Eve, the "two became one."
So Paul sees Jews and Gentiles as two parts of humanity that have
been united in Christ, the new Adam. We have here the imagery

of both a new Temple and a new Adam, strikingly similar to the description of the *yahad* as a "Temple of Adam" in the Scrolls.[12]

Paul continues to describe the Church:

> So then you are no longer strangers and sojourners, but you are fellow citizens with the holy ones and members of the household of God, built upon the foundation of the apostles and prophets, Christ Jesus himself being the cornerstone, in whom the whole building is joined together and grows into a holy temple in the Lord; in whom you also are built into it for a dwelling place of God in the Spirit. (Eph 2:19–22 RSV *alt.*)

This resonates strongly with the theology of the covenant community at Qumran. For example, a text that we have looked at several times before has many similarities with this passage from Ephesians:

> When such men as these come to be in Israel, then shall the party of the *Yahad* truly be established, an "eternal planting" (*Jub* 16:26), a temple for Israel, and—mystery!—a Holy of Holies for Aaron; true witnesses to justice, chosen by God's will to atone for the land and to recompense the wicked their due. They will be "the tested wall, the precious cornerstone" (Isa 28:16), whose foundations shall neither be shaken nor swayed, a fortress, a Holy of Holies for Aaron, all of them knowing the Covenant of Justice and thereby offering a sweet savor. They shall be a blameless and true house in Israel, upholding the covenant of eternal statutes. They shall be an acceptable sacrifice, atoning for the land. (1QS 8:4–10)

We have here an amazing correlation of images and terms: in both Ephesians and the *Community Rule,* the respective communities are a "temple," a "house," built on a "cornerstone" and "foundations," and described as "holy." If we bring in the near context of Ephesians, we find parallels for other elements of the *Community Rule*. The Rule describes the community as a "mystery" (Heb. *sôd*),[13] and Paul likewise speaks of his insight into "the *mystery* hidden for ages in God" that "through the *church* the manifold wisdom of God might now be made known" (Eph 2:9–10), later adding, "this *mystery* is a profound one . . . it refers to Christ and the Church" (5:32). The *Community Rule* speaks of the members of the *yahad* "upholding the *covenant*," and Paul says that before entering the Church, the Gentiles were "strangers to the *covenants*" (2:12), but they are strangers no more. The members of the community offer "a sweet savor" and are "an acceptable sacrifice" (1QS 8:8–10), whereas Paul calls Christians to imitate Christ, who was "a fragrant offering and sacrifice to God" (5:1–2). The Spirit functions prominently in both communities: earlier the Rule speaks of the "Spirit pervading God's true society" that atones for sin, so that one may be "joined to His truth by His Holy Spirit" (1QS 3:6–7), and Paul speaks of the Church as "having access in one Spirit to the Father" (2:18) and as "the dwelling place of God in the Spirit" (2:22).

We could identify dozens of other close parallels between Ephesians and the Scrolls—particularly the *Community Rule*—both at the level of language and at the level of concepts; for example, the Rule refers to the members of the *yahad* as "children of light,"[14] and Paul tells the Ephesians, "once you were darkness, but now you are light in the Lord: walk as children of the light" (5:8). However, the similarities we have identified suffice to make our point. The members of the Qumran *yahad* and the early Christians both understood their communities to be predestined to holiness of life by the plan of God, who also revealed to them divine wisdom and raised them to heavenly realms where they participate in worship with the angels. Both communities composed a new, holy, mysterious, and Spirit-infused Temple of human beings, a mystical "new Adam," replacing the defiled old Temple in Jerusalem, and replacing its ineffective sacrifices with spiritual sacrifices and atonement for all God's people, the "children of light."

What explains this heavily Essene-like theology in an epistle addressed to a city in Asia Minor? Interestingly, Acts 19:1–7 notes that followers of John the Baptist were in Ephesus and received Christian baptism from Paul, helping to form the nucleus of the Ephesian church. We've already discussed the relationship of the Baptist to Qumran above.

In Christian theology, the subdiscipline that studies the Church is called *ecclesiology*.[15] It is fair to say that the Essene movement, and the Qumran *yahad* in particular, truly had an *ecclesiology*, that is, a well-developed theology of how the covenant community played a role in the salvation of its members, according to God's plan. After all, as noted in chapter 12, although the English term "Church" comes from the Greek *kuriakon doma*, "house of the Lord," the original word for Church in the New Testament is *ekklesia*, "assembly, congregation" (cf. Spanish *iglesia*), which is the direct Greek translation of the Hebrew *qahal*, which the Essenes used as a synonym for their own movement[16] or for the eschatological community of Israel after the arrival of the Messiah(s).[17]

It seems to me that the implications for understanding the New Testament and the origins of the Church are profound. Christian biblical studies continue to be influenced, even dominated, by attitudes inherited from the nineteenth and early twentieth centuries. In those days, before the discovery of the Scrolls, European scholars saw Jesus and Paul as essentially prophets who preached a saving message of faith in Jesus the Messiah, and the imminent end of the world by the arrival of God's supernatural kingdom. Neither Jesus nor Paul could have imagined or intended a Church in its fully Christian sense, according to these scholars, because what was the sense of establishing a new human community when the world was about to end? Therefore, any passages of the New Testament that showed Jesus or Paul placing emphasis on the Church must be insertions written by Christians decades or centuries after the fact, and put into the mouths of Jesus and Paul. Thus, the account of Jesus establishing the Church on Peter (Matt 16:13–20) and the entire Letter to the Ephesians must be late and fictitious. Such was the mind-set of the nineteenth-century scholars, and their modern heirs.

But the Scrolls turn this paradigm on its head. The *Community Rule* was copied perhaps as early as 100 B.C., and it represents a theologically mature document that has already undergone development for decades at least.[18] A century before the birth of Christ, it has a highly developed ecclesiology comparable to that of Paul and other early Christian writers. The fact that the Essenes expected the end of the history and arrival of the Messiah(s) to happen soon did not prevent them from forming a rather elaborate and hierarchically structured community designed to await this imminent event. *If the Essenes could do it, so could Jesus and his Apostles.* "Churchy" passages like Matthew 16:13–20 and much of Ephesians represent creative reuse and recombination of theological concepts that were available and attested in devout Judaism for over a century before the ministries of Jesus and Paul. They are entirely believable in the historical context that they claim for themselves. Ephesians is thoroughly Jewish in its outlook and could stem entirely from Paul's formation in the Palestinian Judaism of his youth, without needing reference to Greek philosophies or concepts. Likewise, Matthew 16:13–20 is thoroughly Jewish and is shot through with Palestinian Jewish concepts like the Temple being built on a rock that blocked the shaft to Hades, and the exercise of the *halakhic* (legal) authority to "bind and loose."[19] As noted German scholars Otto Betz and Rainer Riesner put it: "A comparison with the Qumran texts shows that New Testament expressions and notions which many people regarded as Greek and late are, rather, *Palestinian and early.*"[20]

That is not to say that Jesus' movement was just a form of Essenism, or that Paul was simply copying the Essenes, because there were notable differences, too, not the least of which would be the divinity of Jesus and the abandonment of the ceremonial law! Nonetheless, the fact that many of Jesus' followers were familiar with, or had been part of, "new covenant communities" at Qumran or elsewhere made possible the very rapid formation of the external structures and practices of the early Church that we see reflected in Acts, the Epistles, and the Apostolic Fathers. Once again, the Scrolls help make the origins of Christianity more understandable in their ancient historical context.

Paul's emphasis on the Church in the Epistle to the Ephesians has caused many scholars to dispute his authorship of the letter. Ideas about the Church were supposed to be later developments within Christianity. However, what Paul says about the Church in Ephesians compares very well with what the Scrolls say about the Essenes' sacred community. In light of the Scrolls, Ephesians fits seamlessly into the Judaism of Paul's day and even earlier. This removes a major objection to the authenticity of his letter.

For Further Reading

Hoehner, Harold W. "Did Paul Write Galatians?" Pages 150–169 in *History and Exegesis: New Testament Essays in Honor of Dr. E. Earle Ellis for His 80th Birthday.* Edited by Sang-Won (Aaron) Son. New York: T & T Clark, 2006. Hoehner demonstrates that the same kinds of literary arguments used to dispute Paul's authorship of Ephesians could also be turned against Galatians with devastating effect. However, the authenticity of Galatians is seldom if ever disputed, because Galatians suits the theological agendas of modern biblical scholarship, whereas Ephesians does not.

O'Connor, Jerome Murphy, and James H. Charlesworth, editors. *Paul and the Dead Sea Scrolls.* New York: Crossroad, 1990. See especially the contributions by Karl Georg Kuhn, "The Epistle to the Ephesians in Light of the Qumran Texts" (pp. 115–131), and Franz Mussner, "Contributions Made by Qumran to the Understanding of the Epistle to the Ephesians" (pp. 159–178).

White, Benjamin L. *Remembering Paul: Ancient and Modern Contests over the Image of the Apostle.* New York: Oxford University Press, 2014. See especially chapter 2, "Capturing Paul: F. C. Baur and the Rise of the Pauline Captivity Narrative," pp. 20–41. White shows how Baur first opposed the authenticity of Ephesians because it did not fit his philosophical-historical model of early Christian development. Later, he marshaled literary arguments to support the conclusion he had already embraced.

CHAPTER 15

The Scrolls, the Reformation, and Church Unity

MOST PRACTICING CHRISTIANS TODAY WOULD AGREE THAT one of the biggest tragedies of modern Christianity is its divisions. There are upward of fifty thousand different Christian denominations in the world. In antiquity, however, the Church was not so divided. For the first thousand years of Christian history, there were sects that split off, to be sure, but the vast majority of the Church stayed intact and "in communion"—that is, recognizing each other as fellow Christians and able to share sacraments together.

The first permanent split was in 1054, when a variety of factors led to a break in communion between the Latin-speaking Western Church and the Greek-speaking Eastern Church, giving rise to what we now call Roman Catholicism and Eastern Orthodoxy. Then, within the Western Church, a whole series of divisions exploded in the 1500s in what we call the Reformation. We remember Martin Luther (1483–1546) as the figure associated with the beginning of this schism. His nailing of the famous "95 Theses" to the door of the church in Wittenberg in 1517 started a public debate that led to the breakup of Western Christianity and the rift between Protestantism and Catholicism that continues to this day.[1]

What bearing do the Scrolls have on the Reformation? It's hard to believe that Jewish documents from the first century would be relevant to theological debates fifteen hundred years later, but they actually are.

One of the central theological ideas of Martin Luther was the concept "salvation by faith alone," or *sola fide*. What exactly this slogan means can vary significantly depending on who is using it, but for Luther, it meant that one's *faith* in Christ was the sole determining factor in one's salvation, and one's *works*—that is, one's behavior and actions—did not contribute to one's being saved. In his more extreme moments, Luther would argue that one could continue to commit even heinous crimes and, provided one's faith in Christ's atoning sacrifice on the cross remained strong, one would still go to heaven.[2]

I was trained in evangelism by a man who embraced the more extreme form of "salvation by faith alone." I remember one autumn day we were going door to door in the neighborhood around our downtown church, and a middle-aged woman invited us up to her second-floor apartment. We sat down on her tattered couches and began to explain the Gospel using the well-known "Roman Road" method.[3] The woman wanted to receive Jesus as her savior, so we prayed with her, and it was a beautiful experience. However, as soon as the prayer was done, my trainer began to ask the woman, "So now that you've received Jesus, if you went out and shot someone tomorrow, would you still be saved?" and when she tentatively said, "No?" he replied, "Yes! You would! Because salvation is by faith alone, and once saved, always saved!"

I did then—and still do—have serious reservations about presenting the Gospel that way. It's a fringe approach, since most Protestants would insist that true faith inevitably shows itself in holy behavior, and therefore a life of sin is a contradiction to true faith in Christ. Nonetheless, salvation, for these believers, is not based on good behavior but comes "by faith alone."

Where did Luther get his concept of "faith alone"? His major sources were the letters of Paul, particularly Romans and Galatians, in which Paul contrasts "faith" with "works of the law." Here are some key passages:

> For no human being will be justified in his sight by *works of the law,* since through the law comes knowledge of sin. (Rom 3:20)

> [We] know that a man is not justified by *works of the law* but through faith in Jesus Christ, even we have believed in Christ Jesus, in order to be justified by faith in Christ, and not by *works of the law,* because by *works of the law* shall no one be justified. (Gal 2:16)

> For all who rely on *works of the law* are under a curse; for it is written, "Cursed be everyone who does not abide by all things written in the Book of the Law, and do them." (Gal 3:10)

The key question is: what does "works of the law" mean? For Christians, the "law" in religious conversation usually means the Ten Commandments, which are a summary of the moral law. That's essentially how Luther read these passages, and concluded that it was only faith in Christ that saved a person, and the moral law (i.e., the Ten Commandments) had nothing do with it, since it could not "justify" someone (Gal 2:16) and in fact led to a curse (Gal 3:10).[4]

Why hadn't someone seen this before, and why wasn't "salvation by faith alone" preached in the Church for the first fifteen hundred years of her existence? The problem is that elsewhere in his writings, Paul *does* say that "works" play a role in salvation. For example, in his Letter to the Romans, Paul insists:

For *he will render to every man according to his works*: to those who by patience in well-doing seek for glory and honor and immortality, he will give eternal life; but for those who are factious and do not obey the truth, but obey wickedness, there will be wrath and fury. (Rom 2:6–8)

Likewise:

For it is not the *hearers of the law* who are righteous before God, but the *doers of the law* who will be justified. (Rom 2:13)

So there seems to be a contradiction in Paul's thought: on the one hand, "doers of the law . . . will be justified" (Rom 2:13), but on the other, "by *works of the law* shall no one be justified" (Gal 2:16).

Earlier commentators, like Thomas Aquinas (1225–1274), noticed these apparent contradictions and suggested that the phrase "works of the law" must have a specialized sense, referring not to the moral law generally but to the *ceremonial and ritual elements* of the Mosaic Law—ritual washings, circumcision, food laws, and so on—which were no longer practiced in the new covenant. Aquinas remarks on Gal 2:16:

It should be known, therefore, that some works of the Law were moral and some ceremonial. The moral, although they were contained in the Law, could not, strictly speaking, be called "works of the Law," for man is induced to them by natural instinct and by the natural law. But the ceremonial works are properly called the "works of the Law."[5]

Paul would be saying, then, that it is faith in Christ—rather than getting circumcised, observing the Sabbath, keeping kosher, and performing other "works of the law"—that *justifies* us, that is, changes our inner being to be right with God.

Aquinas's solution to the apparent contradiction in Paul's thought and writings would be convenient if true—but is this merely a clever explanation, or is there actual evidence to support his interpretation?

Here's where the Dead Sea Scrolls come into play, because among them we found a most remarkable document that contains several theological phrases that otherwise occur only in Paul's letters.

Scholars call this document "4QMMT," "MMT" being an acronym for the Hebrew *Miqsat Ma'asei ha-Torah,* meaning "Some of the Works of the Law." It is a letter written, apparently, from the Essenes to the Pharisees, during a time when the Pharisees enjoyed royal patronage and were given a lot of say in how Judaism was practiced in Jerusalem and the Temple. The Essenes thought the Pharisees had the wrong interpretation of certain religious laws, and wrote to correct them on those points.

The end of the letter is fascinating, because in it we find a cluster of terms also found in the writings of Paul:

> Now, we have written to you some of *the works of the Law,* those which we determined would be beneficial for you and your people, because we have seen that you possess insight and knowledge of the Law. Understand all these things and beseech Him to set your counsel straight and so keep you away from evil thoughts and the counsel of Belial. Then you shall rejoice at the end time when you find the essence of our words to be true. And it will be *reckoned to you as righteousness,* in that you have done what is right and good before Him, to your own benefit and to that of Israel. (4Q398 2:2–8)[6]

Here we have a combination of two phrases, *works of the law* and *reckoned to you as righteousness,* that may not seem that unusual but actually can't be found in ancient literature except Paul's writings, when he is discussing the role of faith and works in salvation. So we read the following statements in Romans:

> For no human being will be justified in his sight by *works of the law,* since through the law comes knowledge of sin. (Rom 3:20)

> For what does the scripture say? "Abraham believed God, and it was *reckoned to him as righteousness.*" . . . To one who does not work but trusts him who justifies the ungodly, his faith is *reckoned as righteousness.* (Rom 4:3–5)

I cannot bring myself to believe that the occurrence of these phrases in both Romans and 4QMMT is a pure coincidence. Rather, it must reflect an ancient Jewish discussion about which "works of the law" were absolutely necessary in order to be "reckoned as righteous" before God.

Still, what does "works of the law" mean in this ancient context? The Essenes conclude 4QMMT by saying, "We have written to you concerning some of the *works of the law.*" Therefore, the topics discussed in the body of the letter were considered "works of the law" by the Essenes. So if we take a look at these topics, we can get an idea of the kinds of things that qualified as "works of the law." And these are the topics:[7]

- The proper liturgical calendar of only 364 days (4Q394 1:1–3)

- Prohibition of Gentile-grown wheat in the Temple (394 1:6–8)

- The proper way to cook the sin-offering (394 1:8–11)

- Prohibition of sacrifices offered by Gentiles (394 1:11–12)

- The proper way to eat the grain portion of the peace-offering (394 1:12–16)

- Proper handling of the corpse of the heifer of the sin-offering (394 1:16–19)

- Proper handling of leather (394 2:2–3)

- How to sacrifice pregnant animals (394 3:7–9)

- Prohibition of marriage for men who are permanently unclean due to physical defect or impure birth (394 3:9–18)

- Exclusion of the blind and lame from the Temple (394 3:19–4:4)

- The purity of liquids poured from one container to another (394 4:5–8)

- Prohibition of dogs from Jerusalem (394 4:8–12)

- Tithing of the produce of fruit trees (394 4:12–14)

- Exclusion of lepers from the Temple precincts and from sacrificial offerings (394 4:14–16)

- Cleanliness regulations concerning human corpses (396 4:1–3)

- Prohibition of marriages between priests and laity (396 4:4–11)

Many of these topics are extremely technical and require some explanation. For example, concerning the purity of liquids poured from one container to another, the issue was this: Suppose one pours milk from a clean pitcher into an unclean cup. Does the uncleanness stay in the cup? Or does it travel backward up the stream of liquid into the pitcher, thus defiling the pitcher? The Pharisees said: It stays in the cup. The Essenes said: It travels up the stream of liquid and defiles the pitcher. The distinction may seem petty, but it makes a huge difference if one is trying to keep one's kitchen ritually clean. This is how technical the discussion of "works of the law" could get!

Look back over our list of sixteen topics described as "works of the law" in 4QMMT. Are these the kinds of things that we would describe as "good works," "works of mercy," or "works of charity"? Are any of them even properly *moral* issues? Absolutely not! Every single issue concerns either ritual cleanliness or liturgical regulation. Nothing pertains to the Ten Commandments or the moral law. According to the traditional Christian division of the Old Law into the civil, ceremonial, and moral precepts,[8] every topic that 4QMMT describes as a "work of the law" would fall under the category "ceremonial." It looks like 4QMMT confirms Aquinas's hunch that "works of the law" had a technical meaning as the ceremonial precepts of the old covenant.[9]

This evidence should not be ignored, because it sheds light on what is really at stake for Paul in Romans and Galatians. The issue between Paul and his opponents in these epistles is not whether good works are necessary for salvation once one has placed one's faith in Christ. The issue is, What causes one to receive the Holy Spirit: placing one's faith in Christ, or observing the ceremonies of the Mosaic Law? As Paul says in Galatians:

> O foolish Galatians! . . . Let me ask you only this: Did you receive the Spirit by *works of the law,* or by *hearing with faith*? . . . Does he who supplies the Spirit to you and works miracles among you do so by *works of the law,* or by *hearing with faith*? (Gal 3:1–2, 5)

And the particular "work of the law" or ceremonial observance at issue is *circumcision,* which is mentioned *a lot* in both epistles:[10]

> Now I, Paul, say to you that if you receive circumcision, Christ will be of no advantage to you. I testify again to every man who receives circumcision that he is bound to keep the whole law. You are severed from Christ, you who would be justified by the law. (Gal. 5:2–4)

Notice that the example Paul gives of someone trying to be "justified by the law" is not a man who tries to love others too much, or someone who gives too many alms, or feeds the poor excessively, but rather someone who gets *circumcised,* which is a matter of ritual cleanliness of the Old Law.

If Paul were arguing against the need for "good works" in the life of the Christian, then he would object to people doing acts of love or mercy in order to try to be saved—something he *never* does. Instead, in at least ten passages throughout his epistles, he attacks the practice of circumcision as if it were a salvific ritual:

> For in Christ Jesus neither circumcision nor uncircumcision is of any avail, but faith working through love. (Gal 5:6)[11]

Scholars have spilled a lot of ink trying to clarify the role of "faith" and "works" in Romans and Galatians, but Paul's basic message does not need to be so difficult to grasp. Paul affirms that God rewards good and punishes evil:

> There will be tribulation and distress for every human being who does evil . . . but glory and honor and peace for everyone who does good. (Rom 2:9)

The problem is, ever since Adam and Eve we have an inborn tendency toward evil:

All men, both Jews and Greeks, are under the power of sin. (Rom 3:9)

We can't do right without the help of God:

For I know that nothing good dwells within me, that is, in my flesh. I can will what is right, but I cannot do it. (Rom 7:18)

The ceremonies of the Old Testament—circumcision, food laws, the Sabbath, and the other "works of the law"—don't help because they don't bestow on us God's Spirit, which comes only through faith in Jesus:

Let me ask you only this: Did you receive the Spirit by *works of the law,* or by *hearing with faith*? (Gal 3:2)

The Holy Spirit enables us to overcome evil and actually do good in our lives, so we can be pleasing to God:

For the law of the Spirit of life in Christ Jesus has set me free from the law of sin and death. For God has done what the law . . . could not do: sending his own Son in the likeness of sinful flesh and for sin, he condemned sin in the flesh, in order that *the just requirement of the law might be fulfilled in us, who walk not according to the flesh but according to the Spirit.* (Rom 8:2–4)

So Christians *do* end up fulfilling the "just requirement of the law," which boils down to the twofold love of God and love of neighbor:

God's love has been poured into our hearts through the Holy Spirit. (Rom 5:5)

Love does no wrong to a neighbor; therefore love is the fulfilling of the law. (Rom 13:10)

The Holy Spirit is the forgotten element in so many arguments between Protestants and Catholics about "justification by faith" and the role of "faith and works." The Holy Spirit is the ultimate reason that Paul can affirm that (1) we need to lead holy lives to be saved, but also that (2) salvation is not our own effort. That's because the change in our behavior, and the growth in holiness, is due not to our effort but to the working of the Holy Spirit in us.

Paul is emphatic that we cannot continue to live in sin and expect to be saved:

If you live according to the flesh you will die, but if by the Spirit you put to death the deeds of the body you will live. . . . We are children of God, and if children, then heirs, heirs of God and fellow heirs with Christ, *provided we suffer with him* in order that we may also be glorified with him. (Rom 8:12–17)

If we allow the Spirit to work in us, we will live; but if we don't, we won't. The Christian life is not simply a "decision for Jesus" and then a trip to heaven when we die. It involves suffering, and in fact, if we don't suffer, we won't be glorified with Christ (Rom 8:17). This agrees with Jesus' own words: "If anyone would come after me, let him deny himself and take up his cross daily and follow me" (Luke 9:23).

It's interesting to note that there are several parallels to Paul's thought in the Scrolls. The Essenes also recognized that one could live a holy life only by the power of God's Spirit:

For *only through the Spirit* pervading God's true society can there be atonement for a man's ways, all of his iniquities; thus only can he gaze upon the light of life and so be joined to His truth by His Holy Spirit, purified from all iniquity. (1QS 3:6–8)

The Essenes also acknowledged that, relying on his own strength, a human being could scarcely do anything but sin. In a passage reminiscent of Paul's famous dictum "All have sinned and fall short of the glory of God" (Rom 3:23), the Qumran Teacher of Righteousness says:

What is mortal man in comparison with this? . . . For he is sinful from the womb and in the guilt of unfaithfulness until old age. I know that man has no righteousness, nor does the son of man walk in the perfect way. (1QHª 12:30–32)

Like Paul moaning, "Wretched man that I am! Who will deliver me from this body of death?" (Rom 7:24), the Teacher of Righteousness says:

I am a vessel of clay and kneaded with water, a foundation of shame and a spring of filth, a melting pot of iniquity and a structure of sin, a spirit of error, perverted without understanding and terrified by righteous judgments. (1QHª 9:23–25)

But Paul rejoices in the gift of the Spirit through Jesus Christ: "The law of the Spirit of life in Christ Jesus has set me free from the law of sin and death!" (Rom 8:2). And the Essene Teacher also knew—probably from Ezekiel 36:26—that the answer to human sin was the gift of God's Spirit:

I know that no one can be righteous apart from You. And I entreat Your favor by that Spirit which You have given me, to

fulfill Your mercy with Your servant forever, to cleanse me by
Your Holy Spirit, and to bring me near by Your grace according to Your great mercy. (1QHª 8:29–30)

* * *

According to the Gospel of John, on the night of the Last Supper,
Jesus prayed for those who would believe in him, that they would
"all be one," so that "the world may know" that Jesus was sent
from the Father (John 17:21). When Christians aren't "one," the
world cannot know the truth about Jesus.

One thing that needlessly divides Christians is this fruitless and
misguided polemic about "salvation by faith alone" versus "works
righteousness," which we have inherited from the Reformation era.
In light of the Dead Sea Scrolls, we can once more read Romans
and Galatians with first-century Jewish eyes—indeed, through Essene eyes—and come to agreement on what St. Paul meant. The
issue at stake in Romans and Galatians is not "salvation by just
believing" versus "doing good works to be saved." The fundamental issue is: How do you receive the Holy Spirit, by having faith in
Jesus or by performing the ceremonies of the Old Testament?
When Paul says, "a man is not justified by *works of the law* but
through faith in Jesus Christ" (Gal 2:16), he means it is through
having faith that the Spirit cleanses and empowers (i.e., "justifies")
us, not by being circumcised or any other Mosaic ceremony. After
all, he wasn't arguing against opponents who were urging everyone
to pray, be kind, and give alms in order to be saved; rather, his opponents were urging people to be circumcised (Gal 5:2–12).

All Christians ought to be able to agree: it is through faith that
we receive the Holy Spirit, and are empowered to live a holy life
(Gal 3:2–5; Rom 8:13).

All Christians ought to be able to agree: a holy life is not optional (Matt 5:48; 1 Pet 1:14–16). All Christians are called to
holiness, and just believing facts about Jesus will not save a person

who continues a sinful life (Matt 7:21; Luke 6:46; James 2:14–17). The way of salvation necessarily involves self-denial and discipleship (Luke 9:23; Rom 8:13, 17).

All Christians ought to be able to agree: we don't save ourselves (Eph 2:8). We don't earn our salvation (Rom 6:23). The Holy Spirit is God's gift, not something we merit (Acts 2:38, 10:45). God gives it to those who trust in him (Gal 3:2, 5), usually through Baptism (John 3:5; Acts 2:38; 1 Cor 12:13). So we never boast about our own accomplishments, because anything good we do is actually the work of God in us (Rom 3:27; Gal 2:20; Eph 2:8–10).

If we could all agree on these points, it would go a long way to "burying the hatchet" of the Reformation that Christians have been wielding against each other for five hundred years. There would still be a large number of other points of disagreement, but it would be a step in the right direction.

The debate over what St. Paul means by "works of the law" played a major role in the breakup of Western Christianity in the Reformation. Now the Scrolls give us the only examples of this theological phrase outside of Paul, and they refer to ritual observances of the Mosaic Law—confirming how Aquinas and other early interpreters understood St. Paul. The Scrolls help us get a better handle on St. Paul's message: faith in Christ, not Mosaic ceremonies, gives us the Holy Spirit, who helps us love God and neighbor so as to fulfill the heart of God's law.

For Further Reading

Abegg, Martin G., Jr. "4QMMT C 27, 31 and 'Works Righteousness.'" *Dead Sea Discoveries* 6, no. 2 (1999): 139–147.

Dunn, James D. G. "4QMMT and Galatians." *New Testament Studies* 43, no. 1 (1997): 147–153.

Schiffman, Lawrence. "Miqsat Ma'asei Ha-Torah." Pages 558–560 in *Encyclopedia of the Dead Sea Scrolls,* Volume 1. Edited by Lawrence H. Schiffman and James C. VanderKam. Oxford: Oxford University Press, 2000.

CHAPTER 16

The Essenes and the Early Church:
What Is the Relationship?

IN THE COURSE OF THIS BOOK WE'VE OBSERVED A WIDE range of similarities between the Essene movement, especially the community it founded at Qumran, and the early Christian community founded by Jesus of Nazareth. It's now time to try to summarize and synthesize what we have learned in these pages. Granted that there are all these parallels between the early Church and the Essene movement: what is the significance of them? In the end, what do these parallels tell us about Jesus, Christianity, and Judaism that we didn't know before?

I would be the first to admit that sometimes our study has given the impression that the relationship between early Christianity and the Essene movement was stronger than it really was. That's because some of the parallels and correlations we have identified can also be found with other forms of Second Temple Judaism. The Essenes, for example, were not the only ancient Israelites who espoused a 364-day liturgical calendar: that calendar was older than their movement and enshrined in documents read widely outside their circles, like *Jubilees* and *1 Enoch*. The Pharisees also formed covenantal societies, *haburîm,* that resembled the Qumran community in certain ways. However, only the Essenes practiced celibacy, so Jesus' words praising those who "made themselves Eunuchs for the sake of the kingdom of heaven" (Matt

19:12) were likely aimed at the Essenes specifically. Likewise, the young man wearing nothing but a single linen garment in the Garden of Gethsemane was certainly an Essene, as this strange practice is attested only among their members. So if the question is, How strong is the relationship between early Christianity and the Essene movement specifically? then each correlation would have to be examined carefully on its own merits. Our purpose has been to use the Scrolls not so much to prove a relationship between Essenism and Christianity but to give us a window into the thought and practice of the Judaism of Jesus' day. The Scrolls are particularly suited for that purpose, because they are the only still-existing physical documents that we know were actually written down during this time period. Furthermore, the community that produced them had, in many ways, a greater similarity to the early Church than to other forms of Judaism.

Now, let's return to the main question of this concluding chapter. Granted there are all these connections between the Essenes and the Christians: what do we make of this fact?

One conclusion scholars have drawn is that Christianity is nothing but a child movement of Essenism, or even a form of Essenism itself. That position has been argued many times over the years, often by persons interested in debunking Christianity.[1] These scholars, or pseudoscholars in some cases, ignore fundamental and obvious differences between Christianity and Essenism that prevent us from describing them as the same movement.[2] The most obvious of these are as follows: (1) the Christian conviction that Jesus of Nazareth is the one Messiah, combining the roles of priest and king; (2) the divinity of the Messiah; (3) the necessity of the suffering, death, and resurrection of the Messiah; and (4) the abrogation of the system of ritual cleanliness instituted by Moses. The Essenes, of course, expected two messiahs, neither of whom was divine; neither of whom would suffer, die, and rise again; and they were firmly committed to ritual cleanliness in both the present age and the age to come. Concerning this latter point, the Essenes really treated ritual cleanliness on the same level that later Christians would treat what is called the "natural law" or the "moral law." In other words, the Essenes considered all of Moses' principles of ritual cleanliness to have been written into the fabric of nature itself, so pigs were unclean *by their nature*, and not simply because they were declared to be so by an authority. This is a radical difference between the Essene and Christian movements. The following teaching of Jesus would have greatly upset Essene sensibilities:

> "Do you not see that whatever goes into a person from outside cannot defile, since it enters, not the heart but the stomach, and goes out into the latrine?" (Thus he declared all foods clean.) (Mark 7:18–19 NRSV, *alt.*)

But even granting that there are several significant doctrinal differences between Essenism and Christianity, some may still be inclined to think that the number of similarities damages Christianity's claim to be a unique revelation from God. The Christian phenomenon, one might argue, can be explained simply as a natural and organic development of certain movements or trends within Second Temple Judaism, without appeal to a special initiative of God.

In response, one could point out, first of all, that no number of parallels between Christian and Essene literature can explain away the unique and remarkable nature of the person and ministry of Jesus of Nazareth. In particular, the accounts of Jesus' miraculous powers are so numerous and belong to such early stages of Christian literature that many Scripture scholars who may not themselves be Christian believers are nonetheless willing to concede that Jesus of Nazareth was, among other things, a miracle worker.[3] Josephus records him as such, and while Josephus was not a Christian himself, he was proud of Jesus as an example of what the Jewish prophetic tradition could produce:

> Now, there was about this time Jesus, a wise man, if it be lawful to call him a man, for he was a doer of wonderful works—a teacher of such men as receive the truth with pleasure. He drew over to him both many of the Jews, and many of the Gentiles. He was the "Christ"; and when Pilate, at the suggestion of the principal men amongst us, had condemned him to the cross, those that loved him at the first did not forsake him, for he appeared to them alive again the third day, as the divine prophets had foretold these and ten thousand other wonderful things concerning him; and the tribe of Christians, so named from him, are not extinct at this day. (*Antiquities* 18:63–64)[4]

So we see that Jesus was known as a miracle worker by his contemporaries, and his greatest miracle was, of course, his own resurrection, the historical evidence for which is very difficult to explain away.[5]

But second, it's not clear that the strong resemblance of the Essene community to the early Church in terms of teaching, practice, and structure truly contradicts anything the Church claims about herself. Indeed, it may actually lend credence to certain Christian claims, especially the claim that the "Gospel" or good news of Jesus was prophesied in a hidden way in the Scriptures of Israel, which Christians commonly call the Old Testament. An aphorism attributed to St. Augustine affirms, "The New is in the Old concealed; the Old is in the New revealed."

Reading the New Testament, one frequently encounters statements insisting that the new revelation brought by Jesus Christ is, in a sense, not new at all, but rather a fulfillment of what had been promised by the prophets. According to the Gospels, Jesus himself insists, "I have come not to abolish [the Law and the Prophets] but to fulfill them" (Matt 5:17). He begins his ministry reading from the prophet Isaiah in Nazareth and insisting he is the fulfillment of Isaiah's prophesies (Luke 4:17–28), and at the end of his ministry he rebukes the two men on the road to Emmaus for being "slow of heart to believe all that the prophets have spoken," and "beginning with Moses and all the prophets, he interpret[s] to them in all the scriptures the things concerning himself" (Luke 24:25, 27).

In Acts, St. Paul insists that believing in the Good News of Jesus Christ involves nothing other than "believing everything laid down by the law or written in the prophets" (Acts 24:14) and that his own preaching is "saying nothing but what the prophets and Moses said would come to pass" (Acts 26:22). And it is not just in Jesus but in the growth of the Church that the prophets are fulfilled, because important decisions about the structure and governance of the Church were also seen as the fulfillment of prophetic Scripture: thus the replacement of Judas by Matthias in the role of Apostle is justified by appeal to Psalms 69:25 and 109:8 (Acts 1:20), and the inclusion of the uncircumcised Gentiles into the early Church by appeal to Amos 9:11–12 (Acts 15:15–18).

But is this true? Do the prophets and Scriptures of Israel—the Christian Old Testament—really testify to the coming of Jesus Christ and the establishment of his Church? If it were true, one would expect that *someone* would have seen it and understood it before the fact.

Therefore, the fact that the Essenes, by their prayer and meditation on the Scriptures of Israel, were able to form themselves into a new covenant community bound together by shared rituals of Spirit-infused water washing and a daily sacred meal of bread and wine in anticipation of the Messiah—in other words, something that looks strikingly like early Christianity—suggests that perhaps the seeds of the structures, practices, and beliefs of the early Church truly *were* contained within the writings of the prophets and the other Scriptures. Construed in this way, the similarities of the two communities would be a confirmation of the Church's claim to be rooted in the Israelite Scriptures.

In any event, all of us who are heirs of the religious tradition of Israel, whether Christian or Jewish, owe a debt of gratitude to these ancient holy men. They were imperfect, to be sure— sometimes given to a religious chauvinism and a contempt for those who disagreed with them. But then, few of us are completely free of this vice. Yet aside from this fault, the Essenes of Qumran were men of prayer, self-denial, and poverty, who dedicated themselves to a demanding lifestyle for the sake of communion with God and the ushering in of the divine kingdom on earth. Tragically, the Roman legions seem to have ignominiously annihilated the Essene community around the time that Jerusalem was fatefully destroyed in A.D. 70. One of the last acts of these pious monks may have been to hide their most treasured possessions—their holy scrolls—in the caves of their community as the Roman legions could be seen approaching in the distance.

Were they a failure? Their purpose in settling in the wilderness east of Jerusalem was to "prepare the way of the Lord" in accordance with Isaiah 40:3. If it is true—as I think likely—that many of those formed or influenced by them later became followers of Jesus of Nazareth, and found that their Essene formation prepared them very well for building up the new covenant *qahal* of Jesus the Christ, then the Qumranites may have succeeded in a way they hadn't expected. They did indeed "prepare the way of the Lord in the desert."

The Essenes were not the "parent" movement of Christianity, but rather the Qumranites and the early Christians were "siblings," both born from the faith of ancient Israel, both communities formed to await the coming Messiah(s). In structure, liturgy, and theology, the Essenes and early Christians were remarkably similar, but they diverged sharply on a few very important matters: the divinity of Christ and the ritual law, for example. The similarities help us to see how many aspects of Christianity thought to be novel are actually rooted in the faith and practice of Israel. It is likely that many of the first Christians came from an Essene background and were well prepared to help organize the early Church.

For Further Reading

Betz, Otto, and Rainer Riesner. "Did the Essenes Turn to Jesus as Messiah?" Pages 141–156 in Betz and Riesner, *Jesus, Qumran, and the Vatican: Clarifications*. Gordon City, NY: Crossroad, 1994.

Cross, Frank Moore, Jr. "The Essenes and the Primitive Church." Pages 197–238 in Cross, *The Ancient Library of Qumran*. Garden City, NY: Doubleday, 1956.

Joseph, Simon. "Beyond the Essenes." Pages 163–169 in Joseph, *Jesus, the Essenes, and Christian Origins: New Light on Ancient Texts and Communities*. Waco, TX: Baylor University Press, 2018.

ACKNOWLEDGMENTS

I would like to express my gratitude to James C. VanderKam and Eugene Ulrich, who introduced me to the non-biblical and biblical scrolls, respectively, during my doctoral studies at the University of Notre Dame. Both were so generous in helping me through academic and practical hurdles during those challenging years of graduate study. John J. Collins's response and comments on a paper of mine concerning the self-conception of the Qumran community were very helpful to me in formulating my ideas on the subject. Gabriele Boccaccini kindly invited me to present at the 2007 Enoch Seminar in Camaldoli, Italy, an event which allowed me to meet many of the top researchers on the Scrolls personally, and exchange ideas with them. The administration and my faculty colleagues at the Franciscan University of Steubenville have graciously allowed me the time away to write this book, covering for responsibilities I was not able to meet. My wife, Dawn, and our children have been very understanding of my physical or mental absence during the throes of this project. Thanks to Gary Jansen, my editor at Image Books, as well as Scott Hahn, Brant Pitre, Michael Barber, John Kincaid, Mike Aquilina, Jeff Morrow, and Michael Thomas for reading and commenting on various parts of the draft. Jeff Morrow and Michael Thomas, in particular, made incisive and very helpful suggestions for the treatment of Paul and the Epistle to the Ephesians.

NOTES

Introduction

1. German scholars F. C. Baur, Rudolf Bultmann, and the so-called Tübingen School were associated with this late dating of John. See discussion in Wally V. Cirafesi, "The Temple Attitudes of John and Qumran in the Light of Hellenistic Judaism," pp. 315–339 in *Christian Origins and Hellenistic Judaism: Social and Literary Contexts for the New Testament* (ed. Stanley E. Porter and Andrew W. Pitts; Texts and Editions for New Testament Study 10/Early Christianity in its Hellenistic Context 2; Leiden: Brill, 2013), here pp. 329–330. See also Raymond Brown, as cited in following note.

2. See Raymond Brown, "The Qumran Scrolls and the Johannine Gospels and Epistles," pp. 183–207 in *The Scrolls and the New Testament* (ed. Krister Stendahl; New York: Harper, 1957), here p. 206.

3. See, for example, the discussion and literature cited in Andreas Köstenberger, *John* (Grand Rapids, MI: Baker, 2004), pp. 6–8.

4. The Church is called a "mystery" by St. Paul in Ephesians 5:32. The Second Vatican Council's Dogmatic Constitution on the Church *Lumen Gentium* speaks of the Church as the "universal sacrament of salvation" (*Lumen Gentium* §48).

Chapter 1: The Archeological Find of the Twentieth Century

1. This appellation for the Scrolls has become ubiquitous. For an example, see "The 20th Century's Greatest Archaeological Discovery," *Fortworth Magazine,* July 2, 2012, http://www.fwtx.com/articles /20th-century%E2%80%99s-greatest-archaeological-discovery-0.

2. The story of the discovery of the Scrolls has been told many times in many publications. An authoritative account, on which I've based my retelling here, may be found in James C. VanderKam and Peter C.

Flint, *The Meaning of the Dead Sea Scrolls* (San Francisco: Harper Collins, 2002), pp. 3–19.

3. Trans. H. Rackham, *Pliny—Natural History II* (Loeb Classical Library; Cambridge, MA: Harvard University Press, 1942), p. 277.

4. Ein Gedi is the settlement that marks the approximate midpoint as one travels from north to south down the western shore of the Dead Sea.

5. On the archeology of Qumran, see Jodi Magness, *The Archeology of Qumran and the Dead Sea Scrolls* (Grand Rapids, MI: Eerdmans, 2002), esp. pp. 163–187: "The archeological evidence attests to only minimal female presence at Qumran" (182).

6. The three lengthy passages are found in *The Jewish War* 2.119–161 (hereafter *War*) and *The Antiquities of the Jews* (hereafter *Antiquities*) 13.171–173 and 18.18–22.

7. See Acts 23:8.

8. See discussion in James VanderKam, "The Identity and History of the Community," pp. 490–499 in vol. 2 of *The Dead Sea Scrolls After Fifty Years* (2 vols.; ed. Peter Flint and James VanderKam; Leiden: Brill, 1999).

9. One often reads the claim that Josephus's description of the Essenes is unreliable, or contrary to the contents of the Scrolls, or irreconcilable with the archeology of Qumran, et cetera. Although Josephus, like every other ancient and modern author, is not immune to bias and error, his description of the Essenes actually accords quite well with the content of the Scrolls and the archeology of Qumran. See especially Todd S. Beall, *Josephus' Description of the Essenes Illustrated by the Dead Sea Scrolls* (Society for New Testament Studies Monograph Series 58; Cambridge, UK: Cambridge University Press, 1988); and Magen Broshi, *Bread, Wine, Walls, and Scrolls* (New York: Sheffield Academic Press, 2001), pp. 71–77.

10. F. Josephus and W. Whiston, *The Works of Josephus: Complete and Unabridged* (Peabody, MA: Hendrickson, 1987), pp. 605 and 607.

11. This is from the Damascus Document, col. 7, ll. 4–7. The Damascus Document is still regularly abbreviated "CD" for the name originally given it ("The Covenant of Damascus"), and so scholars cite this passage as "CD 7:4–7."

12. See discussion in Elisha Qimron, "Celibacy in the Dead Sea Scrolls and the Two Kinds of Sectarians," pp. 287–294 in vol. 1 of *The Ma-*

drid Qumran Congress (2 vols.; Studies on the Texts of the Desert of Judah 11/1; Leiden: Brill, 1992).

13. One cannot help comparing Jesus' teaching: "There is no one who has left house or brothers or sisters or mother or father or children or lands, for my sake and for the gospel, who will not receive a hundred-fold now in this time, houses and brothers and sisters and mothers and children and lands, with persecutions, and in the age to come eternal life" (Mark 10:29–30).

Chapter 2: Waiting for the Messiah

1. See, for example, Ezekiel 43:2.

2. For a readable overview of Jewish messianic expectation in the time of Christ, see Brant Pitre, "What Were the Jewish People Waiting For?" pp. 22–47 in Pitre, *Jesus and the Jewish Roots of the Eucharist: Unlocking the Secrets of the Last Supper* (New York: Doubleday, 2011).

3. For an explanation of this hypothesis, see Jerome Murphy-O'Connor, "The Teacher of Righteousness," pp. 340–341 in vol. 6 of *The Anchor Bible Dictionary* (New York: Doubleday, 1992).

4. See Murphy-O'Connor, "Teacher of Righteousness," p. 341.

5. Michael O. Wise, *The First Messiah: Investigating the Savior Before Christ* (San Francisco: HarperCollins, 1999).

6. I have a more extensive discussion of 11QMelchizedek in my book *The Jubilee from Leviticus to Qumran: A History of Interpretation*, pp. 277–291 (Vetus Testamentum Supplements 115; Leiden: Brill, 2007).

7. For a more thorough discussion of the history of observation and interpretation of the Jubilee Year in ancient Israel, see Bergsma, *The Jubilee from Leviticus to Qumran*, pp. 295–304.

8. Many translations render the last phrase "anoint a most holy place," but the Hebrew is literally "to anoint a holy of holies," which could also be a most holy person.

9. The NRSV renders it as "to the coming of an anointed prince," but "Messiah, a prince" is just as faithful to the Hebrew.

10. In rendering "seven weeks and sixty-two weeks," I follow the Septuagint (the ancient Greek translation) and, indeed, all the ancient translations. The Hebrew punctuation that ends the sentence after "seven weeks" is not attested in antiquity. See discussion in Bergsma,

The Jubilee from Leviticus to Qumran, p. 230, and Roger Beckwith, "Daniel 9 and the Date of the Messiah's Coming in Essene, Hellenistic, Pharisaic, Zealot, and Early Christian Computation," *Revue de Qumran* 10 (1981): 521–542.

11. The Jubilee Year was every fiftieth year, but it was simultaneously year one of the next jubilee cycle. On the counting of the jubilee, see John Bergsma, "Once Again, the Jubilee, Every 49 or 50 Years?" *Vetus Testamentum* 55.1 (2005): 121–125.

12. The translation is from F. García Martínez and E. J. C. Tigchelaar, *The Dead Sea Scrolls Study Edition* (Leiden and New York: Brill, 1997–1998). For a discussion of 4Q246, see Michael Segal, "Who Is the 'Son of God' in 4Q246? An Overlooked Example of Early Biblical Interpretation," *Dead Sea Discoveries* 21 (2014): 289–312.

13. Bargil Pixner, *Paths of the Messiah* (ed. Rainer Riesner; trans. Keith Myrick et al.; San Francisco: Ignatius Press, 2010), pp. 23–26.

14. See Pixner, *Paths of the Messiah*, pp. 24–32.

Chapter 3: The Scrolls, John the Baptist, and Baptism

1. Raymond E. Brown, "The Qumran Scrolls and the Johannine Gospels and Epistles," pp. 183–207, in *The Scrolls and the New Testament* (ed. Krister Stendahl; New York: Harper, 1957), here p. 207.

2. See Otto Betz, "Was John the Baptist an Essene?," pp. 205–214 in *Understanding the Dead Sea Scrolls: A Reader from the Biblical Archeology Review* (ed. Hershel Shanks; New York: Random House, 1992).

3. In the first century, Judea bordered roughly only the southernmost ten miles of the Jordan River. North of that point, Samaria began, and Judeans avoided traveling through Samaritan territory.

4. John 1:23; Matt 3:3; Mark 1:3; Luke 3:4.

5. Ezek 43:1–5, 44:1–2, 46:1–2, 12, 47:1; Isa 41:2, 25, 46:10, 59:19.

6. 4Q405, frags. 20, 21, 22; line 10.

7. James Charlesworth argues that John the Baptist ate like a former Essene: "John the Baptizer and Qumran Barriers in Light of the Rule of the Community," pp. 353–375 in *The Provo International Conference on the Dead Sea Scrolls* (ed. D. W. Parry and E. Ulrich; Studies on the Texts of the Desert of Judah 30; Leiden: Brill, 1999). Against him, James A. Kelhoffer claims that locust eating was common in first-century Palestine. See "Did John the Baptist Eat Like a Former

Essene? Locust-Eating in the Ancient Near East and at Qumran," *Dead Sea Discoveries* 11 (2004): 293–314. However, all of Kelhoffer's evidence comes from times or locations that are remote from first-century Palestine, for example, Assyrian reliefs from the 700s B.C. depicting roasted locusts, and even older materials. This would be like citing Chaucer to show that eating blackbirds was common in twentieth-century England. For the time period of Qumran, Kelhoffer can cite only the *Letter of Aristeas* and Philo, but these are apologetic works defending the rationality of the Mosaic Law to a classical audience, not direct attestations of Jewish culinary practice. The cleanliness of locusts *is* discussed in the Mishnah and other rabbinic traditions; however, not only do these postdate the first century, but it is frequently the case that the rabbis would debate the application of the law to merely theoretical or highly unlikely scenarios. So it is difficult to make a direct connection between the Mishnah and actual first-century practice.

8. The following scholars show strong Qumran influence on the early chapters of Luke: Daniel R. Schwartz, "On Quirinius, John the Baptist, the Benedictus, Melchizedek, Qumran, and Ephesus," *Revue de Qumran* 13 (1988): 635–646; Stephen Hultgren, "'4Q521,' the Second Benediction of the 'Tefilla,' the "Hasidim,' and the Development of Royal Messianism," *Revue de Qumran* 23 (2008): 313–340; Hultgren, "4Q521 and Luke's *Magnificat* and *Benedictus*," pp. 119–132 in *Echoes from the Caves: Qumran and the New Testament* (ed. Florentino García Martínez; Studies on the Texts of the Desert of Judah 85; Leiden: Brill, 2009); and George J. Brooke, *Qumran and the Jewish Jesus: Reading the New Testament in Light of the Scrolls* (Cambridge: Grove Books, 2005).

9. Aramaic is the language of ancient Syria, and is closely related to Hebrew. Jews in Jesus' day spoke Aramaic in daily life, and true Hebrew had become reserved for worship and scholarship.

10. The translation is from F. García Martínez and E. J. C. Tigchelaar, *The Dead Sea Scrolls Study Edition* (Grand Rapids, MI: Eerdmans, 1999).

11. For a good annotated bibliography on the relationship between John the Baptist and the Essenes, including scholars both "pro" and "con" on the possibility that John was formed at Qumran, see Robert L. Webb, "John the Baptist," pp. 418–421, in *Encyclopedia of the Dead Sea Scrolls,* vol. 1 (ed. Lawrence Schiffman and James VanderKam; New York: Oxford University Press, 2000), here p. 421. I am well

aware that some scholars dispute any connection between John and the Essenes (e.g., Hartmut Stegemann, *The Library of Qumran: On the Essenes, Qumran, John the Baptist, and Jesus* [Grand Rapids, MI: Eerdmans, 1998], pp. 211–227; and Joan E. Taylor, *The Immerser: John the Baptist Within Second Temple Judaism* [Grand Rapids, MI: Eerdmans, 1997]). Those who dispute a relationship between John and Qumran argue that the points of connection could be part of a more broadly shared Jewish heritage, or independently derived from the Jewish Scriptures or tradition. In response, I and many others (including Betz, Brownlee, Charlesworth, Robinson, and Scobie) would argue that some parallels are too specific simply to be part of the shared heritage (e.g., the prominence of Isa 40:3 in the self-understanding of both the Qumran community and John) and that the probability of *so many* parallels arising merely coincidentally without direct contact is rather small. James Charlesworth's review of Joan E. Taylor (*Dead Sea Discoveries* 8 [2001]: 208–211) gives a good sense of the differences of approach between the two sides of this debate.

Chapter 4: The Scrolls, John the Apostle, and Baptism

1. See Benedict XVI's rich reflection on the phrase "lamb of God" in *Jesus of Nazareth: From the Baptism in the Jordan to the Transfiguration* (San Francisco: Ignatius Press, 2008), pp. 20–24.

2. Although scholars typically deny that John the Apostle wrote the Gospel of John, I have never found their arguments convincing. For defenses of John's authorship of the Gospel that bears his name, see Craig Blomberg, *The Historical Reliability of John's Gospel: Issues and Commentary* (Downers Grove, IL: InterVarsity, 2001), pp. 17–67; and Craig S. Keener, *The Gospel of John: A Commentary* (Grand Rapids, MI: Baker, 2003), pp. 81–115.

3. Raymond Brown tentatively proposes this scenario as an explanation for the strong similarities between the fourth Gospel and the Scrolls. See "The Qumran Scrolls and the Johannine Gospels and Epistles," pp. 183–207 in *The Scrolls and the New Testament* (ed. Krister Stendahl; New York: Harper, 1957), here p. 207.

4. See especially the seminal essay marking the turning point in the study of the Gospel of John brought about by the discovery of the

Scrolls: William Foxwell Albright, "Recent Discoveries in Palestine and the Gospel of John," pp. 153–171 in *The Background of the New Testament and Its Eschatology* (ed. W. D. Davies and D. Daube; Cambridge, UK: Cambridge University Press, 1964).

5. John's mother tongue would have been Jewish Aramaic, the spoken language of Palestinian Jews in the first century. Aramaic (ancient Syriac) is closely related to Hebrew and has many of the same rhythms, idioms, and characteristics. Jewish Aramaic was further influenced by biblical Hebrew, since the Jews continued to read the Scriptures in Hebrew. Scholars debate how much Hebrew was employed as a spoken language in the Jewish populace in antiquity.

6. See James H. Charlesworth, "A Critical Comparison of the Dualism in 1QS 3:13–4:26 and the 'Dualism' Contained in the Gospel of John," pp. 76–106 in *John and the Dead Sea Scrolls* (ed. James H. Charlesworth; New York: Crossroad, 1990).

7. Cf. 1QHodayot[a] 21:14–16.

8. For discussion of these matters, see Cecilia Wassen, "The Use of the Dead Sea Scrolls for Interpreting Jesus's Action in the Temple," *Dead Sea Discoveries* 23 (2016): 280–303.

9. Translation from F. García Martínez and E. J. C. Tigchelaar, *The Dead Sea Scrolls Study Edition* (2 vols.; Leiden and New York: Brill, 1999), p. 89.

10. See Mark 12:10; Luke 20:17; Acts 4:11; 1 Pet 2:7.

11. For further reading on this whole topic of the term "Jew" (Gk. *ioudaios,* Heb. *yehudi*), see John S. Bergsma, "Qumran Self-Identity: 'Israel' or 'Judah'?" *Dead Sea Discoveries* 15 (2008): 172–189.

12. See the defense of this etymology in James C. VanderKam, "Identity and History of the Community," pp. 487–533 in vol. 2 of *The Dead Sea Scrolls after Fifty Years: A Comprehensive Assessment* (2 vols.; ed. Peter W. Flint and James C. VanderKam; Leiden: Brill, 1999).

13. See *The Testament of the Twelve Patriarchs: Testament of Benjamin* 10:7: "Then shall we also rise, each one over our tribe, worshipping the King of heaven."

14. On being the true Israel, see 1QS 5:5; 8:9; on deceit, see 1QS 10:22.

15. According to Josephus, after a year's probation, candidates were admitted to the "waters of purification" (*War* 2:137–138).

16. See Joseph Jacobs and H. G. Friedmann, "Tabernacles, Feast of," *The Jewish Encyclopedia,* vol. 3 (ed. Isidore Singer; New York: Funk & Wagnalls, 1906), http://www.jewishencyclopedia.com/articles/14185 -tabernacles-feast-of.

17. I divide the Greek clauses of John 7:37–38 differently than most English translations, as follows: "If any one thirst, let him come to me, and let him drink who believes in me. As the scripture has said, 'Out of his heart shall flow rivers of living water.'" It makes better sense in light of the whole Gospel of John to understand Jesus as presenting himself here as the source of living water. See discussion in Raymond E. Brown, *The Gospel According to John I–XII* (Anchor Bible 29; Garden City, NY: Doubleday, 1966), p. 320.

18. 1QHa 3:28; 9:23; 11:25; 12:30; 17:16; 19:6; 21:30, 37; 22:12, 18; 23:27; 25:31.

19. 1QHa 20:27–29; 20:35; 21:12; 23:13–14; 4Q264:8–10; 4Q428 4:2.

20. This hypothesis is virtually proven by Daniel Frayer-Griggs, "Spittle, Clay, and Creation in John 9:6 and Some Dead Sea Scrolls," *Journal of Biblical Literature* 132 (2013): 659–670.

21. Most English translations smooth out the man's response as "I am he" or "I am the man," but in Greek his response is simply *ego eimi,* "I am!"

22. See the Mishnah, tractates *Middot* 3:2–3; *Yoma* 5:6; *Letter of Aristeas* §§88–91; and David Gurevich, "The Water Pools and the Pilgrimage to Jerusalem in the Late Second Temple Period," *Palestine Exploration Quarterly* 149 (2017): 103–134, esp. bottom of p. 128.

23. On Eden as the first temple, see Gregory Beale, *The Temple and the Church's Mission: A Biblical Theology of the Dwelling Place of God* (Downers Grove, IL: IVP Academic, 2004).

24. See Raymond Brown, "The Qumran Scrolls and the Johannine Gospels and Epistles," pp. 206–207 in *The Scrolls and the New Testament* (ed. Krister Stendahl; New York: Harper, 1957).

25. As recognized already by W. F. Albright, "Recent Discoveries in Palestine and the Gospel of St. John," pp. 153–171 in *The Background of the New Testament and Its Eschatology* (ed. W. D. Davies and D. Daube; Cambridge, UK: Cambridge University Press, 1964).

26. William H. Brownlee, "Whence the Gospel of John?," pp. 166–194 in *John and the Dead Sea Scrolls* (ed. James Charlesworth; New York: Crossroad, 1990), here p. 185.

Chapter 5: Baptism Today

1. In traditional Christianity, represented by the ancient traditions such as Roman Catholicism or Greek Orthodoxy, a sacrament is not merely a symbolic act but a sign that *actualizes* what it *symbolizes*. In other words, a sacrament does what it symbolizes to the person who receives it.

2. *War* 2:138 (2.8.7), in Greek: *katharôterôn tôn pros hagneian hudatôn.*

3. Joseph Fitzmyer, "The Role of the Spirit in Luke-Acts," pp. 165–184 in *The Unity of Luke-Acts* (ed. J. Verheyden; Leuven: Peeters, 1999), here p. 182.

4. Commenting on the use of water at Qumran, Jewish scholar Joseph Baumgarten comments: "Far from being merely external acts . . . these purifications were viewed *as the means* by which the holy spirit restores the corporate purity of Israel." See Baumgarten, "The Purification Rituals in DJD 7," pp. 199–209 in *The Dead Sea Scrolls: Forty Years of Research* (ed. Devorah Dimant and Uriel Rappaport; Studies on the Texts of the Desert of Judah 10; Leiden: Brill, 1992), here p. 208.

5. On Baptism as the new circumcision in Paul, see Scott McKnight, *It Takes a Church to Baptize: What the Bible Says About Infant Baptism* (Grand Rapids, MI: Brazos Press, 2018), pp. 52–53.

6. The best quotes on infant baptism from the Fathers, including this one from Hippolytus, are helpfully gathered by McKnight in *It Takes a Church to Baptize,* pp. 16–18. The witness of Hippolytus is highly significant, since he was raised near Jerusalem in a Jewish-Christian household, and the traditions he conveys often have an Essene air about them.

7. See McKnight, *It Takes a Church to Baptize,* p. 17.

8. See Hannah K. Harrington, "Purification in the Fourth Gospel in Light of Qumran," pp. 117–138 in *John, Qumran, and the Dead Sea Scrolls: Sixty Years of Discovery and Debate* (ed. Mary L. Coloe and Tom Thatcher; Atlanta: Society of Biblical Literature, 2011). Harrington is gentle in her expressions, speaking of Jewish water washings as "anticipating" the work of the Spirit, but the primary source texts simply conflate the two. Harrington is accommodating her language to modern sensibilities and metaphysics. Nonetheless, her conclusion about Jewish attitudes toward ritual washing is absolutely correct: "By submitting to ritual ablutions, individuals were making the passage from divine judgment and death to a life approved by God as his elect" (pp. 137–138).

Chapter 6: Did Qumran Have a "Eucharist"?

1. Justin Martyr, *First Apology,* ch. 66, translation from volume 1 of *The Apostolic Fathers with Justin Martyr and Irenaeus* (ed. A. Roberts, J. Donaldson, and A. C. Coxe; Buffalo, NY: Christian Literature Company, 1885), p. 185.
2. See Saul Lieberman, "The Discipline in the So-Called Dead Sea Manual of Discipline," *Journal of Biblical Literature* 71 (1952): 199–206.
3. See Orit Shamir and Naama Sukenik, "Qumran Textiles and the Garments of Qumran's Inhabitants," *Dead Sea Discoveries* 18 (2011): 206–225.
4. See Jodi Magness, "Were Sacrifices Offered at Qumran? The Animal Bone Deposits Reconsidered," *Journal of Ancient Judaism* 7 (2016): 5–34.
5. Sometimes in these hymns, "My God" is substituted for "My Lord" in the initial statement of thanksgiving.
6. This is the F. García Martínez and E. J. C. Tigchelaar translation from *The Dead Sea Scrolls Study Edition,* vol. 1 (Grand Rapids, MI: Eerdmans, 1999), p. 83.
7. See Frank Moore Cross, *The Ancient Library of Qumran* (Garden City, NY: Doubleday, 1958), p. 231; as well as Lieberman, "Discipline in the So-Called Dead Sea Manual of Discipline," esp. p. 201.
8. As Lieberman points out in "Discipline in the So-Called Dead Sea Manual of Discipline."
9. See Matthew Black, *The Scrolls and Christian Origins* (Brown Judaic Studies 48; New York: Scribner, 1961), pp. 105, 113.
10. Mishnah, tractate *Sukkah,* 4.9. See Herbert Danby, *The Mishnah* (Oxford: Oxford University Press, 1933), p. 179.
11. This is a commonplace in scholarship. For one example, see Joseph Ratzinger/Benedict XVI, *Jesus of Nazareth: From the Baptism in the Jordan to the Transfiguration* (San Francisco: Ignatius Press, 2008), p. 171. See discussion in Brant Pitre, *Jesus and the Last Supper* (Grand Rapids, MI: Eerdmans, 2015), pp. 444–446.

Chapter 7: When Was the Last Supper?

1. See Bart Ehrman, *Jesus Interrupted: Revealing the Hidden Contradictions in the Bible (And Why We Don't Know About Them)* (San Francisco: HarperOne, 2010), pp. 25–27.

2. See Bargil Pixner, *Paths of the Messiah* (ed. Rainer Riesner; trans. Keith Myrick et al.; San Francisco: Ignatius Press, 2010), p. 240; and Darrel Bock, *Luke 9:51–24:53* (Grand Rapids, MI: Baker, 1996), pp. 1711–1712.

3. See Gen 24:14–20; Exod 2:16; 1 Sam 9:11; John 4:7, 28.

4. As noted by I. Howard Marshall, cited by Bock, *Luke,* p. 1711.

5. Contra Bock, *Luke,* p. 1711, who concludes the man must have been a servant, without ever considering the possibility he was Essene.

6. See Bargil Pixner, "The Essene Quarter in Jerusalem," pp. 192–219 in Pixner, *Paths of the Messiah.*

7. See Pixner, "The Essene Quarter," pp. 213–215.

8. CD 12:1–2: "A man may not lay with a woman in the city of the Temple, defiling the city of the Temple by their uncleanness."

9. Philo, *Every Good Man Is Free,* ch. 12, §79.

10. Orit Shamir and Naama Sukenik, "Qumran Textiles and the Garments of Qumran's Inhabitants," *Dead Sea Discoveries* 18 (2011): 206–225, here p. 215.

11. Shamir and Sukenik, "Qumran Textiles," pp. 214–216.

12. Shamir and Sukenik, "Qumran Textiles," p. 206.

13. See Raymond Brown, vol. 1 of *The Death of the Messiah: From Gethsemane to the Grave* (2 vols.; New York: Doubleday, 1994), pp. 297–304, for a summary of the history of interpretation of this passage.

14. See Pixner, *Paths of the Messiah,* pp. 239–252, 319–367.

15. In what follows, I am drawing on the well-known work of Annie Jaubert, *The Date of the Last Supper* (New York: Alba House, 1965), and more recently Stéphane Saulnier, *Calendrical Variations in Second Temple Judaism: New Perspectives on the "Date of the Last Supper" Debate* (*Journal for the Study of Judaism* Supplement Series 159; Leiden: Brill, 2012).

16. Saulnier, *Calendrical Variations,* pp. 22–30.

17. See James C. VanderKam, *The Dead Sea Scrolls Today* (2nd ed.; Grand Rapids, MI: Eerdmans, 2010), pp. 54–58.

18. See Saulnier, *Calendrical Variations,* pp. 234–238, 244–245.

19. Jaubert, *Date of the Last Supper.*

20. See Pixner, *Paths of the Messiah,* p. 240.

21. So argues Brian Capper, "The New Covenant in Southern Palestine at the Arrest of Jesus," pp. 90–116 in *The Dead Sea Scrolls as Back-*

ground to Postbiblical Judaism and Early Christianity (ed. James R. Davila, Studies on the Texts of the Desert of Judah 46; Leiden: Brill, 2003).

22. Mark 14:1–2; Luke 22:2; Matt 26:3–5; John 11:47–53.

23. Philo, *Every Good Man Is Free*, §78.

24. See James C. VanderKam and Peter W. Flint, *The Meaning of the Dead Sea Scrolls* (San Francisco: HarperCollins, 2002), pp. 276–281.

25. Pixner, *Paths of the Messiah,* pp. 319–359.

26. Pixner, *Paths of the Messiah,* pp. 192–219.

27. Pixner, *Paths of the Messiah,* pp. 213–215.

28. Boaz Zissu, "'Qumran Type' Graves in Jerusalem: Archeological Evidence of an Essene Community?" *Dead Sea Discoveries* 5 (1998): 158–171.

29. Pixner, *Paths of the Messiah,* p. 208.

30. Pixner, *Paths of the Messiah,* pp. 250–252.

31. Reinhard Pummer, *The Samaritans: A Profile* (Grand Rapids, MI: Eerdmans, 2016).

32. Reinhard Pummer, "Synagogues—Samaritan and Jewish: A New Look at Their Differentiating Characteristics," pp. 51–74 in *The Samaritans in Historical, Cultural and Linguistic Perspectives* (ed. Jan Dušek; Studia Judaica 110, Studia Samaritana 11; Berlin: De Gruyter, 2018).

33. John S. Bergsma, "Qumran Self-Identity: 'Israel' or 'Judah'?" *Dead Sea Discoveries* 15 (2008): 172–189.

34. See Annie Jaubert, "The Calendar of Qumran and the Passion Narrative in John," pp. 62–74 in *John and the Dead Sea Scrolls* (ed. James H. Charlesworth; New York: Crossroad, 1990).

35. Saulnier, *Calendrical Variations,* p. 55.

36. Saulnier, *Calendrical Variations,* pp. 34–35.

37. Pixner, *Paths of the Messiah,* pp. 250–252.

38. My good friend and collaborator Brant Pitre has written an impressive defense of the traditional Maundy Thursday—Good Friday—Holy Saturday chronology of Jesus' Passion and death (*Jesus and the Last Supper* [Grand Rapids, MI: Eerdmans, 2015], pp. 251–375). He argues against the calendrical solution offered here. The greatest weakness in Pitre's tour de force, in my opinion, is the implausibility of fitting all the trials of Jesus and other Passion events into twelve

hours between midnight Thursday and noon Friday—and that on a Passover. Nonetheless, if my own proposal were someday disproven, I would embrace Pitre's hypothesis above the other available solutions.

Chapter 8: Putting It All Together: Reading the Last Supper in Light of the Scrolls

1. Joseph Bayly, *The Gospel Blimp and Other Stories* (Elgin, IL: David C. Cook, 1983), pp. 121–123.

2. See Brant Pitre, *Jesus and the Last Supper* (Grand Rapids, MI: Eerdmans, 2015), pp. 255–256 and elsewhere.

3. The expression "when they would sacrifice the Passover" in Mark 14:12 is a classic example of an impersonal third-person plural, a common construction in both Hebrew and Greek that has the force of a passive: "when the Passover was sacrificed." See Steven Thompson, *The Apocalypse and Semitic Syntax* (Cambridge, UK: Cambridge University Press, 1985), pp. 18–22. Luke, who is a better Greek stylist, changes Mark's colloquial expression into a true passive in Luke 22:7. It cannot be demonstrated from these indefinite expressions that the Apostles actually sacrificed a lamb—they could mean nothing more than that this was the day when custom or law required the sacrifice. I understand both verses as references to Jesus as the true Passover lamb.

4. See Lawrence Schiffman, "Community Without Temple: The Qumran Community's Withdrawal from the Jerusalem Temple," pp. 267–284 in *Gemeinde ohne Tempel: Zur Substituierung und Transformation des Jerusalemer Tempels und seines Kults im Alten Testament, antiken Judentum und frühen Christentum* (ed. Beate Ego et al.; Wissenschaftliche Untersuchungen zum Neuen Testament 118; Tübingen: Mohr Siebeck, 1999).

5. See Jodi Magness, "Were Sacrifices Offered at Qumran? The Animal Bone Deposits Reconsidered," *Journal of Ancient Judaism* 7 (2016): pp. 5–34.

6. Philo, *Every Good Man Is Free,* §§78–79.

7. To observe the synonymity of "bless" and "give thanks," compare Matt 14:19 with John 6:11.

8. The Greek is *eis tên emên anamnêsin.*

9. See Gen 9:15, 9:16; Exod 2:24, 6:5; Lev 26:42, 45; Deut 4:31; 1 Chr 16:15; Ps 105:8, 106:45; Ezek 16:60; Luke 1:54, 72.

10. This is my own definition, but it is congruent with the discussion in O. Michel, "*mimnêskomai* etc.," pp. 675–683 in vol. 4 of *Theological Dictionary of the New Testament* (ed. G. Kittel, G. W. Bromiley, and G. Friedrich; Grand Rapids, MI: Eerdmans, 1964).

11. On the theology of liturgical remembrance, see Scott Hahn, "The Persistence of Memory: Anamnesis and Actualization," pp. 144–157 in *Letter & Spirit: From Written Text to Living Word in the Liturgy* (New York: Image, 2005).

12. On the definition of a covenant, see Gordon P. Hugenberger, *Marriage as a Covenant: Biblical Law and Ethics as Developed from Malachi* (Vetus Testamentum Supplements 54; Leiden: Brill, 1994), pp. 168–215.

13. Damascus Document 6:19, 8:21, 19:33, 20:12; 1QpHab 2:3; 4Q269 frag. 4, col. 2, ln. 1.

14. See John S. Bergsma, "Damascus," pp. 702–708 in *Theologisches Wörterbuch zu den Qumrantexten, Band 1* (ed. Heinz-Josef Fabry and Ulrich Dahmen; Stuttgart: Kohlhammer, 2011).

15. Admission to the "pure food of the Many" and the "drink of the Many" was the last stage of initiation: Josephus, *War* 2:137–142; cf. 1QS 6:16–23. After a year the initiate was allowed to partake of the food; after a second year, also the drink.

16. See discussion in Pitre, *Jesus and the Last Supper,* pp. 444–446.

17. See Matt 16:28; Mark 14:24; Exod 24:8.

18. Matt 26:28; Mark 14:24.

19. The Hebrew is *rab* or *rabbim;* see 1QS 6:18, 20–21, 25; 7:3.

20. See 1QSᵃ 2:11–15.

21. Philo, *Every Good Man Is Free,* §§78–79.

22. See 1QS 2:24–25; 1QS cols. 5–6 generally, esp. 1QS 6:9–10.

23. See discussion in John Bergsma and Scott Hahn, "Covenant," pp. 151–166 in *The Oxford Encyclopedia of Biblical Theology* (ed. Kathleen Dell et al.; Oxford: Oxford University Press, 2015).

24. 2 Sam 5:1–3; Ps 89:3–4. See Bergsma and Hahn, "Covenant," p. 158; W. J. Dumbrell, "The Davidic Covenant," *Reformed Theological Review* 39 (1980): 40–47; and Jon D. Levenson, *Sinai and Zion: An Entry into the Jewish Bible* (San Francisco: Harper & Row, 1985), pp. 97–101.

25. 1QS^a 2:15–16.
26. Justin Martyr, *The First Apology of Justin,* p. 185 in vol. 1 of *The Apostolic Fathers with Justin Martyr and Irenaeus* (ed. A. Roberts, J. Donaldson, and A. C. Coxe; Buffalo, NY: Christian Literature Company, 1885).

Chapter 9: Celibacy in the Scrolls

1. Dan Brown, *The Da Vinci Code* (New York: Doubleday, 2003).
2. For example, in Hebrew, the term *saris* covers both concepts, e.g., Gen 39:1; Isa 56:3–4.
3. There is no historical basis for this theory about the origin of priestly celibacy, but it is a commonly repeated opinion among non-Catholic Christians in America.
4. Nothing is ever said about a wife or children for Elijah and Elisha. The biblical narrative depicts them as single men wholly devoted to their prophetic ministry.
5. Jer 16:1–4; Ezek 24:15–28.
6. Lev 15:18, 22:1–6.
7. *War* 2:120.
8. *Hypothetica* 11:14.
9. Trans. H. Rackham, *Pliny—Natural History II* (Loeb Classical Library; Cambridge, MA: Harvard University Press, 1942), p. 277.
10. Notably Paul Heger, "Celibacy in Qumran: Hellenistic Fiction or Reality? Qumran's Attitude Toward Sex," *Revue de Qumrân* 26 (2013): 53–90.
11. Philo does also describe as celibate another, very Essene-like group of Jews known as the *therapeutae,* and devoted a treatise to them (*On the Contemplative Life*). But the *therapeutae* included women. Outside of Judaism, the only classical group thought to have practiced celibacy was the Pythagoreans.
12. Yigael Yadin, *The Temple Scroll,* vol. 1 (Jerusalem: Israel Exploration Society, 1983), pp. 288–289; Elisha Qimron, "Celibacy in the Dead Sea Scrolls and the Two Kinds of Sectarians," pp. 287–294 in vol. 1 of *The Madrid Qumran Congress* (2 vols.; Studies on the Texts of the Desert of Judah 11/1; Leiden: Brill, 1992); Magen Broshi, "Essenes at Qumran? A Rejoinder to Albert Baumgarten," *Dead Sea Discoveries* 11 (2007): 25–33.

13. Jodi Magness, *The Archeology of Qumran and the Dead Sea Scrolls* (Grand Rapids, MI: Eerdmans, 2002), esp. pp. 163–187: "The archeological evidence attests to only minimal female presence at Qumran" (p. 182).

14. See Joseph E. Zias, "The Cemeteries of Qumran and Celibacy: Confusion Laid to Rest?" *Dead Sea Discoveries* 7 (2000): 220–253, esp. pp. 230–237, where he points out that several skeletons thought by archeologists to be female are anomalously tall for women in first-century Palestine, raising grave doubts that they have been correctly sexed.

15. On the distinction between the concepts "clean" and "holy" in the Old Testament, see John Bergsma and Brant Pitre, *A Catholic Introduction to the Bible: Old Testament* (San Francisco: Ignatius Press, 2018), pp. 210–211.

16. See discussion in Qimron, "Celibacy in the Dead Sea Scrolls," pp. 289–294.

17. Heb. *bêth ha-'elohim,* so frequently in 1–2 Chronicles and Ezra–Nehemiah.

18. The Holy of Holies is where national atonement was performed on Yom Kippur, the holiest day of the Jewish liturgical year. On Qumran as an alternate Temple and its atoning role, see Lawrence Schiffman, "Community Without Temple: The Qumran Community's Withdrawal from the Jerusalem Temple," pp. 267–284 in *Gemeinde ohne Tempel: Zur Substituierung und Transformation des Jerusalemer Tempels und seines Kults im Alten Testament, antiken Judentum und frühen Christentum* (ed. Beate Ego et al.; Wissenschaftliche Untersuchungen zum Neuen Testament 118; Tübingen: Mohr Siebeck, 1999).

19. This is a quote by Bishop Genethlius, which was ratified by the members of the council. See Christian Cochini, *Apostolic Origins of Priestly Celibacy* (trans. Nelly Marans; San Francisco: Ignatius Press, 1990), p. 5; emphasis mine.

20. See Cochini, *Apostolic Origins,* pp. 3–13.

21. Quoted in Cochini, *Apostolic Origins,* p. 9.

22. See Herbert Thurston, "Celibacy of the Clergy," in vol. 3 of *The Catholic Encyclopedia* (New York: Robert Appleton, 1908), pp. 481–488, esp. pp. 484–485.

23. See Magen Broshi, "Was Qumran, Indeed, a Monastery?: The Consensus and Its Challengers, an Archaeologist's View," in Broshi,

Bread, Wine, Walls and Scrolls (Sheffield, UK: Sheffield Academic Press, 2001), pp. 259–273.

Chapter 10: Marriage in the Scrolls

1. Mishnah, tractate *Gittin* §9.10. See Herbert Danby, *The Mishnah* (Oxford: Oxford University Press, 1933), p. 321. Here is the entire section: "The School of Shammai say: A man may not divorce his wife unless he has found unchastity in her, for it is written, *Because he hath found in her* indecency *in anything*. And the School of Hillel say: [He may divorce her] even if she spoiled a dish for him, for it is written, *Because he hath found in her indecency in* anything. R. Akiba says: Even if he found another fairer than she, for it is written, *And it shall be if she find no favour in his eyes.*"

2. James C. VanderKam, *Dead Sea Scrolls Today* (2nd ed.; Grand Rapids, MI: Eerdmans, 2010), p. 154.

3. CD 13:15–17 mentions that a man should consult the Overseer (*mebaqqer*) of the community on a matter of divorce. This is the only mention of divorce in the Scrolls. Aharon Shemesh remarks, "If this passage did not exist, we would assume Qumranic *halakhah* did not recognize divorce in any form," and quotes Mark 10 as a parallel example of Second Temple Jewish halakhic interpretation that did not recognize divorce ("Marriage and Marital Life in the Dead Sea Scrolls," pp. 589–600 in *The Dead Sea Scrolls and Contemporary Culture* [ed. Adolfo Roitman, Lawrence Schiffman, and Shani Tzoref; Studies on the Texts of the Desert of Judah 93; Leiden: Brill, 2011], here p. 591, n. 7). It could be that the Essenes permitted divorce but not remarriage, similar to the early Church, which permitted separation of spouses but not remarriage (1 Cor 7:10–11).

4. Aharon Shemesh points out that the fragmentary text 4Q270 frag. 2, col. 2, ll. 15–17, appears to be a prohibition of intercourse during pregnancy ("Marriage and Marital Life in the Scrolls," p. 596), but too many words are missing to prove the point.

5. See James C. VanderKam and Peter W. Flint, *The Meaning of the Dead Sea Scrolls* (San Francisco: HarperCollins, 2002), pp. 184–185.

6. See VanderKam and Flint, *Meaning of the Dead Sea Scrolls,* pp. 178–180.

7. VanderKam and Flint, *Meaning of the Dead Sea Scrolls,* pp. 178–179, 194–199.

8. In Latin, *sine ulla femina, omnia venere abdicata,* in Pliny, *Natural History* 5:73.

9. See John Bergsma and Brant Pitre, *A Catholic Introduction to the Bible: Old Testament* (San Francisco: Ignatius Press, 2018), pp. 28–31, 462–463.

10. The quote is actually attributed to the orator Apollodoros, and quoted in Demosthenes, Oration 59, §122, *Against Neaera,* available online from Perseus Digital Library, http://artflsrv02.uchicago.edu/cgi-bin/perseus/citequery3.pl?dbname=GreekSept18&getid=1&query=Dem.%2059.

11. This can be seen from the fact that Plato's dialogue on the maturation of love, *Phaedrus,* takes as its focus not a husband and wife but an adult male lover and his adolescent beloved. A convenient edition is Plato, *Phaedrus* (trans. Christopher Rowe; New York: Penguin, 2005).

12. See Mark Vernon, "Plato's Dialogues, part 4: What Do You Love?," August 24, 2009, *The Guardian,* https://www.theguardian.com/commentisfree/belief/2009/aug/24/plato-dialogues-philosophy.

13. This is the point of Plato's Socratic dialogue *Phaedrus.* See note 11 for a print edition.

14. See Plato, *Timaeus,* §§42a–b, 90e, *Laws,* §781b, *Republic,* 455d; Aristotle, *History of Animals,* §608b1–14; see discussion of classical Greek views of women in Nicholas D. Smith, "Plato and Aristotle on the Nature of Women," *Journal of the History of Philosophy* 21 (1983): 467–478.

15. Strabo, *Geography,* bk. 8, chap. 6, sec. 20, available online from the University of Chicago: http://artflsrv02.uchicago.edu/cgi-bin/perseus/citequery3.pl?dbname=GreekSept18&getid=1&query=Str.%208.6.20.

16. See Marguerite Johnson, "The Grim Reality of the Brothels of Pompeii," *The Conversation,* December 12, 2017, http://theconversation.com/the-grim-reality-of-the-brothels-of-pompeii-88853.

17. See 4Q502, published by Maurice Baillet, *Qumrân grotte 4.III (4Q482–4Q520)* (Discoveries in the Judaean Desert 7; Oxford: Clarendon, 1982), pp. 81–205; also discussed by Shemesh, "Marriage and Marital Life," pp. 592–594.

18. See Bergsma and Pitre, *A Catholic Introduction to the Bible: Old Testament,* pp. 612–613.

19. 4Q416 frag. 2, col. 4, ll. 3–4.

20. See discussion in Shemesh, "Marriage and Marital Life," p. 598.

21. Scholars think 4Q415 and 4Q416 may have been one text. See Shemesh, "Marriage and Marital Life," pp. 598–599.

22. See Sue Blundell, *Women in Ancient Greece* (Cambridge, MA: Harvard University Press, 1995), pp. 119–120.

23. 4Q415 2:1–8.

24. Blundell, *Women in Ancient Greece,* pp. 121–122: "'Love and marriage' is a scenario largely absent from the literature of the classical period."

25. For example, Aristotle's somewhat chauvinist views on the relations between men and women should be tempered by acknowledging that he urges husbands to treat their wives well, and not to sleep with other women (in *Economics* 1344a.1, available from Perseus Digital Library, http://artflsrv02.uchicago.edu/cgi-bin/perseus/citequery3.pl?dbname=GreekSept18&getid=1&query=Arist.%20Oec.%201344a).

Chapter 11: Priesthood and the Scrolls

1. See Emanuelle Main, "Sadducees," pp. 812–816 in vol. 2 of *Encyclopedia of the Dead Sea Scrolls* (ed. Lawrence H. Schiffman and James C. VanderKam; Oxford: Oxford University Press, 2000).

2. See Jerome Murphy-O'Connor, "Teacher of Righteousness," pp. 340–341 in vol. 6 of *The Anchor Bible Dictionary* (New York: Doubleday, 1992).

3. See discussion in Michael Knibb, "Teacher of Righteousness," pp. 918–921 in vol. 2 of *Encyclopedia of the Dead Sea Scrolls.*

4. The "strangers" may have been those in the process of initiation.

5. This word, *mebaqqer,* is a participle formed from the verbal root *baqer,* "to look, to inquire," and it is in the Hebrew intensive stem, giving it the sense "one who seeks or looks intently or carefully: inspector, supervisor, overseer." The Greek *episkopos* is almost an exact translation.

6. From *epi,* "over," and *skopos,* "look, watch," i.e., "one who watches over something."

7. See Glen W. Barker, "1 John," pp. 291–358 in vol. 12 of *The Expositor's Bible Commentary* (ed. Frank E. Gaebelein; Grand Rapids, MI: Zondervan, 1981), here p. 320.

8. Gk. *katholike ekklesia,* "universal church."

9. Gk. *ekklesia.* As we will discuss further, *ekklesia* is the Greek equivalent of *qahal,* "congregation," which the Qumranites used as a synonym for *yahad* in reference to their own community.

10. Jean Daniélou, *The Dead Sea Scrolls and Primitive Christianity* (Baltimore: Helicon Press, 1958), pp. 118–121.

11. 1 Clement 40:1–41:1, emphasis mine.

Chapter 12: Priesthood in the Gospels

1. The Hebrew is *mamlekhet kohanîm.* In 1 Pet 2:9, this is rendered "royal priesthood," but the wording of Rev 1:5–6 seems to understand it as "kingdom of priests."

2. Sermon 108, PL 52, 499–500; Office of Readings for Tuesday of the 4th Week of Easter.

3. Jacob Neusner, *A Rabbi Talks with Jesus* (New York: Doubleday, 1993), p. 83; emphasis mine.

4. For example, the "precious cornerstone" of Isa 28:16 (also cited by the Qumran community, 1QS 8:7) or the "stone cut out by no human hand" of Dan 2:34.

5. In Hebrew, "House of God" is *bêth-el* or *bêth-ha-'elohîm.* The latter phrase is used frequently in the Books of Chronicles as a title for the Temple. The Hebrew for "Holy House" is *bêth-qôdesh,* which is used as a Temple image in 1QS 9:6.

6. See CD 7:17, 14:18.

7. See 1QS^a 1:25, 2:4; 1QM throughout.

8. In some languages, the word for "church" reflects the original Greek *ekklesia*: for example, the Spanish *iglesia.* In English, however, the word "church" derived from the Greek *kuriakon doma,* "the Lord's house," which was shortened to *kirk* in Germanic languages, eventually becoming the English "church."

9. In Hebrew, this rock was called the *eben shettiyyah,* the "foundation stone." See Curtis Mitch and Edward Sri, *The Gospel of Matthew* (Grand Rapids, MI: Baker, 2010), pp. 208–209.

10. For the concept of a human temple, observe how 4Q174 1:6 speaks of a *miqdash 'adam,* a "Temple of Adam" or "Temple of Humanity."

11. See W. F. Albright and C. S. Mann, *Matthew* (Anchor Bible 26; New York: Doubleday, 1971), pp. 196–197.

12. The garments mentioned in Isa 22:21 are priestly clothing. In Isa 22:20, the office of the royal steward is filled by a certain "Eliakim son of Hilkiah." All of the Hilkiahs mentioned in the Hebrew Bible (there are several) are Levites, so it appears to be a preferred name within the tribe of Levi. We may presume that Eliakim was a Levite.

13. See the commentary on this verse by Rabbi Kaufmann Kohler in "Binding and Loosing," p. 215a in vol. 3 of *The Jewish Encyclopedia* (ed. Isidore Singer; New York: Funk & Wagnalls, 1906), http://www .jewishencyclopedia.com/articles/3307-binding-and-loosing.

14. Kohler, "Binding and Loosing," p. 215a.

15. For example, the document 4QMMT, "On Some Works of the Law," is a letter rebuking the Pharisees for incorrect interpretations or applications of the Mosaic Law.

16. On Levi as the one to bind and loose, see 5Q13 1:7–8: "and Levi You [. . .] and You appointed him to bind [and loose]." Admittedly, only "to bind" is extant, but I reconstruct "to loose" in the gap following because the context is detailing the duties of the priestly tribe of Levi. The insistence to live by the judgments of the Zadokites is from the Rule of the Congregation, 1QS^a 1:1–2.

17. This is my own translation. I derive the rendering "as my memorial sacrifice," from the Greek of 1 Cor 11:25, *eis tên emên anamnêsin*, and the fact that Psalms 37:1 (38:1 ET) and 69:1 (70:1 ET) are both titled *eis anamnêsis* in the Septuagint, often translated "for the memorial sacrifice." See the comments on *anamnêsis* in Pablo Gadenz, *The Gospel of Luke* (Grand Rapids, MI: Baker Academic, 2018), pp. 355–356, 358–359.

18. On the role of the Davidic king in worship and his priestly character, see Hans-Joachim Kraus, *Theology of the Psalms* (trans. Keith Crim; Minneapolis: Fortress Press, 1992), pp. 107–123, esp. pp. 110, 115–116.

19. This is the literal Hebrew: the sons of David were *kohanîm*, "priests." Without justification, some English translations, not recognizing the priestly role of the Davidic monarchy (see Kraus in note 18), render *kohanîm* as "officers" or something similar.

20. See Lev 4:20, 26, 31, 35; 5:10, 13, 16, 18; 6:7; 19:22; Num 15:25, 28.

Chapter 13: Priesthood in the Early Church

1. See, for example, William S. Kurz and Peter Williamson, *The Acts of the Apostles* (Grand Rapids, MI: Baker, 2013), p. 42: lots are a "biblical method of determining God's will, *especially for assigning the duties of priests.*"
2. Gk. *cheirotoneô*, from *cheir-*, "hand," and *teinô*, "extend, stretch."
3. The Greek word for "presbytery" here is *presbuterion*.
4. Irenaeus of Lyon, *Irenaeus Against Heresies*, p. 497 in vol. 1, *The Apostolic Fathers with Justin Martyr and Irenaeus* (ed. A. Roberts, J. Donaldson, and A. C. Coxe; Buffalo, NY: Christian Literature Company, 1885).
5. Irenaeus, *Irenaeus Against Heresies*, p. 415.
6. See discussion in Michael Knibb, "Teacher of Righteousness," pp. 918–921 in vol. 2 of *Encyclopedia of the Dead Sea Scrolls* (ed. Lawrence H. Schiffman and James C. VanderKam; Oxford: Oxford University Press, 2000).

Chapter 14: Did St. Paul Write Anything About the Church?

1. For example, Markus Barth, *Ephesians 1–3* (Anchor Bible 34; New York: Doubleday, 1974); Bo Reicke, *Re-Examining Paul's Letters: The History of the Pauline Correspondence* (Harrisburg, PA: Trinity Press International, 2001); Frank Thielman, *Ephesians* (Baker Exegetical Commentary on the New Testament; Grand Rapids, MI: Baker, 2010), among many others.
2. Markus Barth (1915–1994), well-known Swiss New Testament scholar, son of the more famous Karl Barth (1886–1968), one of the most influential Protestant theologians of the twentieth century. Markus wrote the Ephesians commentary in the prestigious Anchor Bible commentary series. See publication information in note 1.
3. For a fuller discussion of the role of F. C. Baur in developing the "consensus" that Ephesians and other letters are deutero-Pauline, see Benjamin L. White, *Remembering Paul: Ancient and Modern Contests over the Image of the Apostle* (Oxford: Oxford University Press, 2014), esp. chapter 2, "F. C. Baur and the Rise of the Pauline Captivity Narrative," pp. 20–41. Strikingly, White's volume is a revision of his dissertation directed by Bart Ehrman (pp. xii, xvi).

4. See Eta Linnemann, *Biblical Criticism on Trial: How Scientific is "Scientific Theology"?* (Grand Rapids, MI: Kregel, 2001), pp. 74–99, esp. the lists on pp. 91–99.

5. See Harold H. Hoehner, "Did Paul Write Galatians?," pp. 150–169 in *History and Exegesis: New Testament Essays in Honor of Dr. E. Earle Ellis for His 80th Birthday* (ed. Sang-Won Son; New York: T & T Clark, 2006).

6. Drawing on the rhetorical principles of Cicero (106–43 B.C.), St. Augustine (A.D. 354–430) describes these three styles and their use in his work *De Doctrina Christiana* (On Christian Doctrine), book 4, chapters 17–26, and actually gives examples of each of the styles from various passages of St. Paul's epistles. Thus, the educated reader in antiquity was well aware of the fact that the same orator could employ different styles as the situation and his personal preference dictated. See Augustine, *On Christian Doctrine,* pp. 586–595 in vol. 2 of *St. Augustine's City of God and Christian Doctrine* (ed. P. Schaff; trans. J. F. Shaw; Buffalo, NY: Christian Literature Company, 1887).

7. As suggested by Reicke, *Re-Examining Paul's Letters,* p. 55.

8. Reicke, *Re-Examining Paul's Letters,* p. 52.

9. See Crispin H. T. Fletcher-Louis, *All the Glory of Adam: Liturgical Anthropology in the Dead Sea Scrolls* (Studies on the Texts of the Desert of Judah 42; Leiden: Brill, 2002).

10. The Hebrew for "instructor" is *maskil*. In my opinion, *maskil* is just another title for the *mebaqqer* or "Overseer," because the description of the *maskil*'s duties in the Scrolls duplicates duties assigned to the *mebaqqer*.

11. For example, compare the Greek Septuagint with the Hebrew Masoretic Text for Psalm 8:6.

12. 4Q174 1:6.

13. There is ambiguity concerning whether the Hebrew *sôd* here means "mystery, secret counsel" or "foundation." In any event, close parallels to Paul's language of "mystery" in Ephesians can be found in many other parts of the Scrolls; for example, in 1QHodayot[a], the Teacher of Righteousness remarks, similarly to Paul, that "you have opened within me knowledge in the *mystery* (Heb. *raz*) of Your insight" (1QH[a] 20:16). (The term *raz* is an Aramaic word borrowed into Qumran Hebrew, where it occurs very frequently.)

14. In Hebrew *b'ney 'ôr*: see 1QS 1:9; 2:16; 3:13, 24, 25.

15. This can be pronounced, eh-KLEE-zee-AH-luh-jee, or eh-KLAY-zee-AH-loh-jee.

16. See CD 7:17, 12:6, 14:18; 4Q169 3:7; etc.

17. See 1QS^a 1:24–25, 2:4; 1QM throughout.

18. See Michael A. Knibb, "Rule of the Community," pp. 793–797 in vol. 2 of *Encyclopedia of the Dead Sea Scrolls* (ed. Lawrence H. Schiffman and James C. VanderKam; Oxford: Oxford University Press, 2000).

19. See Curtis Mitch and Edward Sri, *The Gospel of Matthew* (Grand Rapids, MI: Baker, 2010), pp. 208–209.

20. Otto Betz and Rainer Riesner, *Jesus, Qumran, and the Vatican: Clarifications* (New York: Crossroad, 1994), p. 155.

Chapter 15: The Scrolls, the Reformation, and Church Unity

1. "Theses" in this context were theological propositions. Nailing them to the door of the church was not by itself a rebellious act, because many public announcements were nailed to the church door, which functioned as a community bulletin board. Luther's Ninety-Five Theses, surprisingly, are not anti-Catholic. He was still thinking within the bounds of Catholic theology when he composed them. Only later did he begin to embrace opinions that could not be reconciled with Catholic theological definitions.

2. For example, this quote from one of Luther's letters: "Be a sinner, and let your sins be strong, but let your trust in Christ be stronger, and rejoice in Christ who is the victor over sin, death, and the world. We will commit sins while we are here, for this life is not a place where justice resides. . . . No sin can separate us from Him, *even if we were to kill or commit adultery thousands of times each day*" (Letter no. 99, August 1, 1521, from Wartburg, to Melanchthon, translated by Erika Flores from vol. 15 of *Dr. Martin Luther's Sämmtliche Schriften* [ed. Johannes Georg Walch; St. Louis: Concordia Publishing House, 1880–1910], cols. 2585–2590; emphasis mine.

3. This Gospel presentation method, popular among American Evangelicals, relies on reading or quoting several verses from Romans concerning sin, faith, and salvation.

4. Commenting on Gal 2:16 and "works of the law," Luther says: "Here Paul is not speaking about the ceremonial law, but of the whole law, for the ceremonial law was as much the law of God as was the moral law" (Martin Luther, *Galatians* [ed. Alister McGrath and J. I. Packer; Wheaton, IL: Crossway Books, 1998], p. 91).

5. Thomas Aquinas, *Commentary on Saint Paul's Epistle to the Galatians* (trans. F. R. Larcher; Albany, NY: Magi Books, 1966), chap. 4, lecture 2; available online at https://dhspriory.org/thomas/SSGalatians .htm#24.

6. The Qumran documents numbered 4Q394–398 are all partial copies of the entire document known as 4QMMT. For precision, I need to make reference to the documents by their numbers.

7. There appear originally to have been twenty-four topics at issue; I list here the sixteen that can most clearly be reconstructed from the extant copies of 4QMMT. See discussion in the works cited in "For Further Reading."

8. See Thomas Aquinas, *Summa Theologica*, I–II, Q. 99, "Of the Precepts of the Old Law," esp. article 3, "Whether the Old Law Comprises Ceremonial, Besides Moral, Precepts?" John Calvin follows the same traditional division: see his *Institutes of the Christian Religion*, bk. 2, chap. 7, esp. sec. 16.

9. Scrolls scholar Martin Abegg concludes: "It is clear that Luther's reaction to medieval scholasticism, which has been traditionally projected on Judaism in antiquity, is not supported by an examination of the only Jewish community for which record exists that used the vocabulary reflected in Paul's discussions of law and righteousness" ("4QMMT C 27, 31 and 'Works Righteousness,'" *Dead Sea Discoveries* 6 [1999]: 139–147, here pp. 146–147).

10. See Rom 2:25–3:1, 3:30, 4:9–12; Gal 2:3–12, 5:2–12, 6:12–15.

11. See also Rom 2:25–3:1, 3:30, 4:9–12; 1 Cor 7:19; Gal 2:3–12, 5:2–12, 6:12–15; Eph 2:11; Phil 3:3; Col 2:11; Tim 1:10.

Chapter 16: The Essenes and the Early Church

1. The French biblical scholar Ernest Renan was one of the first to claim that Christianity was just a form of Essenism. Edmund Wilson, a literary critic writing for the *New York Times* and fierce opponent of

Christianity, published a series of articles on the Dead Sea Scrolls in *The New Yorker* magazine between 1947 and 1969, all with a strong anti-Christian edge. See discussion in James C. VanderKam and Peter W. Flint, *The Meaning of the Dead Sea Scrolls* (San Francisco: HarperCollins, 2002), pp. 321–345, esp. pp. 321–322.

2. A good overview and debunking of sensationalist claims can be found in James H. Charlesworth, "The Dead Sea Scrolls and the Historical Jesus," pp. 1–74 in *Jesus and the Dead Sea Scrolls* (ed. James H. Charlesworth; New York: Doubleday, 1992).

3. See Brant Pitre, *The Case for Jesus: The Biblical and Historical Evidence for Christ* (New York: Image, 2016).

4. Scholars refer to this famous testimony of Josephus to Jesus as the *Testimonium Flavianum*. The authenticity of part or all of the passage has been challenged, but there is no manuscript evidence that any part of the passage is an interpolation. See the extensive discussion in John P. Meier, *A Marginal Jew: Rethinking the Historical Jesus, Volume One: The Roots of the Problem and the Person* (Anchor Bible Reference Library; New York: Doubleday, 1991), pp. 59–68. Meier defends the authenticity of most of the passage, excising only a few phrases as interpolations. Meier's reconstruction is reasonable and I could be content with it, but in the absence of manuscript evidence to the contrary, I regard the whole passage as authentic. In my reading, Josephus was not a Christian, but he decided to co-opt the famous Jesus called "Christ" as an impressive example of what the Jewish prophetic tradition could produce.

5. See Gary R. Habermas and Michael Licona, *The Case for the Resurrection of Jesus* (Grand Rapids, MI: Kregel, 2004).

ABOUT THE AUTHOR

JOHN BERGSMA, PhD, is a professor of theology at the Franciscan University of Steubenville and a senior fellow at the St. Paul Center for Biblical Theology. Twice voted Faculty of the Year by graduating classes at Franciscan University, Bergsma holds three degrees in ancient languages and theology from Calvin College and Seminary and a doctorate in ancient Christianity and Judaism from the University of Notre Dame. A specialist in the Old Testament and the Dead Sea Scrolls, Bergsma has published several popular and educational books on Scripture and the Christian faith, as well as dozens of technical articles in peer-reviewed journals and essay collections. He and his wife, Dawn, live with their children in Steubenville, Ohio.